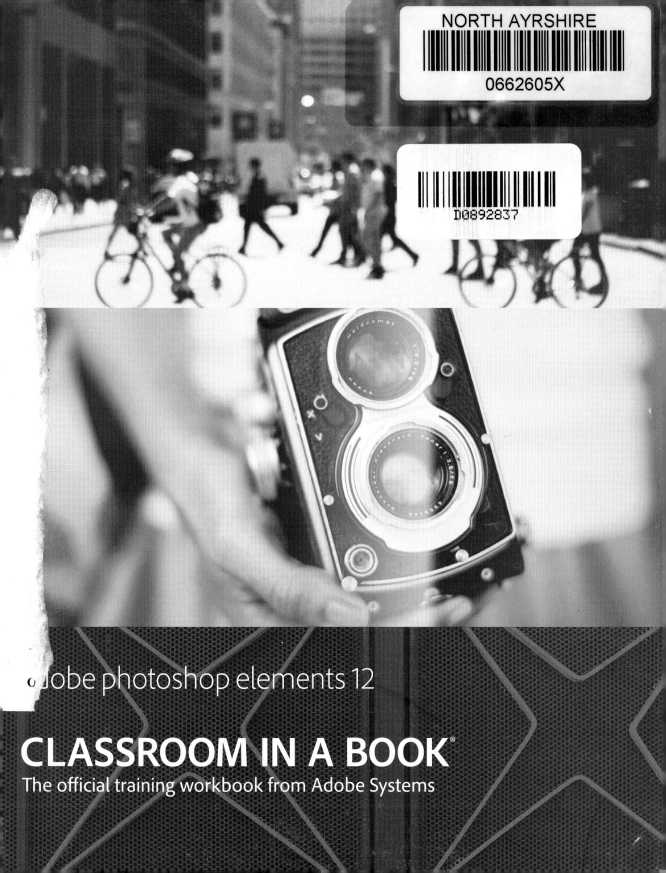

adobe photoshop elements 12

CLASSROOM IN A BOOK®

The official training workbook from Adobe Systems

WHERE ARE THE LESSON FILES?

Purchasing this Classroom in a Book gives you access to the lesson files that you'll need to complete the exercises in the book, as well as other content to help you learn more about Adobe software and use it with greater efficiency and ease. The diagram below represents the contents of the lesson files directory, which should help you locate the files you need. Please see the Getting Started section for full download instructions.

Adobe Press

Find information about other Adobe Press titles, covering the full spectrum of Adobe products, in the Online Resources file.

Lesson files

Each lesson has its own folder inside the Lessons folder. You will need to copy these lesson folders to your hard drive before you can begin each lesson.

Online resources

Links to Adobe Community Help, product Help and Support pages, Adobe certification programs, Adobe TV, and other useful online resources can be found inside a handy HTML file. Just open it in your web browser and click on the links, including a special link to this book's product page where you can access updates and bonus material.

CONTENTS

GETTING STARTED

Adobe® Photoshop® Elements 12 delivers image-editing tools that balance power and versatility with ease of use. Whether you're a home user or hobbyist, a professional photographer or a business user, Photoshop Elements 12 makes it easy to produce good-looking pictures, share your stories in sophisticated creations for both print and web, and manage and safeguard your precious photos.

If you've used an earlier version of Photoshop Elements, you'll find that this Classroom in a Book® will teach you advanced skills and provide an introduction to the many new and improved features in this version. If you're new to Adobe Photoshop Elements, you'll learn the fundamental concepts and techniques that will help you master the application.

About Classroom in a Book

Adobe Photoshop Elements 12 Classroom in a Book is part of the official training series for Adobe graphics and publishing software developed with the support of Adobe product experts. Each lesson is made up of a series of self-paced projects that will give you hands-on experience using Photoshop Elements 12.

See "Accessing the Classroom in a Book files" on the next page for detailed instructions on downloading the sample photographs and other resources used for the lessons in *Adobe Photoshop Elements 12 Classroom in a Book*.

What's new in this edition

This edition covers many new features in Adobe Photoshop Elements 12, including enhancements to the Quick edit mode, advanced content-aware tools, and mobile albums that enable you to access all of the photos in your Photoshop Elements library on your smart phone or tablet, wherever you are.

New exercises will show you how easy it is to correct a photo with the intuitive Auto Smart Tone tool, how to correct flash effects in photos of your pets, reposition objects seamlessly with the Content-Aware Move tool, and how to take advantage of enhanced integration with Adobe Revel™ for online sharing.

Prerequisites

Before you begin the lessons in this book, make sure that you and your computer are ready by following the tips and instructions on the next few pages.

Requirements on your computer

You'll need about 900 MB of free space on your hard disk—around 400 MB for the lesson files and up to 550 MB for the work files that you'll create as you work through the exercises.

Required skills

The lessons in this book assume that you have a working knowledge of your computer and its operating system. Make sure that you know how to use the mouse and the standard menus and commands, and also how to open, save, and close files. Can you scroll (vertically and horizontally) within a window to see content that may not be visible in the displayed area? Do you know how to use context menus, which open when you right-click (Windows) / Control-click (Mac OS) items?

> **Note:** In this book, the forward slash character (/) is used to separate equivalent terms and commands for Windows / Mac OS, in the order shown here.

If you need to review these basic and generic computer skills, see the documentation included with your Microsoft® Windows® or Apple® Mac® OS X software.

Installing Adobe Photoshop Elements 12

Before you begin the lessons in *Adobe Photoshop Elements 12 Classroom in a Book*, make sure that your system is set up correctly and that you've installed the required software and hardware. You must purchase the Adobe Photoshop Elements 12 software separately.

For system requirements and instructions for downloading, installing, and setting up the software, refer to the topics listed under the header "Up and running" at http://helpx.adobe.com/photoshop-elements.html.

Accessing the Classroom in a Book files

In order to work through the exercises in this book, you'll need to download the sample image files and other resources from your Account page at peachpit.com.

You can either download the entire Lessons folder before you begin, or download the files for individual lessons as you need them. Keep the lesson files on your computer until you've completed all the exercises.

Your Account page is also where you'll find any updates to the lessons or to the work files. Look on the Lesson & Update Files tab to access the most current content.

Downloading the Lesson files

1   Point your web browser to www.peachpit.com/redeem, and enter the code found at the back of this book. If you don't yet have a Peachpit.com account, follow the prompts to create one.

2   Click the Lesson & Update Files tab on your Account page to see a list of downloadable files. Click the links to download either the entire Lessons folder or the work folders for individual lessons to your computer.

3   Create a new folder named **PSE12CIB** inside the *username*/My Documents (Windows) or *username*/Documents (Mac OS) folder on your computer.

4   If you downloaded the entire Lessons folder, drag the downloaded folder into the PSE12CIB folder on your hard disk. If you downloaded the work folder for an individual lesson, first create a Lessons folder inside the PSE12CIB folder; then, drag the downloaded folder to your PSE12CIB/Lessons folder.

Creating a work folder

Now you need to create a folder for the work files that you'll produce as you work through the lessons in this book.

1   In Windows Explorer (Windows) / the Finder (Mac OS) open the Lessons folder inside the new PSE12CIB folder on your hard disk.

2   Choose File > New > Folder (Windows) / File > New Folder (Mac OS). A new folder is created inside the Lessons folder. Type **My CIB Work** as the name for the new folder.

Creating an Adobe ID

When you install Adobe Photoshop Elements 12 (Mac OS) or launch the program for the first time (Windows), you'll be asked to create an Adobe ID to register your product online.

If you were off-line and skipped this step, Photoshop Elements will prompt you at startup. You can take advantage of one of these opportunities, or register from the Photoshop Elements Editor by choosing Help > Sign In.

Creating an Adobe ID is free and only takes a minute. Your Adobe ID will streamline your customer support experience, making it easy to make new purchases, or retrieve a lost serial number.

With an Adobe ID, you'll also be able to log into community forums and user groups and get full access to free trial downloads, hundreds of free product extensions, members-only white papers and downloads, and more.

Note: The sample images are provided for your personal use with this book. You are not authorized to use these files commercially, or to publish or distribute them in any form without written permission from Adobe Systems, Inc. and the individual photographers or other copyright holders.

Note: In this book, the forward arrow character (>) is used to denote submenus and commands found in the menu bar at the top of the workspace or in context and options menus; for example, Menu > Submenu > Command. The forward slash character (/) is used to separate equivalent keyboard shortcuts and commands for Windows / Mac OS, in the order shown here.

About catalog files

Photoshop Elements stores information about your images in a library catalog file, which enables you to conveniently manage the photos on your computer. The catalog file is a central concept in understanding how Photoshop Elements works. Photoshop Elements doesn't actually "import" your images at all; for each image you import Photoshop Elements simply creates a new entry in the catalog that is linked to the source file, wherever it is stored. Whenever you assign a tag or a rating to a photo, or group images as an album, the catalog file is updated. All the work you put into organizing your growing photo library is recorded in the catalog.

As well as digital photographs, a catalog can include video and audio files, scans, PDF documents, and any presentations and layouts you might create in Photoshop Elements, such as slide shows, photo collages, and CD jacket designs.

The first time you launch Photoshop Elements it automatically creates a default catalog file (named My Catalog) on your hard disk. Although a single catalog can efficiently handle thousands of files, you can also establish separate catalogs for different purposes if that's the way you prefer to work.

In the first lesson in this book you'll create and load a new, dedicated catalog into which you'll import the lesson sample images. In this way, it will be easy to keep your own photo library separate from your lesson files.

In the first three lessons, you'll learn a number of different ways to add files to your catalog, together with a variety of techniques for tagging, marking, and organizing your images, and for sorting and searching your catalog. You'll be able to practice these new skills when you import lesson files to your Classroom in a Book catalog at the beginning of each chapter.

Additional resources

Adobe Photoshop Elements 12 Classroom in a Book is not intended to replace the documentation that comes with the program or to be a comprehensive reference for every feature. Only the commands and options used in the lessons are explained in this book. For comprehensive information about program features and tutorials, please refer to these resources:

Adobe Photoshop Elements 12 Help and Support Point your browser to http://helpx.adobe.com/photoshop-elements.html where you can browse and find Help and Support content on adobe.com.

Adobe Photoshop Elements 12 product home page www.adobe.com/products/photoshop-elements.html

Adobe Forums forums.adobe.com lets you tap into peer-to-peer discussions, questions and answers on Adobe products.

Adobe TV tv.adobe.com is an online video resource for expert instruction and inspiration about Adobe products, including a How To channel to get you started with your product.

Resources for educators www.adobe.com/education offers a treasure trove of information for instructors who teach classes on Adobe software. Find solutions for education at all levels, including free curricula that use an integrated approach to teaching Adobe software and can be used to prepare for the Adobe Certified Associate exams.

Free trial versions of Adobe Photoshop Elements 12 and Adobe Premiere Elements 12 The trial version of the software is fully functional and offers every feature of the product for you to test-drive. To download your free trial version, go to http://www.adobe.com/downloads.html.

1 A QUICK TOUR OF PHOTOSHOP ELEMENTS

Lesson overview

This lesson provides an overview of Photoshop Elements that will familiarize you with the basic components of the workspace while introducing many of the tools and procedures you'll use to import, manage, and edit your digital images.

The exercises in this lesson will step you through some of the skills and concepts basic to the Photoshop Elements workflow:

- Creating and loading Catalogs
- Importing media
- Reconnecting missing files
- Reviewing and comparing photos
- Switching between the Organizer and the Editor
- Switching modes in the Editor
- Working with panels and the Panel Bin
- Customizing the workspace
- Using Photoshop Elements Help

 You'll probably need between one and two hours to complete this lesson. If you haven't already done so, download the Lesson 1 work files from the Lesson & Update Files tab of your Account page at www.peachpit.com.

Welcome to Adobe Photoshop Elements 12!
Take a quick tour and get to know the Photoshop
Elements workspace—you'll find all the power and
versatility you'd expect from a Photoshop application
in an easy-to-use, modular interface that will help you
keep your media files organized while you take your
digital photography to a new level.

How Photoshop Elements works

Note: Before you start this lesson, make sure that you've set up a folder for your lesson files and downloaded the Lesson 1 folder from your Account page at www.peachpit.com, as detailed in "Accessing the Classroom in a Book files" in the chapter "Getting Started" at the beginning of this book.

Photoshop Elements has two primary workspaces: the Elements Organizer and the Editor. You can think of the Organizer as a library and browser for your photos and other media files, and the Editor as a digital darkroom and workshop where you can adjust and enhance your images and create presentations to showcase them.

1 Start Photoshop Elements.

By default, the Welcome screen opens whenever you start Photoshop Elements, serving as a convenient entry point to either of the workspace modules.

2 Click the Options button (⚙) at the upper right of the Welcome screen, and then click to open the On Start Always Launch menu.

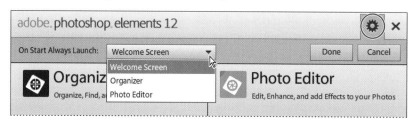

If you change the default launch option, you can always access the Welcome screen from the Help menu. For now, you can leave the default setting unchanged.

3 Click Cancel, or click the Options button (⚙) again, to hide the options bar.

This tour—like the Photoshop Elements workflow—begins in the Organizer, where you can import, sort, group, search, and share your photos.

4 Click the Organizer button to launch the Elements Organizer module. If you see a welcome message offering a choice of import options, click Cancel.

The library catalog file

Behind the scenes, Photoshop Elements stores information about your images in a library catalog file, which enables you to conveniently manage all the photos and media files on your computer without ever leaving the Organizer. The catalog file is a central concept in understanding how Photoshop Elements works. Photoshop Elements doesn't actually "import" your images at all, but instead simply registers them in the catalog. For each image you import Photoshop Elements creates a new catalog entry; a link to the original or *source file*, wherever it is stored.

All the work you put into organizing your growing photo library is recorded in the catalog file; whenever you assign a tag or a rating to a photo, or group images in a stack or an album, the catalog is updated.

As well as digital photographs, a catalog can include video and audio files, scans, PDF documents, and any presentations and layouts you might create in Photoshop Elements, such as slide shows, photo collages, and CD jacket designs.

Creating a catalog for working with this book

The first time you launch Photoshop Elements, a default catalog file (named My Catalog) is automatically created on your hard disk. Although a single catalog can efficiently handle thousands of files, you can also establish separate catalogs for different purposes—if that's the way you prefer to work. In this exercise you'll create and load a dedicated catalog to handle the sample files used for the lessons in this book, making it easy to keep them separate from your own photos.

1 When the Organizer has opened, choose File > Manage Catalogs. In the Catalog Manager dialog box, click New. Don't change the location setting, which specifies who can access the catalog file and where it is stored.

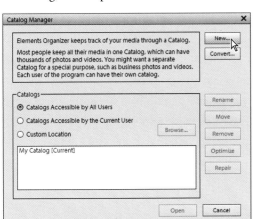

> **Note:** On Mac OS, you may see slightly different location options from those shown in the illustration at the left.

2 Type **CIB Catalog** in the Enter A Name For The New Catalog dialog box. Disable the option Import Free Music Into This Catalog, if necessary, and then click OK.

Your new catalog is loaded in the Organizer. If you are ever unsure which catalog is currently loaded, you can always check the catalog name displayed in the lower right corner of the Organizer workspace.

> **Tip:** You can launch the Catalog Manager without using the menu command by simply clicking the name of the current catalog in the lower right corner of the Organizer workspace.

Now that you have a catalog created specifically to manage the sample files that you'll use for the lessons in this book, you're ready to put some photos into it.

Importing media

Before you can view, organize, and share your photos and other media files in Photoshop Elements, you first need to import them into the Organizer in order to link them to your catalog.

You can bring photos into Photoshop Elements from a variety of sources and in a number of different ways.

1   Click the Import button, at the upper left of the Organizer workspace. The options in the Import menu vary slightly, depending on your operating system.

 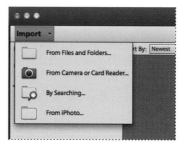

Import options on Windows   Import options on Mac OS

2   Click the Import button again to close the menu.

Getting photos from files and folders

If your image files are already on your computer hard disk—as is the case for the Classroom in a Book sample photos—you can either drag them directly into the Elements Organizer workspace from Windows Explorer or the Mac OS Finder, or import them from within Photoshop Elements using a menu command.

The import options that are listed in the Import button menu can also be accessed from the File menu.

1   Choose File > Get Photos And Videos > From Files And Folders.

2   In the Get Photos And Videos From Files And Folders dialog box, navigate to and open the Lessons folder inside your PSE12CIB folder. Open the Lesson 1 folder; then, click once to select the subfolder Import 1.

3   Make sure that the options Automatically Fix Red Eyes and Automatically Suggest Photo Stacks are disabled (*see the illustration on the next page*); then, click Get Media.

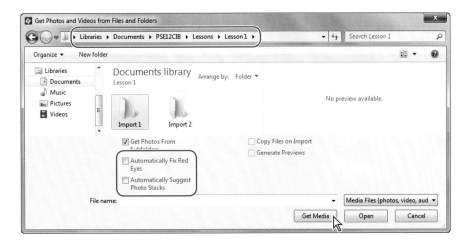

The Getting Media dialog box displays a progress bar as the photos are imported.

4 The Import Attached Keyword Tags dialog box appears, indicating that the photos you're importing have already been tagged with keywords. Check the box beside Lesson 01 tag in the Keyword Tags list to confirm it for import, and then click OK.

● **Note:** You'll learn more about keyword tags in Lesson 3.

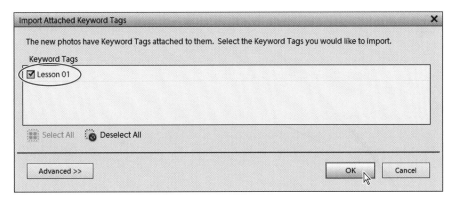

5 Thumbnails of the six imported photos appear in the Organizer's Media Browser pane. Choose View > Details. Note that each image's capture time is now displayed below its thumbnail, together with a blue tag badge indicating that the photo has attached keywords.

6 Repeat steps 1 through 4 for the folder Lessons \ Lesson 1 \ Import 2, but this time, choose From Files And Folders from the Import button menu.

Exploring the Organizer workspace

The Elements Organizer is an integral part of both Adobe Photoshop Elements and Adobe Premiere Elements video editing software. You can import, manage, and view both photos and video in the Elements Organizer, which serves as a hub, allowing seamless integration of the two editing applications.

In the Organizer, the main work area is the Media Browser pane. This is where you'll review, sort, organize, and search your photos and other media files. The bars just above the image thumbnails display information about the selection of photos currently on view; in this case, the lower bar displays the date and time of the last import. If the Media Browser was showing the results of a catalog search, the lower bar would detail the search criteria shared by that selection of images.

1 To clear the Last Import filter and view all twelve photos in your catalog, click the Clear button at the right of the search results bar above the image thumbnails, and then click the Back button at the left of the actions bar above that.

The search results bar closes. The header in the actions bar indicates that the Media Browser is now displaying all of the media files in your catalog (*see the illustration below*). By default, the images are sorted by capture date, from newest to oldest.

2 Choose Oldest from the Sort By menu at the left of the actions bar to reverse the order. Note that you can also sort your photos by name or import batch.

Once you've spent a little time organizing your catalog by tagging your photos, you can use the view picker above the sorting bar to move between the People, Places, and Events views, quickly filtering the images in the Media Browser so that it displays only those photos that feature the faces, locations, or occasions that matter to you. The currently active view is the Media view, which is unfiltered.

You can use the text search box (located in the menu bar on Windows, or in the application window header on Mac OS) to conduct a text search, or choose from a range of other search options in the associated menu.

Note: Until you've tagged your photos for faces, locations and events, the People, Places and Events views will remain empty. You'll learn more about these views and searching your photo library in Lessons 2 and 3.

The left panel will list any albums that you create to group your photos, and also provides quick and easy access to all the files and source folders on your computer. The default My Folders view lists only your *managed folders*: those folders that contain files that you've already imported to your Photoshop Elements catalog.

3   To see your folders in tree hierarchy view, click the folder hierarchy icon (📇-) to the right of the My Folders view. You can expand folders in order to drill down in the hierarchy by clicking the boxes (Windows) or arrows (Mac OS) beside them. To expand the tree even further, right-click / Control-click the Lessons folder and choose Show All Subfolders from the context menu. You can now see all of the subfolders inside the Lessons folder, rather than just those that contain files managed by your catalog.

Tip: If the left panel is not wide enough to display the folder names in the tree hierarchy, move the pointer over the panel's right edge and drag to the right with the double-arrow cursor.

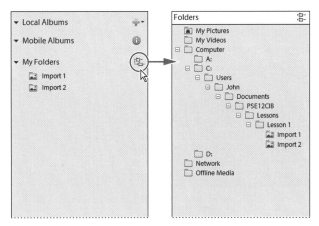
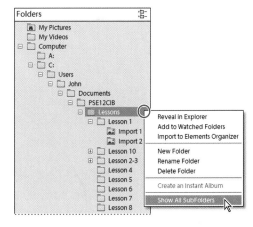

In the Folders view, you can drag and drop files and folders to new locations on your hard disk, and create, rename, and delete folders on your computer without leaving the Organizer. The catalog file tracks all your work in the Folders view, making it easy to manage your media library from the ground up, and helping to avoid the hassle of locating and reconnecting missing files.

When you select a folder in the Folders view, that folder becomes the image source, rather than your entire catalog, so the Media Browser displays only the photos contained in the selected folder. Any filter or search—including the People, Places, and Events views—will be applied only to the images in the selected folder. The Media view will display the unfiltered contents of the selected folder.

4   Click the folder list icon (⌷) at the top of the Folders view to return to the "flat" My Folders view. Click between your managed folders to see their contents isolated in turn in the Media Browser. Click All Media, at the left of the Sort By menu above the image thumbnails, to view all of the photos in your catalog.

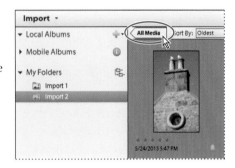

The Task Bar across the bottom of the workspace presents an array of tools, giving you one-click access to some of the most common Organizer tasks.

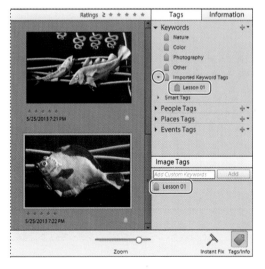

Note: The Slide Show, Editor, and Instant Fix buttons are covered later in this lesson. You'll learn how to use the Add People, Add Places, and Add Event buttons in Lesson 2.

5   Toggle the button at the far left of the Task bar to hide and show the left panel. The Undo / Redo and Rotate buttons are self explanatory; click the arrow beside each of these tools to see the variant. Experiment with the full range of the Zoom slider to change the size of the image thumbnails. Leave the thumbnails set to a large enough size to see the blue keyword tag badges.

6   Select any thumbnail in the Media Browser, and then click the Tags / Info button at the right of the Task Bar to open the right panel group. The Image Tags panel at the bottom shows that the selected image is tagged with the Lesson 01 keyword. Expand the Keywords list at the top of the Tags panel; then, expand the Imported Keyword Tags category to see the Lesson 01 tag nested inside.

Above the right panel, at the upper right of the Organizer workspace, are the Create and Share buttons.

7 Click the Create and Share buttons in turn and examine the options.

You can choose from the Create menu to begin a variety of photo projects to share and showcase your images, from personalized greeting cards to stylish photo books and slide shows.

The Share menu offers a range of ways to share your photos and videos with friends, family, and clients, or show them off to the world at large. Burn a DVD, publish to online sharing sites, attach your images to an e-mail, or upload an online album.

● **Note:** The Slide Show project and the Photo Mail option in the Share menu are not supported on Mac OS.

8 Double-click any thumbnail in the grid, or select it and press Ctrl+Shift+S (on Windows) / Command+Shift+S (on Mac OS) to see the image enlarged. Use the arrow keys on your keyboard to cycle through the photos in the single image view. Double-click the enlarged image to return to the thumbnail grid view.

▶ **Tip:** You can use the controls below the enlarged image to add either a text or audio caption to a photo.

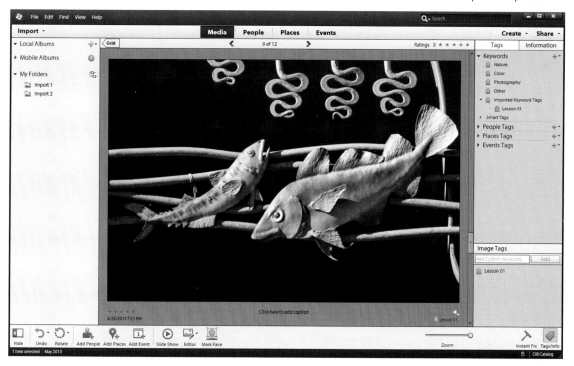

Reviewing and comparing images

Photoshop Elements provides several options for quickly and easily reviewing and comparing your photos in the Organizer. The Full Screen and Side By Side views let you examine images at any level of magnification—without the distraction of image windows, panels, and menus. In both of these views you can apply keywords, add photos to albums, and even perform a range of one-click editing tasks.

Viewing photos in Full Screen mode

You can use the Full Screen view to inspect and assess your photos in detail, or to effortlessly present a selection of images as an instant slide show.

1 Click to select a single thumbnail image in the Media Browser, and then choose View > Full Screen. Avoid moving the pointer for a few moments until the control bar and the Quick Edit and Quick Organize panels disappear.

2 Move the pointer over the full screen image to see the control bar again. Move the pointer over the gray tabs at the left of the screen to open the Quick Edit and Quick Organize panels. Move the pointer into the center of the screen; the control bar and panels disappear again after a few moments' inactivity.

The Film Strip below the main image shows all the photos from the Media Browser; if you had entered Full Screen mode with multiple images selected, the Film Strip would display only the selected photos.

▶ **Tip:** If you don't see the Film Strip, press Ctrl+F / Command+F on your keyboard, or click the Film Strip button in the Full Screen view's control bar.

3 Use the arrow keys on your keyboard, and then the Previous Media and Next Media buttons (flanking the triangular Play button at the left of the control bar), to move backwards and forwards through the images in the Film Strip.

▶ **Tip:** You can use the Slide Show button (▶) in the Task Bar to start the slide show from the standard Media view.

4 To start the slide show, press the spacebar, or show the control bar by moving the pointer over the image, and then click the Play button. To stop the slide show, press the spacebar again, or click the Pause button in the control bar.

5 In the control bar, click the Theme and Settings buttons in turn to set a variety of options for the slideshow and the Full Screen view. Choose a style for transitions between slides, select an audio file to replace the default sound track, and set the slide show to repeat. Play the slide show to see the effects of your settings.

▶ **Tip:** If you choose either Pan and Zoom or 3D Pixelate transitions in the Theme dialog box, you'll need to press the Esc key on your keyboard to stop the slide show, rather than the spacebar or the Pause button in the control bar.

6 Stop the slide show. Toggle the Film Strip, Fix, and Organize buttons to show and hide the Film Strip and the Quick Edit and Quick Organize panels.

Comparing photos side-by-side

The Side By Side viewing mode lets you keep one image fixed on one side of a split screen while you cycle through a selection of photos on the other—great for comparing composition and detail or for choosing the best of a series of similar shots.

1 Show the Film Strip, if necessary, and then click to select the first photo in the series. Click the View button in the control bar to see the alternative view options; then, choose the Side By Side view.

The photo you selected is displayed at the left of the screen, and the next photo in the series is shown on the right. By default, the image on the left—image #1—is active, as indicated by the blue border around the photo in the split-screen view. Any organizing or editing operation you perform will affect only the active image.

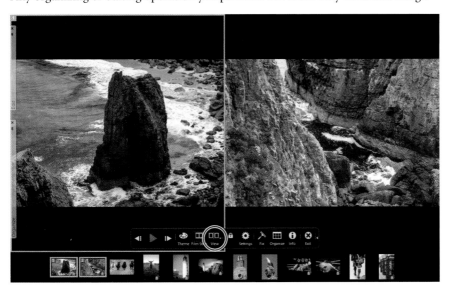

2 With the photo on the left—image #1—still active, click the first photo of the lighthouse in the Film Strip. The new selection becomes the new #1 image.

3 Click the photo on the right of the split screen—image #2—to make it active. Click the forward navigation (Next Media) button () in the control bar, or press the right arrow key on your keyboard, to move the #2 preview to the second lighthouse photo, while the image on the left remains fixed.

4 Click either image repeatedly to toggle between fit-to-view and 100% magnification. To compare detail at higher magnification, zoom in and out in the active image using the scroll-wheel on your mouse—or by pressing the Ctrl / Command key together with the plus (+) or minus (-) key. Drag the zoomed photo with the hand cursor to see a different portion of the image.

5 To synchronize panning and zooming between the two photos, click the lock icon to the right of the View button in the full screen view control bar.

6 Click the View button and select the second split-screen layout from the fly-out menu—the horizontally divided Above And Below view.

7 Click the Exit button () at the right of the control bar, or press the Esc key on your keyboard to close the split screen view and return to the Organizer.

Reconnecting missing files to a catalog

When you bring a photo into Photoshop Elements, the name and location of the file is recorded in the catalog. If you wish to move, rename, or delete a photo that is already in your catalog, it is best if you do it from within the Elements Organizer.

If you move, rename, or delete a file in the Windows Explorer / Mac OS Finder after it has been added to the catalog, Photoshop Elements searches your computer for the missing file automatically, and will usually do a great job finding it—even when the file has been renamed; however, you need to know what to do if the automatic search fails. If a file cannot be located, the missing file icon (⬛) appears in the upper left corner of its thumbnail in the Media Browser to alert you that the link between the file and your catalog has been broken.

Tip: To avoid the problem of files missing from your catalog, use the Move and Rename commands from the File menu, and the Edit > Delete From Catalog command to move, rename, or delete files from within Photoshop Elements, rather than doing so outside the application.

1   Switch to the Windows Explorer / Mac OS Finder by doing one of the following:

   •   On Windows, minimize the Elements Organizer by clicking the Minimize button (⬛) at the right of the menu bar, or simply click the Elements Organizer application button on the Windows taskbar.

   •   On Mac OS, click the Finder icon the Dock, or hold down Command; then press and release the Tab key, repeatedly if necessary, to select the Finder icon in the Application Switcher.

2   Open an Explorer / Finder window, if there's not one already available. Navigate to and open your Lessons folder. Drag the Lesson 1 folder out of the Lessons folder to the Recycle Bin / Trash. Do not empty the Recycle Bin / Trash.

3   Switch back to the Organizer, and then choose File > Reconnect > All Missing Files. Photoshop displays a message to let you know it's busy searching for the missing files. We don't expect the files to be found in the Recycle Bin / Trash, so you can stop the automatic search by clicking the Browse button.

The Reconnect Missing Files dialog box opens—as it would have done, had the search run its course without Photoshop Elements locating the missing files.

4   For this exercise, you won't follow the re-linking process through to completion, but you should take this opportunity to inspect the dialog box thoroughly (*see the illustration on the next page*).

At the upper left of the Reconnect Missing Files dialog box is a list of all missing files. Below the list, a preview displays a thumbnail of the currently selected missing file. To the right, you can browse the contents of your computer.

When you select a candidate, you'll see a preview thumbnail below the Locate The Missing Files pane, opposite the missing file preview, enabling you to visually verify the photo as a match, even if its name has been changed.

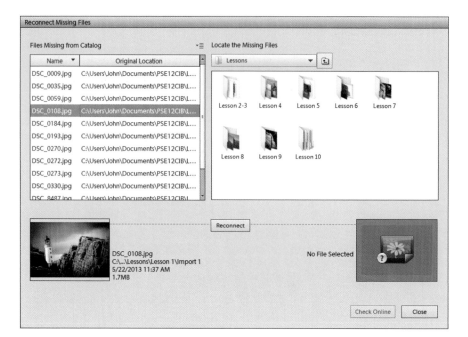

Note: Once you've created one or more Mobile Albums, which are stored online at Adobe Revel, the Check Online button becomes available, making it possible to reconnect missing files with their online copies.

5   Once you've verified a file or series of files to be reconnected, you can click the Reconnect button. For now, click Close to cancel the operation. Note that all of the thumbnails in the Media Browser now display the missing file icon (█).

6   Switch back to the Explorer / Finder; then, drag the Lesson 1 folder out of the Recycle Bin / Trash and return it to your Lessons folder.

Note: The missing file icons may persist until you next change the view or execute another command.

7   Switch back to the Organizer and choose File > Reconnect > All Missing Files. Photoshop briefly displays a message to let you know that there are no missing files to reconnect.

Switching between the Organizer and the Editor

Although the Instant Fix panel in the Organizer and the Quick Edit panel in the Full Screen view offer one-step tools for some of the most common editing tasks, you'll switch to the Editor for more sophisticated editing.

1   Select any two photos in the Media Browser.

Tip: Alternatively, right-click / Control-click either of the selected images, and choose Edit With Photoshop Elements Editor from the context menu.

2   To open the selected images in the Editor, either choose Edit > Edit With Photoshop Elements Editor, or click the Editor button (█) in the Task Bar.

You can switch back to the Organizer from the Editor just as easily, by clicking the Organizer button (█) in the Task Bar at the bottom of the Editor workspace.

The Editor workspace

The Editor provides a comprehensive, yet intuitive editing environment, with a choice of editing modes to satisfy users of any level of expertise, and a flexible workspace that can be customized to suit the way you prefer to work.

1   If your workspace arrangement differs from the illustration below, click the word Expert in the mode picker at the top of the workspace, and then choose Window > Reset Panels. If you don't see the photo thumbnails below the main image, click the Photo Bin button in the lower left corner of the Editor window.

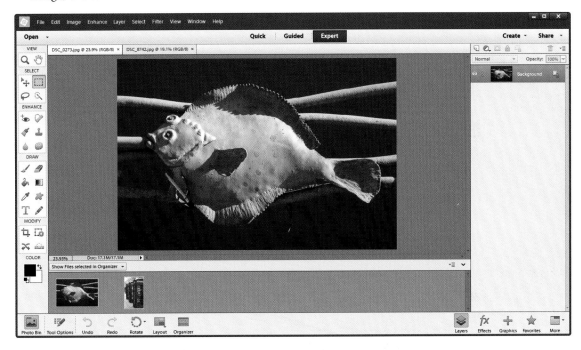

The central work area in the Editor is the Edit pane, where you'll adjust and enhance your images, and preview the projects and presentations that you create to showcase them.

2   In the edit mode picker immediately above the Edit pane, click Quick to enter Quick Edit mode. Note the simplified tool bar at the left. The right panel presents easy-to-use controls for six common image editing operations; click the small arrow beside each of the Quick Edit options in turn to expand and collapse the controls.

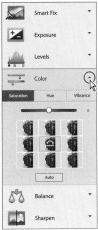

3 Click Guided in the edit mode picker above the Edit pane to switch to Guided Edit mode. The tool bar now hosts only the View tools; once you choose a guided task from the list, the tools you'll need for that operation are presented in the right panel together with easy step-by-step instructions that will help you learn as you work.

4 Click the arrows to the right of the Touchups, Photo Effects, and Photo Play categories in the right panel to collapse and expand the guided edit listings. Click to initiate a few of the procedures from each of the three guided edit categories. Read briefly through the steps and instructions for each operation, such as the Perfect Portrait procedure illustrated at the right; then, click Cancel to return to the list.

5 Click Expert in the edit mode picker to switch back to the Expert mode.

6 Below the Edit pane is the Photo Bin, which provides easy access to the images you're working with, no matter how many files you have open. Double-click each of the thumbnails in the Photo Bin in turn to bring that photo to the front in the Edit pane, making it the active image.

7 Choose Preferences > General from the Edit / Adobe Photoshop Elements Editor menu. On the General tab of the Preferences dialog box, click the check box to activate the option Allow Floating Documents In Expert Mode; then, click OK.

8 Drag whichever image is foremost by its name tab, away from its docked position to float above the Editor workspace.

9   Explore the options for arranging image windows that are available from the Window > Images menu, and from the menu on the Layout button (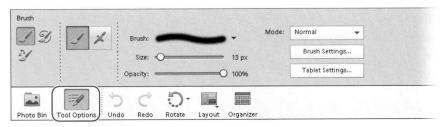) in the Task Bar at the bottom of the Editor workspace. You may wish to go back to the Organizer and open more files to develop a feel for the way you prefer to work with your image windows.

10 When you're done, choose Preferences > General from the Edit / Photoshop Elements Editor menu and disable floating documents in expert mode; then, click OK to close the Preferences dialog box.

The Edit mode tool bar includes tools for making precise selections, fixing image imperfections, drawing, painting, adding text, and creating special effects, conveniently grouped by function. You can hide and show the tool bar to free up screen space as you work by choosing Tools from the Window menu.

11 Click the Tool Options button in the Task Bar at the bottom of the Editor workspace to hide the Photo Bin and show the Tool Options pane in its place. In the tool bar, click to activate several of the tools in turn, noting the settings and controls available for each in the Tool Options pane.

12 Click the Photo Bin button at the left of the Task Bar to show the Photo Bin.

Working with panels and the Panel Bin

To the right of the Edit pane is the Panel Bin. In its default Basic mode, the Panel Bin displays one panel at a time.

1   Use the buttons in the Task Bar below the Panel Bin to switch the Panel Bin between the Layers, Effects, Graphics, and Favorites panels. The illustration at the right shows the Effects panel.

2   Click the More button (not the triangle beside it) at the far right of the Task Bar. The rest of the Editor panels appear in a tabbed group floating 'above' the workspace. Click the More button again to hide the floating panels; then, click the small triangle beside the More button and choose the Histogram from the menu. The floating panels group appears once more: this time, with the Histogram panel foremost.

You can also show and hide the floating panels by choosing any panel other than the Layers, Effects, Graphics, and Favorites panels from the Window menu.

3   Drag the Histogram panel out of the tabbed panel group by its name tab, and then drag the Navigator panel onto the tab bar of the Histogram panel, releasing the mouse button when the Histogram's tab bar is highlighted in blue.

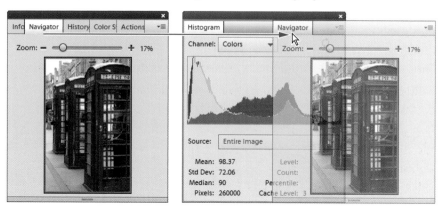

4   To close the Color Swatches panel, drag it free of the original group and click the close button (x) in its header bar (at the right on Windows, at the left for Mac OS), or click the small menu icon to the right of the name tab and choose Close from the panel's Options menu. Collapse the grouped Info, History, and Actions panels by double-clicking the name tab of any panel in the group.

5   To dock the two floating panel groups, drag the collapsed group onto the lower edge of the Histogram / Navigator group and release the mouse button when you see a blue line highlighting the connection between the two groups.
    To expand the lower group, click the name tab of any of the collapsed panels.

Tip: Single floating panels can also be grouped by docking them one above the other in this manner.

Note: Photoshop Elements remembers which panels you have dismissed, and the way you've grouped those that you use most often; your arrangement will persist until you use the Reset Panels command or switch between Basic and Custom modes.

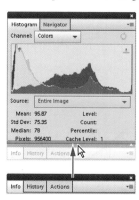
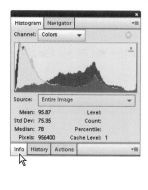
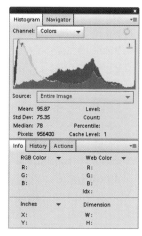

6   To separate the two tabbed panel groups again, drag the collapsed group away by its tab bar (not by any of the three name tabs).

Customizing the Panel Bin

If you're a dedicated user of the Expert editing mode, you may prefer to switch the workspace from Basic to Custom mode. The most important difference between the two working modes is that in Custom mode the panel bin can store and display more than one panel at a time—so you can dock your favorite floating panels in the Panel Bin, keeping them clear of the work area and ready at your fingertips without the need to use menu commands. You can group and arrange the panels you use most often in the Custom mode Panel Bin just as you did with floating panels in Basic mode. Panels left floating behave in the same way they do in Basic mode.

1 Click the small arrow beside the More button at the far right of the Task Bar and choose Custom Workspace from the pop-up menu.

In Custom mode, the Layers, Effects, Graphics, and Favorites buttons disappear from the Task Bar below the Panel Bin. The panels accessed by those buttons in the Basic mode—the Layers, Effects, Graphics and Favorites panels—are now docked in the Panel Bin by default; accessible by clicking their name tabs at the top of the Panel Bin. Other panels can be opened from the Window menu or from the menu on the More button at the far right of the Task Bar.

2 Choose Window > Navigator to open the floating panel group. Drag the Histogram panel out of the tabbed panel group by its name tab onto the tab bar of the Panel Bin, beside the four default tabs. Release the mouse button when the Panel Bin's tab bar is highlighted in blue.

3 Create a floating tabbed group containing the Navigator, History, and Actions panels, and then close the remaining panels. Drag the new panel group to the bottom edge of whichever panel is currently foremost in the Panel Bin and release the mouse button when you see a blue line indicating the new position.

4 Choose File > Close All to close both of the open images. Bring the Editor window back to the front; then, close it by clicking the Close button (in the top right corner of the workspace on Windows, at the upper left on Mac OS).

Getting help

Help is available in several ways, each one useful in different circumstances:

Help in the application The complete user documentation for Adobe Photoshop Elements is available from the Help menu, in the form of HTML content that displays in your default browser. This documentation provides quick access to information on using the various features in Photoshop Elements.

Help on the Web Even without invoking the Help menu commands, you can access the most comprehensive and up-to-date documentation and community discussions on Photoshop Elements via your default browser. Point your browser to http://helpx.adobe.com/photoshop-elements.html.

Help PDF Help and manuals are also available as PDF documents, optimized for printing; look for the PDF links under "Help and tutorials" on the main Photoshop Elements Help page (http://helpx.adobe.com/photoshop-elements.html).

Links in the application Within the Photoshop Elements application there are links to additional help topics, such as the hot-linked tips associated with specific panels and tasks. Look for the question mark icons.

Navigating Help

▶ **Tip:** If you search for a phrase, put quotation marks around the phrase. Make sure that your search terms are spelled correctly. If a search term doesn't yield results, try searching a synonym; for example "photo" instead of "picture."

Depending on which module you're working in, choose Help > Elements Organizer Help or Help > Photoshop Elements Help, or simply press the F1 key.

Click a topic heading in the table of contents. Click the plus sign (+) to the left of a topic heading to see its sub-topics. Click a topic or sub-topic to display its content. Type a search term in the Search text box under Adobe Community Help at the upper left of the Help page, and then press Enter on your keyboard.

Additional resources

Adobe Photoshop Elements 12 Classroom in a Book is not meant to replace the documentation that comes with the program, nor to be a comprehensive reference for every feature. Additional resources are listed in detail at the end of the Getting Started chapter in this book; please refer to these resources for comprehensive information and tutorials about program features.

You've reached the end of the first lesson. Now that you know how to import images, understand the concept of the catalog, and are familiar with the essentials of the Photoshop Elements interface, you're ready to start organizing and editing your photos in the next lessons.

Before you move on, take a few moments to read through the review questions and answers on the next page.

Review questions

1 What are the primary workspaces and working modes in Adobe Photoshop Elements?

2 What is a catalog file?

3 What are keyword tags?

4 How can you select multiple thumbnail images in the Media Browser?

Review answers

1 Photoshop Elements has two primary workspaces: the Elements Organizer and the Editor. You'll work in the Organizer to locate, import, manage, and share your photos, and use the Editor to adjust your images and to create presentations to showcase them. The Editor offers three editing modes: Quick edit, Guided edit, and Expert mode. Both the Organizer and the Editor provide access to the Create and Share modes.

2 A catalog file is where Photoshop Elements stores information about your images, enabling you to conveniently manage the photos on your computer from within the Organizer. For each image you import, Photoshop Elements creates a new entry in the catalog file. Whenever you assign a tag or a rating to a photo, or group images in an album, the catalog file is updated. All your work in the Organizer is recorded in the catalog file.

  As well as digital photographs, a catalog can include video and audio files, scans, PDF documents, and any presentations and layouts you might create in Photoshop Elements such as slide shows, photo collages, and CD jacket designs. A single catalog can efficiently handle thousands of files, but you can also create separate catalogs for different types of work.

3 Keyword tags are labels with personalized associations that you attach to photos, creations, and video or audio clips in the Media Browser so that you can easily organize and find them.

4 To select images that are in consecutive order in the Media Browser, click the first photo in the series, and then hold down the Shift key and click the last. All the photos in the range that you Shift-clicked will be selected. To select multiple non-consecutive files, hold down the Ctrl / Command key as you add files to the selection.

2 IMPORTING AND SORTING PHOTOS

Lesson overview

As your photo library grows, it becomes increasingly important that you have effective ways to organize and manage your pictures on your computer so that those valuable memories are always accessible. Adobe Photoshop Elements makes it easy to import photos from a variety of sources and provides powerful tools for organizing and searching your collection, including the People, Places, and Events views, where you can intuitively sort and search your images for the faces, locations, and happenings that mean the most to you.

This lesson will get you started with the essential skills you'll need to import images and keep track of your expanding image collection:

- Importing images from folders on your computer

- Importing photos from a digital camera

- Acquiring embedded images from a PDF

- Navigating the Media view

- Tagging faces and sorting photos in the People view

- Sorting photos by location in the Places view

- Grouping photos of special occasions in the Events view

 You'll probably need between one and two hours to complete this lesson. If you haven't already done so, you'll need to download the combined work files for Lessons 2 and 3 from the Lesson & Update Files tab of your Account page at www.peachpit.com.

Import photos to your catalog, and then explore the new People, Places, and Events views. You'll discover the many ways that the Organizer can help you to manage your image library so that you can always find exactly the photo you want, exactly *when* you want it—no matter how big your catalog, or across how many folders your media files are scattered.

Getting started

● **Note:** Before you start this lesson, make sure that you've set up a folder for your lesson files and downloaded the Lesson 2-3 folder from your Account page at www.peachpit.com, as detailed in "Accessing the Classroom in a Book files" in the chapter "Getting Started" at the beginning of this book. If you skipped Lesson 1, you'll also need to create a work catalog, and then download and import the Lesson 1 sample images in order to follow this lesson as written (see "Creating a catalog for working with this book" and "Getting photos from files and folders" in Lesson 1).

In this lesson you'll be working in the Elements Organizer, where you'll learn a variety of ways to import media into your catalog and begin to sort your image library.

1 If Photoshop Elements is still running from the previous exercise, switch to the Organizer now—if not, start Photoshop Elements, and then click the Organizer button to launch the Elements Organizer module.

2 Check the name of the current catalog, which is displayed in the lower right corner of the Organizer workspace. On Windows, you can also see the catalog name displayed in a tooltip that appears when you hold the pointer over the Elements Organizer icon at the upper left of the Organizer window.

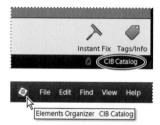

3 If the CIB Catalog that you created in Lesson 1 is not currently loaded, choose File > Manage Catalogs. Select the CIB Catalog from the list in the Catalog Manager dialog box, and then click Open.

4 If you don't see the CIB Catalog listed in the Catalog Manager, refer to "Creating a catalog for working with this book" in Lesson 1.

Getting photos

Before you process, print, or share your photos, the first step is to bring them into your catalog via the Elements Organizer. The Organizer provides a convenient, centralized workspace where you can browse, sort and manage all the images in your library, no matter where the files are stored on your computer.

In the following exercises you'll import the images for this lesson into your new catalog using a variety of different methods.

Perhaps the most direct and intuitive way to bring media files into the Organizer and add them to your catalog is to use the familiar drag-and-drop technique.

Dragging photos from Windows Explorer

1 Minimize the Organizer by clicking the Minimize button () at the right of the Organizer menu bar, or simply click the Elements Organizer application button on the Windows taskbar.

2 Open the My Computer window in Windows Explorer; either double-click the shortcut icon on your desktop, or choose My Computer from the Start menu.

3 Locate and open the PSE12CIB \ Lessons folder on your hard disk, and then open the downloaded subfolder named Lesson 2-3.

4 Inside the Lesson 2-3 folder you'll find three sub-folders: drag the subfolder Import 3 out of the Windows Explorer window and hold it over the Elements Organizer application button on the Windows taskbar.

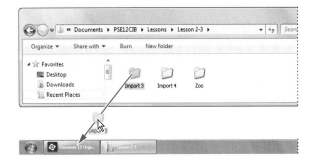

5 Wait until the Organizer becomes the foreground application; then, drag the Import 3 folder onto the Media Browser pane in the Organizer and release the mouse button. Skip to "Importing attached keyword tags" on the next page.

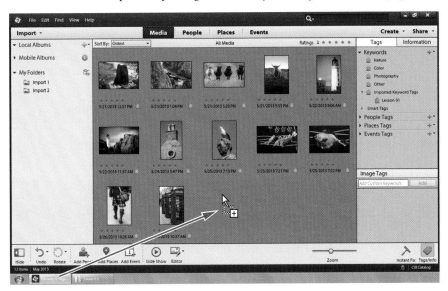

▶ **Tip:** If you can arrange the Windows Explorer window and the Organizer application window on your screen so that you can see both at once, you can simply drag the folder (or individual media files) directly from the Windows Explorer window into the Organizer, rather than going via the Windows taskbar.

Dragging photos from the Mac OS Finder

1 There are several ways to switch to the Finder on Mac OS. For this exercise, we'll use the Application Switcher. Hold down the Command key; then, press and release the Tab key. Continuing to hold down the Command key, click the Finder icon; then, release the Command key.

2 In the Finder, press Command+N to open a new Finder window. Navigate to and open the PSE12CIB / Lessons folder on your hard disk, and then open the downloaded subfolder named Lesson 2-3.

3 Inside the Lesson 2-3 folder are three subfolders: Import 3, Import 4, and Zoo. If necessary, move the finder window enough to see the Elements Organizer workspace behind it; then, drag the Import 3 subfolder onto the Media Browser pane and release the mouse button.

4 Photoshop Elements briefly displays a dialog box while searching inside the Import 3 folder for files to import; then, the Import Attached Keyword Tags dialog box opens. Click the Organizer workspace to bring it back to the front.

Importing attached keyword tags

Whenever you import photos that have already been tagged with keywords, the Import Attached Keyword Tags dialog box will appear, giving you the opportunity to specify which tags you wish to import with your images.

1 In the Import Attached Keyword Tags dialog box, click Select All; then, click OK.

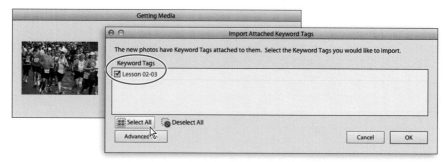

2 The Getting Media dialog box displays a progress bar as the Organizer imports the keywords. The Media Browser now shows only the newly imported images.

3 Make sure that the Details option is checked as activated in the View menu. Each thumbnail in the Media Browser is marked with a blue tag badge indicating that it has keywords attached.

4 If necessary, click the Tags/Info button at the right of the Task bar below the Media Browser to open the Tags, Image Tags, and Information panels. In the Tags panel, click the triangle beside the Imported Keyword Tags category to expand it and see the newly imported Lesson 02-03 tag nested inside, together with the keyword that you imported in the previous lesson.

Tip: If you still don't see the blue badges on the thumbnails in the Media Browser after activating View > Details, use the Thumbnail Size slider above the Media Browser to increase the size of the thumbnails.

5 Click the Back button at the upper left of the Media Browser, or the Clear button at the right, to display all the media in your catalog in the Media Browser.

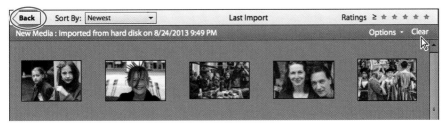

Automatically fixing red eyes during import

The term "red eye" refers to a phenomenon common in flash photography, where the light of the flash is reflected by the retinas at the back of the subject's eyes, so that the pupils appear red instead of black. In most cases, Photoshop Elements can fix the problem automatically during the import process, saving you the effort of further editing. This can be a substantial advantage when you're importing large numbers of images shot indoors or at night, such as photos from social occasions.

You'll import the photo for this exercise with the From Files And Folders menu command, as you did for the images in Lesson 1.

1 Click the Import button in the upper left of the Organizer workspace and choose From Files And Folders from the menu. Alternatively, choose File > Get Photos And Videos > From Files And Folders.

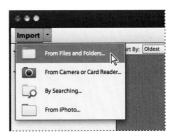

2 In the Get Photos And Videos From Files And Folders dialog box, navigate to and open the PSE12CIB / Lessons / Lesson 2-3 folder. Open the subfolder Import 4; then, click once to select the file Red_Eyes.jpg.

3 Click the check box to activate the Automatically Fix Red Eyes option. Make sure that the Automatically Suggest Photo Stacks option is disabled; then, click Get Media.

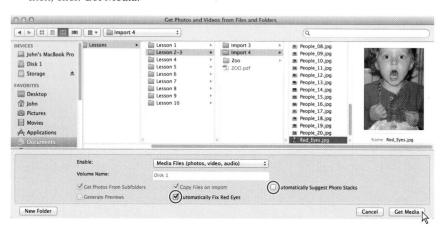

4 In the Import Attached Keyword Tags dialog box, click Select All; then, click OK.

5 The newly imported image appears in the Media Browser. If you don't see the name of the image file below the thumbnail, choose View > File Names.

The corrected photo has been stacked on top of the original in a *Version Set*. You can identify a Version Set by the badge in the upper right corner of the thumbnail, and also by the extension to the file name, which shows that the image has been edited. You'll learn more about working with Version Sets in Lesson 3.

▶ **Tip:** For some images, the automatic red eye fix may not be so effective; more tools and techniques for correcting the effect are discussed in Lesson 5.

6 Click the arrow at the right of the thumbnail once to expand the Version Set, and then again to collapse it.

Searching for photos to import

This import method is useful when you're not sure exactly where on your hard disk you've stashed your photographs and other media files over the years. You can run a search of every folder on your entire hard disk, or limit the search to a defined subset, such as your Documents folder. For the purposes of this exercise, you'll narrow the search to just a small branch of your folder hierarchy.

1   In the Organizer, choose File > Get Photos And Videos > By Searching. Under Search Options in the Get Photos And Videos By Searching dialog box, choose Browse from the Look In menu.

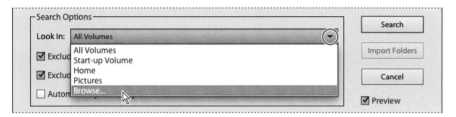

2   In the Browse For Folder / Select Folder For Search dialog box, locate and select your Lessons folder, and then click OK.

3   Under Search Options in the Get Photos And Videos By Searching dialog box, make sure the Automatically Fix Red Eyes option is disabled; then, click the Search button located at the upper right of the dialog box.

4   The Search Results box lists all folders inside the Lessons folder. Select the folder **Lessons / Lesson 2-3 / Import 4**. The preview pane at the right shows thumbnails of the contents of the selected folder. Click Import Folders.

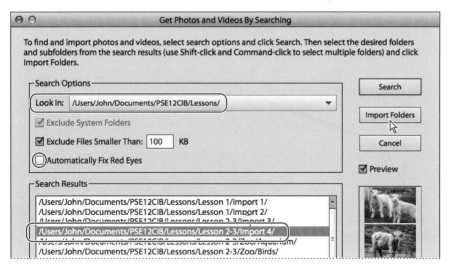

5   In the Import Attached Keyword Tags dialog box, activate the check box to confirm the Lesson 02-03 tag for import, and then click OK.

6 When the import process is complete, the Getting Media dialog box displays a message to let you know that two of the files in the Import 4 folder (the red eyes photo and its edited copy) were already in the catalog, and were therefore not imported. Each file that was not imported is listed, together with the reason it was excluded. Click OK.

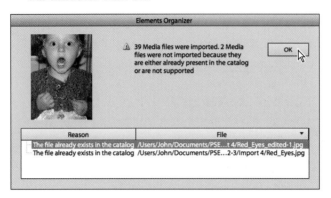

Importing images from iPhoto

On Mac OS, Photoshop Elements makes it easy to import your favorite photos, events, and albums from iPhoto. Click the Import button at the upper left of the Organizer workspace and choose From iPhoto. The Import From iPhoto dialog box gives you the option to bring your iPhoto events into Photoshop Elements, where they will be converted to albums. iPhoto albums will be imported by default.

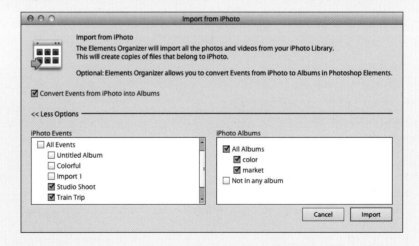

If you don't wish to import your entire iPhoto library, click More Options to specify which events and albums you want. The source folders for the photos imported from your iPhoto library will be added to the Folders panel.

Importing from a digital camera

If you have a digital camera or memory card at hand with your own photos on it, you can step through this exercise using those images. Alternatively, you can follow the process by reading through the steps and referring to the illustrations in the book, and then return to work through this set of exercises when you are prepared.

1 Connect your digital camera or card reader to your computer, following the manufacturer's instructions. If you're working on Mac OS, skip to step 3.

2 On Windows, the Auto Play dialog box may appear. You could choose the option Organize And Edit Using Adobe Elements Organizer 12 (and even specify this as the default action when you connect a camera), but for the purposes of this lesson, simply click the Close button to dismiss the dialog box. If the Photo Downloader dialog box appears automatically, you can skip to step 4; otherwise, continue to step 3.

> **Tip:** You can set AutoPlay to import to Elements Organizer by default. The AutoPlay dialog box will no longer appear when you connect your camera, but you can access the settings at any time on the Hardware And Sound pane in the Windows Control Panel.

3 Click the Import button at the upper left of the Organizer workspace and choose From Camera Or Card Reader.

4 In the Photo Downloader dialog box, choose the name of your connected camera or card reader from the Get Photos From menu.

5 Accept the default target folder listed beside Location, or click Browse / Choose to designate a different destination for the imported files.

6 From the Create Subfolder(s) menu, choose Today's Date (yyyy mm dd) as the folder name format; the Location path reflects your choice.

> **Tip:** On Windows, you can activate the Automatic Download option to have the Photo Downloader download your photos automatically whenever a camera or card reader is connected to your computer, using the default settings from your Elements Organizer Preferences.

7 Make sure that the Rename Files menu is set to Do Not Rename Files, and the Delete Options menu is set to After Copying, Do Not Delete Originals. If you're working on Windows, deactivate the Automatic Download option.

8 Click Get Media.

That's all there is to it!

With these basic Photo Downloader settings, the photos will be copied from your camera to a folder named with today's date, inside your default Pictures folder. Your photos will retain their camera-generated file names.

Advanced Photo Downloader options

In this exercise you'll explore some advanced options for importing photos from your camera that will help to keep your growing image library organized.

You can set up your camera import so that Photoshop Elements will automatically apply tags and create groups during the import process, which means that your images will already be organized by the time they arrive in your catalog!

If you have a digital camera or memory card at hand with your own photos on it, you can step through this first exercise using those images, otherwise, simply read through the process and refer to the illustrations in the book, and then return to this exercise when you are prepared.

▶ **Tip:** To get the best results from this exercise, your import should include several batches of pictures taken at different times on the same day.

1   Repeat steps 1 through 5 from "Importing from a digital camera" on the previous page to open the Photo Downloader, specify your camera as the import source, and accept the default destination for the downloaded files.

2   Without making any other changes to the settings, click the Advanced Dialog button in the lower left corner of the dialog box.

In advanced mode, the Photo Downloader Dialog displays thumbnail previews of all the photos on your camera's memory card, and also offers options for processing, tagging, and grouping your images during the import process.

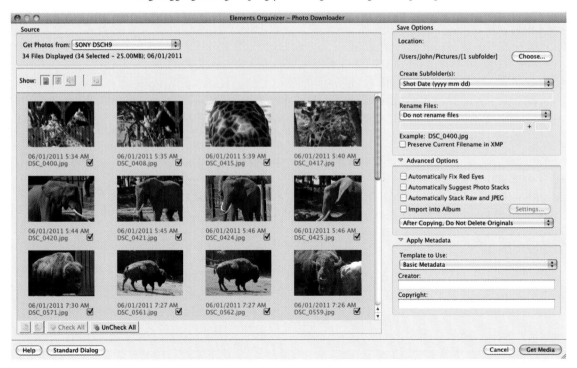

You can exclude a photo from the selection to be imported from your camera by clicking the check box below its thumbnail to remove the check mark.

In the next steps you'll set up the automatic creation of subfolders for the files copied from your camera and apply keyword tags to the images as they are imported.

3   Under Save Options, choose Custom Groups (Advanced) from the Create Subfolder(s) menu. Your selection is reflected in the Location pathname.

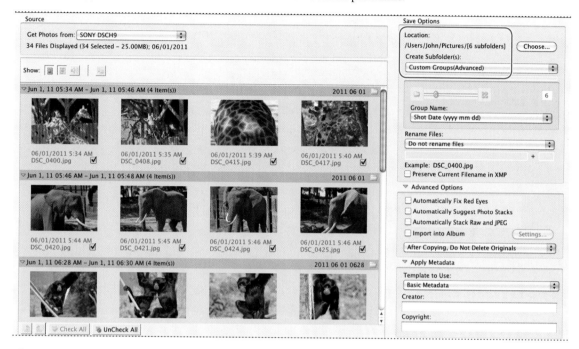

The images have been automatically divided into groups, based on capture time and date. A slider below the Create Subfolder(s) menu enables you to adjust the subdivision and the box to the right of the slider shows the resulting number of groups. In our example, the automatic capture time grouping has produced six groups.

4   Experiment by moving the slider to the left to generate fewer groups (subfolders) or to the right to generate more. Scroll down the list of thumbnails to review the effect of the slider on the grouping of your photos. Note that the number of groups created is displayed in the box to the right of the slider.

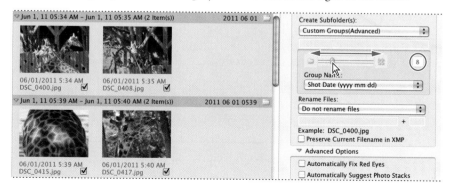

5 Next you'll specify custom names for the subfolders that will be automatically created to separate your grouped photos. From the options in the Group Name menu, choose Shot Date (yyyy mm dd) + Custom Name.

6 Click the Custom Name field at the right of the separator bar above each group in turn and type a descriptive name in the text box. In our example, we used the animal names **Giraffe**, **Elephant**, **Monkey**, and so on.

7 Under Advanced Options, activate the option Import Into Album by clicking the check box, and then click the adjacent Settings button. In the Select An Album dialog box, click the green plus sign icon, and then type a name for the new album. For now, you can click Cancel; you'll learn about creating and working with albums in Lesson 3.

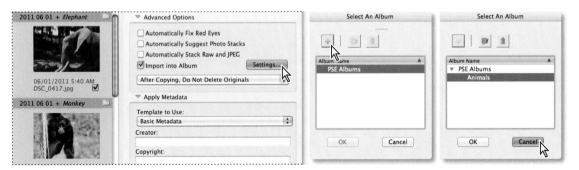

▶ **Tip:** The more you take advantage of these advanced options when importing your photos, the less time and effort you'll need to spend sorting and organizing images, and looking for the photos you want.

8 Click Get Media. The photos are copied to your hard disk, organized in sub-folders named for your custom import groups. If the Files Successfully Copied dialog box appears, click Yes.

The Getting Media dialog box appears briefly while the photos are being imported into your catalog. The imported images appear in the Media Browser and the Folders view now lists the new source subfolders, named according to the custom groups that you set up in the Photo Downloader dialog box.

Using watched folders on Windows

Watched folders are not supported for Mac OS; if you're working on Mac OS, you can skip to "Importing from a PDF document" on the next page.

On Windows, you can simplify and automate the process of keeping your catalog up to date by using watched folders. Designate any folder on your hard disk as a watched folder and Photoshop Elements will automatically be alerted when a new file is placed in—or saved to—that folder. By default, the My Pictures folder is watched, but you can set up any number of additional watched folders.

You can either choose to have any new files that are detected in a watched folder added to your catalog automatically, or have Photoshop Elements ask you what to do before importing the new media. If you choose the latter option, the message "New files have been found in Watched Folders" will appear whenever new items are detected. Click Yes to add the new files to your catalog or click No to skip them.

In this exercise you'll add a folder to the watched folders list.

1 Choose File > Watch Folders.

2 In the Watch Folders dialog box, click the check box to activate Watch Folders And Their Sub-Folders For New Files. Under Folders To Watch, click Add; then, navigate to and select your Lesson 2-3 folder and click OK.

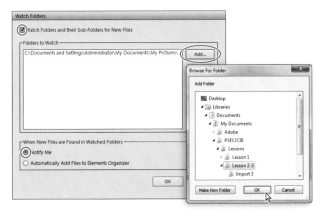

The Lesson 2-3 folder now appears in the Folders To Watch list. To stop a folder from being watched, select it in the list, and then click Remove.

3 Ensure that the Notify Me option is activated, and then click OK to dismiss the Watch Folders dialog box.

Whenever a media file is placed in, or saved to, your Lesson 2-3 folder or any of its subfolders, the Watched Folder Notification will appear, giving you the opportunity to import the file or exclude it. If you add a file to a watched folder when the Organizer is not running, the notification will appear the next time you launch the Organizer.

Importing from a PDF document

Photoshop Elements gives you the option to import either whole pages from a PDF document, or to select and extract just the images you want.

▶ **Tip:** If you can't see the file ZOO.pdf in the Open dialog box, click the Files Of Type menu (Windows) or Enable menu (Mac OS) at the bottom of the dialog box and choose either All Formats / All Readable Documents or Photoshop PDF.

1 Choose Edit > Deselect (Ctrl+Shift+A / Command+Shift+A) to ensure there are no images selected; then, click the Editor button (⬛) in the Task bar. Click Expert in the mode picker at the top of the Editor workspace; then, click the Photo Bin button (⬛) in the Task bar, if necessary, to show the Photo Bin.

2 In Expert mode in the Editor, choose File > Open. In the Open dialog box, navigate to your Lesson 2-3 folder, select the file ZOO.pdf, and then click Open. With Pages activated in the Select pane, choose Fit Page from the Thumbnail Size menu below the preview. Activate the Images option to set the Import PDF dialog box to import Images. Select Large from the Thumbnail Size menu.

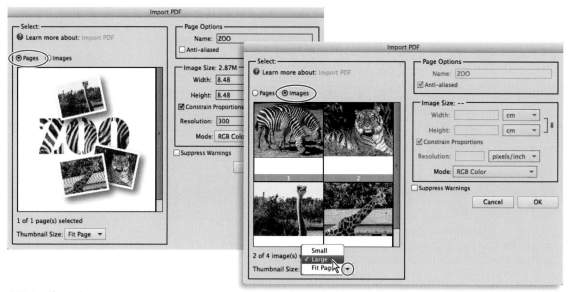

Note: If you choose to import entire pages from a PDF file with more than one page, you can use the same method to multiple-select the pages. Pages are rasterized (converted to bit-mapped graphics) according to your choice of image size, resolution, and color mode. The imported result will be an image similar to that acquired by scanning a printed document.

3 Ctrl-click / Command-click to select the images you wish to import. Click OK.

Each image imported from the PDF file opens in its own document window in the Editor. Thumbnails for the open files appear in the Photo bin below the Edit pane.

If you choose to import entire pages from a PDF file with more than one page, you can use the same method to multiple-select the pages. The pages extracted from the PDF file are rasterized (converted to bit-mapped graphics) at your choice of image size, resolution, and color mode.

4 Choose File > Close All. Click the check box to activate the Apply To All option, and then click No / Don't Save.

5 Choose File > Exit / Adobe Photoshop Elements Editor > Quit to close the Editor and return to the Organizer.

Sorting your photos

When you call one of your favorite photos to mind, chances are that your first thoughts will be of the people in the picture, the location where you shot it, and the occasion that took you there. You can probably answer who, where, and when, or at least two of these questions, for the majority of your photographs. In the new People, Places, and Events views in the Elements Organizer, Photoshop Elements makes it easy for you to sort, tag, and then search the photos in your library in terms of those faces, places, and happenings that mean the most to you.

Up to this point, your time in the Organizer has been spent in the Media view, where you can review all the images in your catalog, or see the contents of a single album or folder. You'll learn more about working in the Media view in Lesson 3; for now, we'll continue our exploration of the Organizer with a look at the People view and a test-drive of Photoshop Elements' powerful face recognition tools.

Automatically finding faces for tagging

Undoubtedly, your growing photo library will include many photos of your family, friends, and colleagues. Photoshop Elements makes it quick and easy to tag the faces in your pictures with the People Recognition feature, taking most of the work out of sorting and organizing a large portion of your catalog.

People Recognition automatically finds the people in your photos and makes it simple for you to tag them. Once you begin using the People Recognition feature, Photoshop Elements learns to recognize the people you've already named and will automatically tag their faces whenever they appear in new photos.

Setting up People Recognition

Both the People Recognition feature, and also the automatic face tagging prompts that it generates, can be disabled. Before continuing with the exercises, you need to make sure that both are activated.

1 In the Organizer, choose Edit > Preferences > Media-Analysis (Windows) / Elements Organizer > Preferences (Mac OS).

2 In the Media-Analysis pane of the Preferences dialog box, make sure that the options Analyze Photos For People Automatically and Analyze Media For Visual Search Automatically are both activated. Click OK to save your settings and close the Preferences dialog box.

3 In the View menu, make sure the People Recognition option is activated.

4 For the purposes of the following exercises, make sure that the Sort By menu at the left of the bar above the Media Browser is set to Oldest.

Tagging faces in the Media Browser

Your first experience of People Recognition will probably be the "Who Is This?" prompt that appears as you move the pointer over a photo in the enlarged single image view in the Media Browser.

● **Note:** Once People Recognition begins to recognize a particular face, the "Who is this?" hint changes to read "Is this Emma?," giving you the opportunity to confirm or cancel automatic tagging.

People Recognition displays these hints to help you identify and tag all the people in your photos. You can ignore or disable the hints if you wish, but remember that the more people you identify, the smarter People Recognition gets at tagging the faces of your friends and family automatically.

1   In the Folders list at the left of the Organizer workspace, click the Import 4 folder. The Media Browser is filtered to display only the contents of that folder.

2   Scroll down in the Media Browser—or reduce the size of the thumbnails using the Zoom slider in the Task bar—to locate the image People_16.jpg; then, double-click the thumbnail to see the photo enlarged in the single image view.

3   Move the pointer over the image; white boxes appear around any faces detected in the photo. People Recognition has found four of the five faces in this picture. Move the pointer over any of the boxes; the "Who is this?" prompt appears.

If you don't see the face tagging boxes when you move the pointer over the photo in single image view, it may be that Photoshop Elements has not yet analyzed your recently imported photos. By default, the auto analysis process is triggered for new images when you click the Add People button to begin batch-tagging the faces in your photos, but for this exercise, you can kick-start it from the single image view.

If you already see the face tagging boxes, read through the next three steps, in case you should encounter this situation in the future; you'll rejoin the action in step 7.

4   To initiate the People Recognition analysis, click the Mark Face button in the Task bar at the bottom of the workspace.

5   An alert message appears to let you know that the photo has not yet been analyzed. Click Yes to start the auto analysis process.

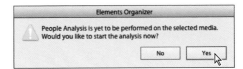

6   A People Recognition dialog box opens, asking you to name or confirm faces; you'll see this again later when you switch to People view. For now, click Cancel.

7   Click the "Who is this?" text below the face tagging box for the girl on the left. Type the name **Emma**, and then press Enter / return to commit the tag.

When you press Enter / return, a blue People tag badge appears briefly in the lower left corner of the enlarged photo, confirming that Photoshop Elements has created a new tag for Emma.

8   Type **Kat** to tag the mother, **Sophie** for the daughter beside her, and **Lilly** for the one shading her eyes. Be sure to press Enter / return to commit each tag.

9   If necessary, click the Tags/Info button at the far right of the Task bar to open the right panel group. Note that the Image Tags panel shows that this photo now has five tags: the keyword tag Lesson 02-03, and the four new *People tags* you created in this exercise.

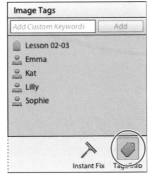

As you can see, People tags display a different badge from the standard keyword tag icon. This makes the photos that are already tagged for people easy to spot in the thumbnail grid.

10 Keep the photo open in single image view for the next exercise.

Tagging undetected faces

The People Recognition analysis occasionally misses faces that are partially obscured, "broken up" by harsh light and shadow, or photographed at an angle or in profile. You can tag undetected people manually in the single image view.

1 Click the Mark Face button in the Task bar below the enlarged image.

2 Drag the new tagging box onto the face that was not detected, and then use the handles on the box to resize it so that it frames the face neatly. Type **Pauline** in the "Who is this?" text box; then, click the green check mark to confirm the tag.

People Recognition will sometimes incorrectly identify a chance arrangement of light and shadow as a face. In this image, this has happened with the folds in the jacket sleeve of the girl on the left.

▶ **Tip:** You can use the same method to cancel the tagging prompt for a stranger's face, so that Photoshop Elements will no longer ask for a name for that person.

3 Click the X button on the extraneous tagging box to dismiss it; otherwise People Recognition will continue to register this pattern as a person not yet named.

4 Press the right arrow key on your keyboard twice to navigate to the black and white photo of a girl seated on a stone lion.

5 Move the pointer over the image and click the "Who is this?" prompt; then, type the letter **L**. A drop-down menu appears, offering the Lilly tag—the only People tag in your catalog that begins with an "L." Click the Lilly tag to accept it.

6 Double-click the image, or click the Grid button (◀ **Grid**) in the bar above the single image view to return the Media Browser to the thumbnail view, which is still filtered to display only the 40 photos the Import 4 folder.

Tagging faces in batches

When you want to do some serious face tagging, you can let People Recognition help you bulk-process your files, rather than working through your catalog one image at a time in single image view. In this exercise, you'll make a start by tagging the people in just a subset of the photos in your catalog.

1   Click the All Media button (All Media) in the bar above the Media Browser.

The Import 4 folder is no longer selected in the Folders list. The Media Browser now displays all of the photographs in your catalog; the file count in the lower left corner of the workspace shows the total number of images in your CIB Catalog.

The file names of the photos you'll use in this exercise all include the word "people." You can start by using a text search to isolate these images in the media Browser.

2   Click in the text search box at the right end of the menu bar (Windows) / the application window header (Mac OS) and type **people**. The search results bar immediately above the Media Browser shows that your catalog has been filtered so that the Media Browser displays only items matching your search.

3   Click the Add People button (👤) in the Task bar below the Media Browser. The first of a sequence of People Recognition dialog box opens.

Add People: first screen - Windows

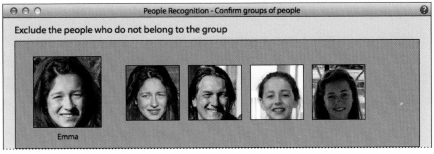

Add People: first screen - Mac OS

Note: Depending on your operating system and how much experimenting you've been doing, the results you see from People Recognition may not be exactly the same as those referred to and illustrated in these exercises. The illustrations at the left show different aspects of the tagging process offered at the very beginning of the Add People procedure on different machines; the sequence of dialog boxes and the order of the faces presented may vary, but the overall process will be the same.

If the first People Recognition screen that you see is the Confirm Groups Of People dialog box, skip ahead to step 7, and then return to step 4 when you encounter the Label People dialog box.

4 Click the "Who is this?" prompt under any of the faces. People Recognition makes tagging suggestions, drawing from names already tagged in your catalog. If you see the name you want, simply click to apply it.

5 If you don't see the right name, start typing in the text box to see existing tags that match the letters you type. Name all of the faces in the first batch; then, click Save at the lower right of the dialog box. If the Label People dialog box presents a new batch of faces, repeat the process. If the Confirm Groups Of People dialog box opens, read through the next step before taking action.

▶ **Tip:** If there is no existing People tag that matches the name you've started typing (as is the case for Tom, the father in this family), finish typing the name and press Enter / return to create the new tag.

6 If you're asked to identify a face you don't know, you can ignore it and try again next time it's presented, or dismiss it so that People Recognition no longer asks for a name. To exclude a stranger's face, move the pointer over the thumbnail and click the X button that appears in the upper right corner, or click the lower right corner of the image and choose from the menu. Use the same menu to reinstate a face excluded by mistake. When you're done, click Save; then, continue the process. Be patient—People Recognition is getting smarter with every click!

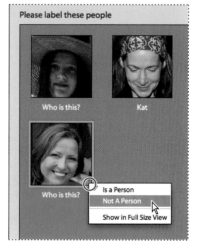

Despite very few photos having been tagged, People Recognition is already learning to recognize the faces in the lesson images; at some point it will switch to Confirm Groups Of People mode, collating groups of faces that match known people, and then offering you the option to exclude faces that don't belong in those groups.

7   To exclude a face that doesn't belong in a proposed group (or multiple selected faces), click the lower right corner of the thumbnail and choose from the menu. Click Save. After two or three cycles, the Label People Dialog box will reappear.

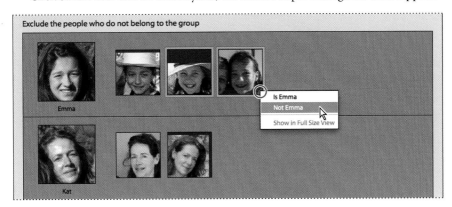

8   In the People Recognition - Label People dialog box, tag as many of the faces as you can. If you need to type a name, be sure to press Enter / return.

People Recognition alternates between its Confirm Groups and Label People modes, until you're presented with a set of dimmed images like those in the illustration below. These may be faces obscured by shadows, hands, or sunglasses—or chance arrangements of light and shadow that have triggered the face detection algorithms. This time you're being asked which images to *include* as faces, rather than exclude.

9   To include one of these images as a face, either click the thumbnail itself or move the pointer over it, click the arrow button, and choose Is A Person from the menu. Use the same menu to exclude a face included mistakenly. Click Save.

10 Photoshop Elements will notify you when the tagging session is completed. Click OK to dismiss the completion message and return to the Media Browser; then, click Clear at the right of the search results bar to clear the "people" text search and see the unfiltered contents of your catalog in the Media Browser.

> **Tip:** Saving your work in small chunks as you go means that you can cancel a long tagging session at any stage in the process, and then pick it up where you left off later.

 **Note:** You'll be returned to the Label People dialog box to tag any faces that you decided to include. Images you ignore or dismiss here will no longer be seen as faces by People Recognition.

Importing Facebook friends as People tags

When it's time to set up a Photoshop Elements catalog for your photos, you can speed up the process of tagging the people in your photos by downloading your Friends list from Facebook. Photoshop Elements converts your Facebook friends to People tags.

The next time you begin to type a name in a tagging box, Photoshop Elements will include the names of any of your Facebook friends that match the letters you've typed in the drop-down menu of existing People tags.

Once you've tagged a photo with the name of a Facebook friend, it will appear in the "Who is this?" suggestions and in the Advanced Search criteria for People, just like any other People tag.

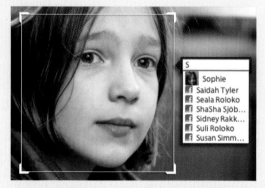

1   Launch your default web browser and log in to your Facebook account. (This step is not essential, but it will make the process smoother: you won't need to switch between the Organizer and your browser to log in later.)

2   In the Media browser, select at least one photo with untagged faces, and then click the Add People button in the Task bar. In the People Recognition – Label People dialog box, click the Download/Update Facebook Friends List To Name People button at the lower left.

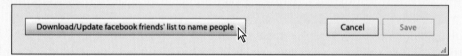

3   Click through the dialog boxes asking you to authorize Photoshop Elements to access your Facebook account. The authorization sequence may vary slightly, depending on your web browser and Facebook account settings, but the process is self-explanatory.

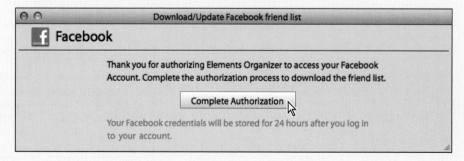

Welcome to the People view

Now that you've tagged a few of the faces in your catalog, you can begin to have some fun in the People view, where your photo library is automatically sorted by personnel, making it easy to answer the first question you're likely to ask about the photo you're looking for: Who?

Note: The People view remains empty until you've tagged at least one person in one photo.

1   Click the word People in the view picker at the top of the Organizer workspace.

With no folder selected, the People view filters your entire catalog and displays a stack of photos for each person you've tagged. By default, the first image tagged with a newly created People tag becomes that person's profile picture—the photo that appears on top of their stack in People view and also on their People tag icon.

2   Move the pointer slowly across each stack thumbnail in turn to quickly browse through all the images tagged with the same name. For each of the People stacks, stop the pointer when you see your favorite photo of that person, and then right-click / Control-click the thumbnail and choose Assign As Profile Picture.

Tip: You can also choose from a People stack's context menu to remove that person's tag from the stack, or to rename the People tag for that person. This can be useful for changing the tags imported from your Facebook friends list so that they display first names only, or for substituting a nickname.

Tagging faces in the People view

If you click the Add People button (👥) in the Task bar now, with no source folder or album selected, People Recognition will scan your entire catalog for every person it can find and initiate another face tagging session. To save time in this exercise, you'll search your catalog for more pictures of just one of our tagged people.

1. Double-click the Sophie stack in the People view. The stack expands so that the People view displays all of the images tagged with Sophie.

Note: In the example illustrated at the right, the Find More command has returned one sure match and a selection of possibilities. You may see a different selection of images, depending on how successfully you identified Sophie earlier.

2. Click the Find More button (👥) in the Task bar. The People Recognition dialog box opens in "Confirming Sophie" mode. Use the techniques you practiced earlier to either confirm faces for tagging or exclude them. Click Save to add your choices to the Sophie stack in the People view.

3. Work your way through any further groups of candidates presented; People Recognition will inform you when all the photos including Sophie have been tagged. Click OK to exit tagging mode.

4. If the expanded People stack shows only thumbnails of Sophie's face, click the switch at the left of the actions bar above the thumbnails to change the view mode from Faces to Photos; the view displays the full photos featuring Sophie.

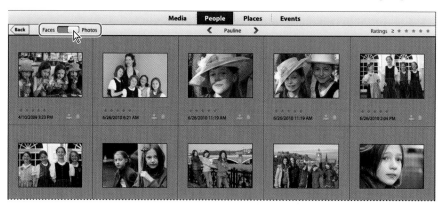

5. Double-click any of the images featuring Sophie to see it enlarged in the single image view. Use the left- and right-arrow keys on your keyboard to navigate through the photos in the stack. When you're done, click the Grid button (Grid) in the bar above the image to see all of the Sophie photos once again. Click the Back button (Back) to see all the People stacks.

Working with People groups

You can make your People tagging more versatile by grouping your tags. You might find photos of the same person by looking in her personal stack, by filtering your Friends group, or by searching a group created for your basketball team.

1 Click the switch at the left of the actions bar to change the viewing mode from People to Group. A header bar above the People stacks indicates that all six people are ungrouped. If you don't see the Groups panel at the right of the workspace, click the Groups button (icon) in the Task bar.

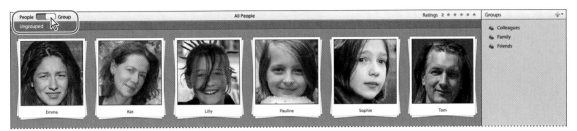

2 Ctrl-click / Command-click to select all six People stacks, and then drag them to the Family group in the Groups panel. The header bar above the People stacks shows that all six people in your catalog are now listed in that group.

3 Click the green Create New People Groups button (icon)—not the arrow beside it—in the header of the Groups panel. In the Add Group dialog box, type **Kids** to name the group and choose Family from the Group menu. Click OK.

4 Select the stacks for the four sisters and drag them to the new Kids group. The stacks in the People view are now divided under two group headers.

5 Right-click / Command-click the Kids group in the Groups list and choose Add Group from the menu. Name the new group **Twins**. "Kids" is already selected as the group inside which the new group will be listed. Click OK.

6 Select the Pauline and Sophie stacks. Drag the Twins tag from the Groups panel onto either of the selected stacks. The People view now shows three groups.

● **Note:** Clicking a group in the Groups list does not filter the stacks displayed in the People view—although it will scroll the view to show you the people in that group amongst the rest. All the stacks in your catalog, or in a selected source folder, are displayed in the People view at all times. The Groups list is not a tool for searching your catalog, but rather an aid to navigating and managing your tags in the People view.

7 Click Media in the view picker at the top of the workspace to return to the Media Browser. You'll learn more about the People view in Lesson 3.

Sorting photos by location

Think of that favorite photo again. You've answered "Who?"—now, lets ask "Where?" Photoshop Elements lets you organize your world in the Organizer's new Places view, where you can put your photographs on the map (quite literally!), making it fun to follow the trail of a family road trip or revisit memories of an exotic vacation.

Adding Places tags to your photos

In this exercise you'll create some new *Places*: saved locations that you can attach to your photos as tags, so that it's quick and easy to find that shot you took … where?

1   In the Media Browser, isolate the images for this lesson by typing the word **run** in the text search box at the top of the workspace. The search results bar above the thumbnails shows that your catalog has been filtered so that the Media Browser is displaying only those photos that match your search. Shift-click, or drag a selection marquee, to select the first ten photos in the Media Browser.

2   Click the Add Places button ( ) in the Task bar below the Media Browser.

3   In the Add Places dialog box, type **Manhattan** in the Search box above the map pane. If the location suggestions menu does not appear quickly, click Search. Choose the suggestion with the most detailed location information so that Photoshop Elements can reference it for tagging: Manhattan, New York, NY, USA.

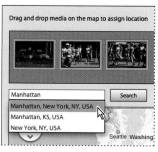

4   The map zooms in and centers on Manhattan. Click the green check mark on the message above the search result pin to add all ten photos to the new location.

5   An image count appears on the new pin, indicating that the operation was successful. Click Done to close the Add Places dialog box.

Note: In the Tags panel, the Manhattan tag is colored differently from the United States and New York tags; this indicates that it's the only tag with GPS data and a marker pin on the Places view map.

In the Media Browser, the selected photos are now marked with map-pin Places badges. Click the Tags/Info button at the far right of the Task bar, if necessary, to open the right panel group. In the Tags panel, Expand the Places Tags category to see the listings for your new Places tags.

Adding photos to a saved location

You can use the Places tags in the Tags panel to search your photos, and also to quickly add more images to a group that you've already placed on the map.

1   In the Media Browser, select the nine photos that have yet to be placed.

2   Drag the United States tag from the Places Tags list in the Tags panel to any of the selected photos. Alternatively, you could drag the photos onto the tag.

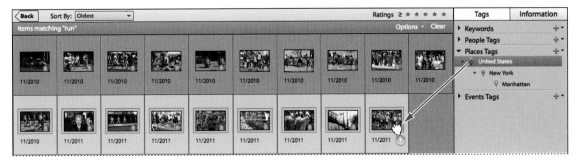

3   Hold the mouse over the Places tag badge on any of the selected photos; a tooltip lists the United States tag. To remove the new tag from all the selected photos, right-click / Control-click the Places tag badge and choose Remove From United States Place.

4   With the nine un-placed photos still selected, drag the Manhattan tag from the Places Tags list to any of the selected photos. Hold the mouse over the Places tag badge; the tooltip shows that applying the Manhattan tag has automatically added all three tags in the hierarchy.

5   Click the Back button (Back) in the bar above the thumbnails to show all of the photos in your catalog in the Media Browser.

A short trip to the Places view

The Places view displays only those images in your catalog that have location data. Now that you've added some Places tags, you can begin exploring.

1   Click the word Places in the view picker at the top of the workspace.

The arrangement of the Places view workspace depends on the way it was left the last time you visited. Follow the directions in the next three steps to set up the workspace to match what's described and illustrated in this exercise.

2   If the right panel is not open in the Places view, click the Map button ( ) at the right of the Task bar below the thumbnail grid.

3   If the Map panel is significantly narrower in relation to the rest of the workspace than it is in the illustration below, move the pointer over the left edge of the panel; then, when the pointer changes to a double-arrow cursor, click carefully on the edge of the map and drag to the left to make it wider.

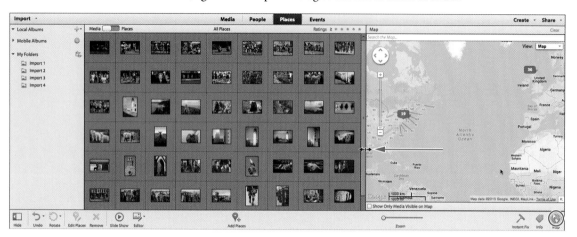

Note: Remember that the Places view can show only those images in your catalog that have GPS location data. The Places view will remain empty until you either place media on the map or import photos that have embedded GPS data.

4   If you don't see two pins on the map, drag the map's zoom slider to the minimum setting or drag the map itself to reposition it. Use the Zoom slider in the Task bar to reduce the size of the thumbnails to see as many images as possible.

The image counts on the map pins show that there are 19 photos placed at New York and another 36 images attached to a pin located in Scotland.

5   Click the pin positioned on Scotland to select all the attached photos in the thumbnail grid. Click the Show Media prompt above the selected pin to filter the Places view so that it displays *only* the photos attached to that pin.

6   Click the All Places button at the left of the actions bar above the thumbnails to see every image in your catalog that is attached to a pin anywhere on the map.

Tip: If ever the map doesn't jump when you tell it to, or a pin seems to get lost in the move, choose View > Refresh.

7   Drag the map to the left so that the USA is moved completely outside the frame, then click any of the unselected New York marathon photos. The map pans so that the view is centered on the Place that you created earlier in the lesson.

Generating Places tags for photos with GPS data

Places tags are created automatically for photos placed on the map using the Add Places command, as you did for the New York photos. However, when you import photos with embedded GPS coordinates—like our 36 Scotland images—Photoshop Elements shows them on the map but does not generate searchable Places tags. If you wish to generate tags for photos like these, you need to edit their location.

1   Click the Scotland pin to select all the associated images, and then click the Edit Places button () in the Task bar.

2   In the Edit Places dialog box, drag the map to center the selected pin. Use the zoom button (+) to zoom in two or three clicks, until the marker splits to show two separate location pins and you can see the names of major cities. Click away from the pins to deselect them both, together with all of the associated images in the Photo Bin.

3   Click the southern pin to select the 18 photos attached to that location; then, type **Edinburgh** in the Search box above the map pane and click Search. Click the location suggestion **Edinburgh, City Of Edinburgh, UK**; then, click the green check icon to confirm the placement of 18 photos at that location.

4   Click the any of the un-selected images in the Photo Bin at the top of the Edit Places window to focus the map on the other location to the north. Click the pin to select all 18 attached photos; then, zoom in by two or three clicks. Drag the location pin north and west to position it slightly closer to the coastline.

5   Click the green check icon to confirm the operation; then click Done to close the Edit Places dialog box. In preparation for the next exercise in the Places view, zoom the map out as far as it will go, and then drag it to the right so that the United Kingdom is no longer visible. Click Media in the view picker to return to the Media Browser; then, choose Edit > Deselect.

In the Tags panel, the new tags are listed under Places Tags. Each level is listed alphabetically; so that United Kingdom appears above United States and Highland above Scotland.

6   Right-click / Control click the tag B8021 (the name of the closest road) and choose Rename. In the New Name box, type **Rua Reidh**.

> **Tip:** Depending on your operating system, you may not see the "Highland" tag listed. This should not affect the overall flow of this lesson, but if you wish to try again, right-click / Control-click the United Kingdom tag and choose Delete; then, repeat this exercise.

Grouping photos as Events

When was your favorite photo taken? Was it at an anniversary dinner? Before your daughter's school concert? Or during a week-long tropical cruise? The new Events view in Elements Organizer helps you tag your photos by occasion, making it even simpler to search your image library for all those precious memories.

Creating Events from the Media Browser

You can select the images from a particular occasion in the thumbnail grid, and then create a new Event to group them, without leaving the Media Browser.

▶ **Tip:** If you don't see the capture dates and file names below the thumbnails, choose View > Details, and then View > File Names.

1 Check the actions bar above the Media Browser to make sure that the Sort By order is set to Oldest. Type **festival** in the text search box at the top of the workspace. The Media Browser shows fifteen photos captured on the same date. Select the first five photos in the series and click the Add Event button ( ) in the Task bar below the Media Browser.

2 In the Add New Event panel at the right type **Medieval Fair** to name the new Event. You won't need to alter the date settings; Photoshop Elements has automatically set both the start and end dates to the capture date of the selected photos. When you click the Add Event button without first selecting a group of photos, you can set the start and end dates manually by clicking the calendar buttons at the right. Click Done at the right of the Task bar to confirm the new Event.

3 In the Tags panel, expand the Events Tags category to see the new event.

4 Select the next 9 photos in the Media Browser, leaving the last image in the series, Festival_15.jpg, un-selected. To add the selected photos to the newly created event, either drag the Medieval Fair tag from the Tags panel to any of the selected images or drag the selection from the thumbnail grid onto the tag.

An invitation to the Events view

Do you like weddings? Sporting events? Street festivals? Road trip vacations? We've got them all ... what are you waiting for?

1 Click Events in the view picker at the top of the Organizer workspace to switch to the Events view. The default view mode is unpopulated until you've saved at least one event—currently, its only occupant is the new Medieval Fair stack.

Right now, you're probably thinking "Where's the promised sports and scenic views? Bring on the bride!" Patience, *please*—we're not yet done with the parade.

2   Move the pointer slowly across the Medieval Fair stack to see all the images in this Event. Stop the pointer when you see your favorite photo from the set. To make this photo the top image in the stack, right-click / Control-click it and choose Set As Cover.

Adding photos to an Event

1   Double-click the Medieval Fair event stack to see all of the photos it contains, and then click the Add Media button (🖼) in the Task bar at the bottom of the workspace.

2   Under Basic at the left of the Add Media dialog box, make sure that All Media is set as the image source. The source images in the Add Media dialog box are ordered from newest to oldest so you'll need to scroll down to find the festival photos. Click to select the image Festival_15.jpg, a rear view of a parade musician in an orange jacket and plumed hat. Click Add Selected Media at the bottom of the dialog box; then, click Done.

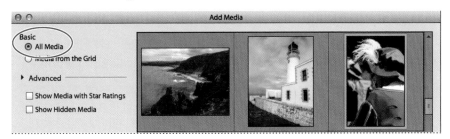

3   Check the image count in the lower left corner of the workspace; there are now 15 images in this Event. Collapse the event by clicking the Back button (◁ Back).

Getting smart about creating Events

You can avoid the effort of locating the images for a new Event manually by letting Photoshop elements find the important occasions in your catalog automatically.

1   Select the Import 3 folder in the left panel; then, click the switch in the actions bar to switch from the default Events view to Smart Events mode.

In Smart Events mode, Photoshop Elements suggests likely Event stacks amongst the photos in your catalog—or in a selected folder—on the basis of capture dates. Smart Events has separated the New York marathon photos into two stacks.

2   Right-click / Control-click each of these stacks in turn and choose Name Event(s) from the context menu. Check the dates on the two stacks and name the new Events **NY Marathon 2010** and **NY Marathon 2011**.

3   The other suggested stack has 19 photos shot at a wedding. Select this stack; then, click the Name Events button (1̲) in the Task bar and name the new Event **Annie's Wedding**. Click OK.

▶ **Tip:** You won't see event names displayed on the stacks in Smart Events mode; they'll become visible when you switch back to the default Events view.

4 Click the Import 4 folder in the left panel. The third smart event stack contains 4 photos dated 6/26/2010 that belong in the Annie's Wedding event. Double-click the stack to expand it; then, select all four images and click Media in the view picker at the top of the workspace to switch to the Media view.

5 Drag the selected photos to the Annie's Wedding tag in the Tags panel; then, click the All Media button (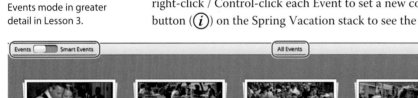) above the Media Browser and click Events in the view picker to return to the Events view in Smart Events mode.

Creating long Events

… And now it's time for that promised road trip.

1 Scroll down, if necessary, to find the five adjacent Smart Event stacks dated 5/21/2013 through 5/26/2013. Shift-click to select all five stacks.

2 Click the Name Events button (1) in the Task bar. In the Name Event dialog box, type **Scottish Road Trip** to name the new Event. Photoshop Elements has already set the start and end dates for the combined Smart Events to the capture dates of the oldest and most recent photos in the selection. Type **you take the high road** in the Description box; then, click OK to create the Event.

3 Click the switch to move from Smart Events mode to the regular Events view.

> **Note:** You'll return to look at the Smart Events mode in greater detail in Lesson 3.

4 Move the pointer slowly across each stack to review the contents, and then right-click / Control-click each Event to set a new cover photo. Click the Info button (*i*) on the Spring Vacation stack to see the description you entered.

5 Click Media in the view picker to switch back to the Media Browser.

Congratulations! In this lesson you've learned a variety of ways to import media files into your Photoshop Elements catalog, and then used the People, Places, and Events views to sort and tag your images so that finding a photo will be as easy as asking "Who, where, and when?" In the next lesson you'll look at ways to add even deeper levels of organization to your catalog and discover how to locate exactly the file you want—the payoff for all this organizing! Before you move on, take a minute or two to read through the review questions and answers on the facing page.

Review questions

1 Name three ways to import photos from your computer hard disk into your catalog.

2 What is a "watched folder"? (Windows users only.)

3 Is there a way to generate searchable Places tags for photos imported with GPS data?

4 How can you add photos to an existing Person, Place or Event?

Review answers

1 This lesson demonstrated three ways to import photos from your hard disk:

- Drag-and-drop photographs from a Windows Explorer / Finder window into the Media Browser pane in the Organizer window.

- In the Organizer, choose File > Get Photos And Videos > From Files And Folders, or choose the same command from the menu on the Import button at the upper left of the workspace.

- Choose By Searching, from either of the menus mentioned above, and then select the folder on the hard disk that you wish Photoshop Elements to search.

2 If you designate a folder on your computer as watched, Photoshop Elements is automatically alerted when new photos are saved or added to that folder. By default, the My Pictures folder is watched.

3 Although Photoshop Elements will pin photos imported with embedded GPS data on the Places view map, it doesn't automatically generate corresponding Places tags as it does for photos that you place manually. To generate searchable tags for these photos, you need to re-locate them on the map. Select the photos in the Places view; then, click the Edit Places button in the Task bar. In the Edit Places dialog box, either move the associated location pin slightly or use the search box to apply a known place name.

4 To add photos to an existing Person, Place or Event from the Organizer, select the photos you wish to include, and then either drag the selection from the Media Browser to the desired tag in the Tags panel, or drag the tag itself to any of the selected images. To add photos to an established Event from the Events view, double-click the Event stack to expand it; then, click the Add Media button in the Task bar at the bottom of the workspace and browse for the photos you wish to add. In the People view, double-click to expand a person's stack, and then click the Find More button in the Task bar.

3 TAGGING, GROUPING, AND SEARCHING PHOTOS

Lesson overview

As your image collection grows larger and larger, keeping track of your photos can be a daunting task. Photoshop Elements delivers sophisticated, intuitive organizing tools that make the job enjoyable.

When the time comes to search and filter your photo library for that special shot that you *know* is in your catalog *somewhere*, the same sophisticated, intuitive tools will make it just as much fun to find it.

In this lesson you'll learn a few more techniques for sorting and grouping your photos, and a variety of ways to search your catalog:

- Using ratings to classify images by quality or usefulness
- Working with keyword tags and categories
- Using Version Sets and Stacks to organize the thumbnail grid
- Grouping photos in Albums
- Searching for people, places, and events
- Managing files in the folders list
- Filtering by date or import batch with the Timeline
- Finding photos by similarity, metadata, and text search

 You'll probably need between one and two hours to complete this lesson. If you haven't already done so, you'll need to download the combined work files for Lessons 2 and 3 from the Lesson & Update Files tab of your Account page at www.peachpit.com.

It's time to reap the rewards for all that sorting, reviewing, tagging, and organizing! Revisit the People, Places, and Events views in search-and-filter mode, where locating the photo you want is as easy as asking "Who, where, and when?" Find out how to set up complex, multi-criteria filters that can be saved and run again whenever you import new images, making it easy to keep your albums up to date.

Getting started

Before you begin this lesson you should complete the Lesson 1 setup exercises "Creating a catalog for working with this book" and "Getting photos from files and folders" and all of the exercises in Lesson 2.

Most of the exercises in Lesson 3 work with sample photos that were imported in the two preceding lessons, and require that your catalog is already organized with the People, Places, and Events tags applied in Lesson 2.

Making it easier to find your photos

In Lesson 2, you made a start on organizing your image library by sorting and tagging the photos in terms of faces, locations, and events. In Lesson 3, you'll learn more ways to order and "mark" your images, and discover how organizing your catalog can pay dividends by making it quick and easy to find the photos you want using the Organizer's search capabilities.

It's a good idea to make several sorting and tagging passes through each batch of photos you import while they're still fresh in your mind, so that they don't get lost in forgotten corners of your hard disk. This becomes an increasingly important strategy as you add more images to your library.

1 In the Organizer, click the Import button at the upper left of the workspace and choose From Files And Folders from the menu.

2 In the Get Photos And Videos From Files And Folders dialog box, navigate to and open the folder Lesson 2-3 and select the subfolder Zoo. Make sure that the option Get Photos From Subfolders is activated the other automatic processing options are disabled; then, click Get Media.

3 In the Import Attached Keyword Tags dialog box, click Select All; then, click OK.

4 The newly imported images appear in the Media Browser. Click the Clear button at the right of the bar above the thumbnails to clear the Last Import filter and view all of the photos in your catalog.

Rating photos

Rating your photos is a simple, yet effective way to add another level of organization to your catalog. With a single click or keystroke, you can mark a photo as one of your best, or relegate it to the bottom shelf—even while you're reviewing your images as a full-screen slideshow. You might choose from your five-star collection for a creative project, select from photos with a rating of three stars or higher for a presentation, or trim your catalog by removing all your un-rated rejects.

1. Make sure that Media is selected in the view picker at the top of the workspace. Click the All Media button (‹ **All Media** ›), or the Back button (‹ **Back** ›) if either is visible in the actions bar above the Media Browser, so that you see all the images in your catalog, rather than a filtered selection or the contents of a single folder.

2. Click the Import 1 folder in the My Folders list in the left panel.

3. In the Media Browser, move the pointer slowly from left to right over the stars beneath your favorite photo in this folder. When you see five yellow stars, click to apply that rating.

4. Select one of the other images in the Media Browser, and then press a number from 1 to 4 on your keyboard to apply that rating. Rate the remaining photos in the Import 1 folder, using whichever method you prefer.

5. To filter the Media Browser to display only those images from the Import 1 folder with three or more stars, click the third star in the Ratings filter at the right of the bar above the thumbnails and choose the appropriate qualifier from the adjacent menu.

6. Click the third star in the Ratings filter once more to deactivate the filter. Select each of the other folders in the My Folders list in turn and rate about half of the photos in each folder. For the folders Import 3 and Import 4, try to rate a selection of images from each of the photo series in each folder.

> **Tip:** The more photos you rate, the better for the demonstration of search features later in this lesson.

7. When you're done, click the All Media button (‹ **All Media** ›) to show all the images in your catalog, rather than the contents of a single folder.

Tagging photos with keywords

Keyword tags are custom labels that you can attach to your photos and other media files, making it possible to sort them—and later, search for them—by personalized associations other than people, places, and events.

Keyword tags make it unnecessary to set up subject-specific folders or rename files with content-specific names. Both of these solutions are inflexible, confining a given photo to a single group. In contrast, you can assign multiple keyword tags to a single photo, associating it with several different groups of images simultaneously, and then use a keyword search to quickly retrieve any of those collections, even if the image files are scattered through different folders on your hard disk.

Keywords provide a perfect solution for tagging images that don't feature people you know, or where the location or event at which the photos were captured is not a particularly relevant association.

For photos that are already tagged for People, Places, and Events, keywords can be used to refine a search. For example, you could use People and Places tags to quickly isolate all your photos of Kat and Tom together in New York, and then use keywords to filter for winter shots captured at night.

Organizing keyword tags and categories

1   If necessary, click the Tags/Info button at the far right of the Task bar to open the right panel group.

2   If you don't see a list of keywords—or at least, the collapsed Keywords header—at the top of the right panel group, click the Tags tab to bring the Tags panel to the front. If necessary, click the arrow at the left of the Keywords header to expand the Keywords list.

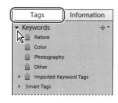

● **Note:** The default category Smart Tags contains tags that can be applied automatically by Photoshop Elements once it has analyzed the images in your catalog. You can activate the Smart Tag analysis on the Media-Analysis tab in the Organizer Preferences.

Photoshop Elements ships with a few default keywords to help get you started. In this exercise you'll convert two of the default keywords to keyword categories by creating sub-categories inside them, and then make a start on organizing your keywords by moving them into a hierarchical arrangement.

3   Select the Nature tag at the top of the Keywords list; then, click the small arrow beside the green plus-sign button (➕) to the right of the Keywords header. Examine the options available in the menu; then, choose New Sub-Category.

4   In the Create New Sub-category dialog box, the selected Nature keyword has been automatically set as the parent category inside which your new tag will be nested. Name the new sub-category **Animals**, and then click OK to create the new Keywords listing and close the Create New Sub-category dialog box.

5   Right-click / Control-click the Nature tag and choose Create New Sub-category. Name the new sub-category **Scenic**, confirm that Nature is set as the parent category, and then click OK.

6 Expand the Imported Keyword Tags category, if necessary, to see all the keyword tags that you've imported together with the lesson images.

7 Ctrl-click / Command-click to group-select the Aquarium, Birds, Bison, Elephant, Giraffe, Monkey, and Siamang keywords that were imported with the photos from the Zoo folder. Drag the seven selected keyword tags to the Animals tag in the expanded Nature category.

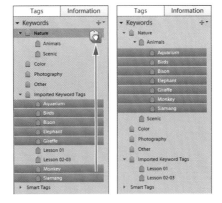

▶ **Tip:** Although this procedure does not add the Nature or Animals keywords to the Zoo photos as tags, searching your catalog for either "parent" keyword will return any image tagged with any of the keywords nested inside these categories.

The Animals tag is converted to a keyword category, with the seven relocated tags nested inside it.

8 Select the Animals category; then, click the small arrow beside the green plus-sign button (➕) at the upper right of the panel and choose New Sub-Category from the menu. In the Create New Sub-category dialog box, name the new sub-category **Mammals**. The selected Animals keyword has been automatically set as the parent sub-category. Click OK.

9 Drag all of the tags in the Animals category other than the Birds keyword to the new Mammals sub-category. Right-click / Control-click the Mammals keyword and choose Create New Sub-Category. Name the new sub-category **Primates**, and then click OK. Drag the Monkey and Siamang tags into the new sub-category.

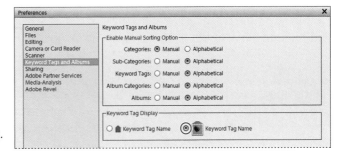

Customizing the Keywords list

You can see that the keyword list will soon become quite complex. Color-coding the categories you use most often, and assigning thumbnail images to the tags in place of the generic tag icons, may make navigating the hierarchy easier.

1 Choose Preferences > Keyword Tags And Albums from the Edit menu on Windows or Preferences from the Elements Organizer menu on Mac OS. In the Keyword Tags And Albums pane of the Preferences dialog box, activate the picture tag option under Keyword Tag Display. Click OK to save the setting.

2   In the Keywords list, right-click / Control-click the Nature category and choose Edit from the Context menu. In the Edit Category dialog box, click Choose Color and choose a color from the picker. Leave the category name unchanged. Scroll the Category Icon menu and click to select an icon; then, click OK to close the Edit Category dialog box.

The Nature category now has a distinctive icon and color-coded badges on its sub-categories and keywords, making it stand out in the list. If you can't see the full keyword names, drag the left edge of the panel group to make it wider. If the edited Nature category changes position in the Keywords list, drag it back to the top.

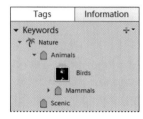

3   Right-click / Control-click the Monkey tag and choose Edit from the menu. In the Edit Keyword Tag dialog box, click Edit Icon.

4   Use the arrows at the sides of the Find button in the Edit Keyword Tag Icon dialog box to cycle through all the photos tagged with the Monkey keyword. When you see the image you want, drag the handles of the bounding box to set a new keyword badge. A thumbnail at the top of the dialog box shows how the image will look applied to a tag icon. Click OK to confirm the new badge image; then click OK to close the Edit Keyword Tag dialog box.

5   Click the arrow beside the plus-sign button (➕) to the right of the Keywords header and choose New Category. In the Create Category dialog box, name the new category **Travel**. Choose a tag badge color and category icon, and then click OK. Right-click / Control-click the new category in the Keywords list and choose Create New Sub-Category. Name the nested sub-category **Family Trips**.

Creating and applying keyword tags

You can also work with keywords in the People, Places, and Events views.

1   Click People in the view picker at the top of the Organizer workspace.

2   In the People view, click All People at the left of the actions bar, if necessary, to see all your People stacks. Double-click the Emma stack to expand it. If you see only faces, click the switch in the actions bar above the thumbnails to switch from the Faces view to the Photos view. Select the image People_12.jpg. If you don't see that image in Emma's stack, you may have tagged it with the wrong person's name; check the other People stacks to locate the photo and select it.

3 With the image People_12.jpg selected in the expanded People stack, click the Info button at the right of the Task bar, and then type **Hill Walking** in the text box at the top of the Image Tags panel. Click Add to apply the new keyword to the selected photo.

Now, you'll use the Places view to locate the other photos shot at the same location.

4 Click Places in the view picker. In the Places view, The map pans to focus on the Scotland marker. Use the zoom button (+) to zoom in by three or four clicks. The marker divides to show two location pins. Click the selected pin (the blue one) to select the rest the photos associated with that location.

> **Tip:** If you prefer to see the thumbnails in image cells as shown below, activate Gridlines in the View menu.

5 Click the Info button, beside the Map button in the Task bar, and then type the letter **H** in the text box at the top of the Image Tags panel. Choose the newly created Hill Walking tag from the pop-up menu of existing tags starting with H. Click Add to apply the new keyword to all the selected photos.

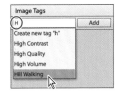

6 Deselect all the photos, then Ctrl-click / Command click to select just the four scenic landscape shots featuring the rocky Scottish coastline.

7 Type the letter **S** in the Image Tags panel text box; then, choose the Scenic tag from the tagging suggestions. Click Add to apply the new keyword to the four selected photos; then, deselect them. Click the Map button to restore the Map panel, and then click Media in the view picker to switch to the Media Browser, where you can organize your new tags.

8 Expand the Travel keyword category, if necessary; then, drag the Hill Walking tag from the category Other into the sub-category Family Trips.

9 Drag the Travel category to the top of the Tags panel and release the mouse button when you see a black line indicating an insertion point just below the Keywords header.

10 Right-click / Control-click the Hill Walking tag and choose Edit from the context menu; then, customize the tag thumbnail as you did in the previous exercise.

You'll end your keyword-tagging expedition in the Events view, where you'll tag all the images from one event, and just a selection of photos from another.

▶ **Tip:** If you don't see names on the image stacks in the Events view, click the switch above the thumbnails to move from Smart Events view to the regular Events mode.

11 Click Events in the view picker. Double-click the Annie's Wedding stack to expand it. Press Ctrl+A / Command+A to select all the photos in this Event; then click the Info button at the right of the Task bar and type **Milestones** in the text box at the top of the Image Tags panel. Click Add to apply the new keyword to all of the selected photos. Click the Back button in the actions bar above the thumbnails grid to collapse the Annie's Wedding stack and see all of the Events in your catalog.

12 Expand the Scottish Road Trip stack by double-clicking it. Select the six images in this Event that feature the Rua Reidh lighthouse. In the Image Tags panel, type **Lighthouse** in the text box; then, click Add to apply the tag.

13 Click Media in the view picker to return to the Media Browser and see your new tags listed in the Keywords list. Press Ctrl+Shift+A (Windows) / Command+Shift+A (Mac OS) to deselect all of the images in the current selection. Set a new thumbnail for the Lighthouse and Milestones keyword tags as you for the other new tags.

Grouping photos

As the number of files in your photo library increases, it can be more difficult to spot the image you want amongst the thumbnails displayed in the Media Browser. Simply grouping some of your images in stacks and version sets can reduce the clutter in the thumbnails grid, effectively simplifying the view by hiding collections of related shots behind a single thumbnail until they're needed.

Working with version sets

A version set groups a photo in its original state with any edited copies that you've generated, so you can find all the edited versions of the image stacked behind a single thumbnail in the Media Browser, rather than scattered through your catalog.

Photoshop Elements automatically creates a version set whenever you edit a photo in the Elements Organizer. When you edit an image from your catalog in the Editor, you can choose whether to create a version set or not in the Save As dialog box.

Grouping your edited files in this way not only makes it much easier for you to find the version you want, but also lets you keep your original, un-edited photo intact, easy to find and ready for a different treatment whenever you want to re-use it.

1   If the All Media button is visible in the actions bar above the thumbnails, click it to ensure that the Media Browser is showing all of the images in your catalog.

2   To isolate the zoo images, select the Nature > Animals sub-category in the Keywords list, and then click the arrow at the right of the Animals tag. Scroll down, if necessary, and select the image DSC_0736.jpg.

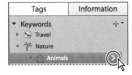

You have just made your first keyword search. With one click, you've retrieved all the photos from your last import, despite the fact that they are spread across seven folders and are tagged with as many separate keywords. The Advanced Search panel has opened above the media browser, offering the opportunity to refine the search, and the search results bar above the thumbnails displays the single search term.

Tip: You'll learn more about using the Advanced Search panel later in this lesson.

Note: The Smart Fix edit corrects the overall color balance and also enhances detail in the brightest and darkest areas of the image.

3   Click the upwards-facing arrow at the right of the Advanced Search panel's header bar to collapse the panel so that only its header remains visible. (Clicking the X button at the far right of the header would close the Advanced Search panel completely, clearing the search terms so that the Media view is unfiltered.)

4   Click the Instant Fix button in the Task bar to open the Photo Fix Options panel. Make sure that the image DSC_0736.jpg is still selected; then, click Smart Fix.

The edited copy is stacked on top of the original photo in a version set. A version set can be identified by a badge (representing a stack of photos overlaid by a paint brush) in the upper right corner of the thumbnail, and by a file name extension indicating that the photo has been edited.

5   Click the Crop button in the Photo Fix Options panel. Drag the handles of the cropping box to crop the image closer around the subjects. Click Done.

6   Click the expand button (▶) to the right of the thumbnail image to see the original and edited images in the version set displayed side by side. Select the original image, DSC_0736.jpg, and click Smart Fix once again.

Tip: If you applied a star-rating to this photo earlier, you'll notice that the edited copies have inherited the same rating. If you think the Smart Fix and Crop operations represent an improvement, increase the rating for your preferred version.

7   There are now three photos in the version stack, with the most recent copy on top. Select the first copy, DSC_0736_edited-1.jpg—the center image in the version set—and choose Edit > Version Set > Set As Top Item. The two edited copies change places in the stack; the older version is now the "cover photo."

8   To see only the topmost photo in the version set, click the collapse button to the right of the original image, or right-click / Control-click any photo in the set and choose Version Set > Collapse Items In Version Set from the context menu. Note the other commands available from the same context menu; these commands can also be found in the Edit > Version Set menu.

About stacks

Scrolling past rows and rows of images of the same subject—when it's not the one you're looking for—can be time-consuming and frustrating. You can reduce clutter in the thumbnail grid and make browsing for photos more enjoyable, and far more productive, by stacking related shots behind a single, distinctive thumbnail.

Glancing along just one row of stacks in the thumbnails grid could save you the effort of scrolling through screen after screen of distracting images.

1 In the Media Browser, Ctrl-click / Command-click to select the four images shot at the aquarium, including the version set you created in the previous exercise.

2 Right-click / Control-click the photo you edited earlier and choose Stack > Stack Selected Photos. The images are stacked, with the edited copy on top, now marked with a stack icon beside its version set badge. Click the arrow at the right side of the stack frame to expand and collapse the stack.

3 Select the four images of elephants, and then right-click / Control-click the photo you'd like to set as the top image and choose Stack > Stack Selected Photos from the context menu. Repeat the process for the four photos of black siamangs from Thailand and the six images of American bison.

Tip: Stacks are particularly useful for managing long series of related images, such as shots taken at sports events with your camera's burst mode or auto-bracket feature. When you take photos this way you end up with many variations of what is essentially the same image—if you stack the series, you'll see only the best shot in the Media Browser.

Stacking photos automatically

You can automate the process of grouping related photos in your catalog by having Photoshop Elements suggest stacks, based on visual similarities between images.

1 Press Ctrl+A / Command+A to select all of the photos in the Media Browser; then, choose Edit > Stack > Automatically Suggest Photo Stacks.

In the Visually Similar Photo Search dialog box, Photoshop Elements presents four groups as potential stacks. Before you go ahead and stack these groups, lets look at the options for tweaking the automatic stacking process manually.

Tip: Experiment with as many of your own photos as possible, so that you'll get a feel for the kind of images that perform best with this feature.

2 To merge the first and second suggested groups—both of which contain photos that feature squirrel monkeys—Shift-click to select the images in either group and drag them to the other.

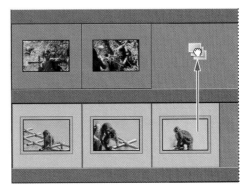

3 Click Unique Photos at the lower left of the Visually Similar Photo Search dialog box. The Unique Photos pane shows any photos from the selection in the Media Browser for which Photoshop Elements has been unable to suggest a stack.

▶ **Tip:** You can simply reverse this process to remove a photo from a group suggested for stacking.

4 Drag the first image in the Unique Photos pane to the top group of five shots featuring squirrel monkeys. Drag the next four images to group them with the two other photos featuring birds, and then add the last two images to the two photos of giraffes in the bottom group.

5 When you stack these groups, the first image in each group will become the top image in the stack. Drag your favorite photo from each group to the first position in that group, and then click the Stack button at the right of the divider bar above the group. Each of the new stacks displays the stacked photos badge.

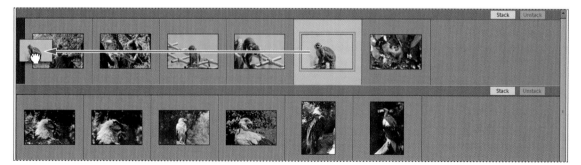

6 Click Done. In the Media Browser, the 34 photos with keywords in the Animals category are now displayed as just seven stack thumbnails. Click the Tags/Info button in the Task bar to reopen the Tags and Image Tags panels. Click Media in the view picker; then click the Back button in the actions bar, if it's visible, to see all of the photos in your catalog.

Tips for working with stacks

You should keep these points in mind when you're working with stacks:

- Combining two or more stacks merges them to form one new stack, with the most recent photo on top of the stack. The original groupings are not preserved.

- Many actions applied to a collapsed stack, such as editing and printing, are applied to the top item only. To apply an action to multiple images in a stack, either expand the stack and group-select the images, or un-stack them first.

- If you edit a photo that you've already included in a stack, the photo and its edited copy will be grouped as a version set nested inside the stack.

- If you apply a keyword tag to a collapsed stack, the keyword tag is applied to all items in the stack. When you run a search on the keyword tag, the top photo in the stack appears in the search results marked with the stack icon. If you want to apply a keyword tag to only one photo in a stack, expand the stack first.

▶ **Tip:** To access stack commands, right-click / Control-click any image in a stack and choose from the Stack sub-menu. Alternatively, select a photo in the stack and choose from the Edit > Stack menu.

Creating albums

Another way of grouping your photos is to organize them into albums. An album is like a *virtual* folder where you can assemble a collection of images that may be drawn from any number of *actual* folders on your hard disk. You might create a new album to collate and arrange the pictures that you intend to include in a creative project such as a photo book or a slideshow, or to group your images of a special interest subject such as flowers, classic cars, or macro photography.

A photo can be included more than one album—the same image might be the first in a New York Architecture album and the last in a National Monuments album. You can also group albums; for example, you might group your New York and San Francisco albums together inside a Vacations album; while your Road Trips album includes the San Francisco album, but not the New York album.

▶ **Tip:** You can achieve similar groupings and sub-groups by using keywords tags, but your Road Trips album may contain only a sub-set of the photos you've tagged with the keyword Road Trips.

The principal advantage to grouping photos in an album rather than using a shared keyword tag is that in an album you can rearrange the order of the photos as you wish. In the Media Browser, each photo in an album displays a number in the upper left corner, representing its place in the order. You can drag photos to change their position within the album, which will effect the order in which they appear in a slideshow or their placement in a project layout.

1   If necessary, click the Tags / Info button in the Task bar to show the Tags panel. In the Keywords list, select the Animals > Mammals > Primates sub-category; then, click the white arrow at the right of the Primates tag to isolate all the images with tags that are included in that category. The grid displays two stacks that you created earlier.

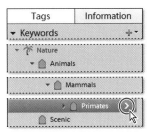

Note: In the latest version of Elements Organizer you can create both *Local* and *Mobile* albums. Local albums contain media that resides only on your computer and con-nected storage media, while Mobile albums are uploaded to Adobe Revel and stored in the cloud where you can access them on your iPhone or iPad, and share them publicly or privately. In this series of exercises, you'll learn the basics by working with Local albums.

In albums, stacks are a special case; you can include a stack in an album, but only the top photo from the stack will appear in a slide show, for instance, unless you expand the stack and select all the photos inside it before you start the slideshow.

You can't rearrange the order of stacked photos in an album, add a selection of photos from a stack to an album without adding the entire stack, or remove a stacked image from your album without removing the rest of the stack.

So, you can start by unstacking the photos in the Primates category.

2   Shift-click to select both of the stacks in the Media Browser, and then choose Edit > Stack > Unstack Photos.

3   Select the best three shots of the black siamangs; then, click the Create New Album Or Album Category button ( ) beside Local Albums at the top of the left panel; make sure you click the green plus sign, not the small arrow beside it.

4   In the New Album panel at the right, type **Monkey Business** as the name for the new album; then, click OK in the Task bar below the panel.

Tip: If you don't see the album badges below the thumbnails in the Media Browser, use the Zoom slider in the Task bar to increase the size of the thumbnails. Hold the pointer over the album badge to see which album or albums a photo belongs to.

5   Expand the Local Albums category in the left panel. Your new album appears in the Local Albums list, and the three siamang photos that you selected for inclusion are marked with green album badges.

Adding more photos to an album

As you add more images to your catalog, you may have new photos that you'd like to add to existing albums—an easy way to sort and organize a fresh import—or perhaps you're assembling a collection for a photo book over several work sessions.

1   With the Media Browser still filtered to show photos with keywords in the Primates category, right-click / Control-click the new album and choose Edit from the context menu. The Edit Album panel opens at the right.

2 Ctrl-click / Command-click to select the best three of the six photos featuring squirrel monkeys. Drag the selected photos into the Content pane in the Edit Album panel; then, click OK in the Task bar.

3 If necessary, click Clear in the search results bar above the thumbnails to clear the Primates filter; then, click the X button at the right of the collapsed Advanced Search panel (right below the stars in the actions bar) to close it. You can now view all of the photos in your catalog. Click the Tags/Info button at the right of the Task bar to close the right panel group, if necessary.

4 Click the Monkey Business album in the Albums list. The Sort By option in the actions bar above the thumbnails grid is set to Album Order: the default setting with the Media Browser filtered to show the contents of an album. Notice the counter in the top left corner of each image, denoting its order in the album.

5 The six photos are arranged in the order in which they were added to the album. Drag the thumbnails to rearrange them, alternating siamangs and squirrel monkeys. When you're done, click the All Media button (**‹ All Media**) in the actions bar so that the Media Browser displays all of the photos in your catalog.

Creating albums from People, Places, and Events

In Lesson 2, you used the People, Places, and Events views as aids to organizing your catalog—and your effort is already paying off. Now you can take advantage of the search and filter aspects of those views to help find the photos you need.

1 Click People in the view picker at the top of the workspace. If necessary, set the switch in the actions bar to Group, rather than People, and click the Groups button ( ) in the Task bar to show the Groups list at the right; then, expand the Family > Kids group. Click the listing for the Twins group to select the Twins group, which contains People stacks for Pauline and Sophie.

> **Tip:** You can drag photos directly to the album in the Albums list, and vice versa, but the Edit command also gives you the opportunity to rename the album, or change its place in the hierarchy of the Albums list.

> **Tip:** Remember: whatever the viewing mode, the People view displays only those of your photos that have already been tagged with People tags.

2   Double-click the Sophie stack. Make sure the switch in the actions bar is set to display Photos, rather than Faces. Ctrl-click / Command-click to select the photos of the twins together without their sisters, and any images of Sophie alone.

3   Click the Create New Album Or Album Category button (➕) beside the Local Albums category, making sure you click the green plus sign, not the small arrow beside it. In the Add New Album panel at the right of the workspace, type **Double Trouble** as the name for the new album; then, click OK in the Task bar.

Your new album appears in the Local Albums list, and the selected photos are now marked with green album badges.

4   Click the Back button in the actions bar to return to the Group view, and then double-click the Pauline stack to expand it. Ctrl-click / Command-click to select any images of Pauline alone and drag them directly to the Double Trouble album in the Albums list. The added photos are marked with green album badges.

You've successfully leveraged the People tags that you attached to your photos in Lesson 2 to perform a simple People search, making use of the various viewing modes in the People view to help locate the photos you needed for the new album.

▶ **Tip:** If you don't see the map or the pins (or Scotland), see steps 1 to 4 in the exercise "A short trip to the Places view" in Lesson 2.

5   Click Places in the view picker at the top of the workspace. In the Places view, click the northern map pin of the two pins positioned on Scotland to select the photos associated with that pin in the thumbnails grid.

6 Scroll down through the thumbnails, if necessary, and Ctrl-click / Command-click the photo DSC_0330.jpg (a rear view of a Scotsman wearing a green kilt) to add it to the selection. Both of the Scotland pins should now be selected, and the image count in the lower left corner of the workspace should show that there are 19 photos selected.

7 Click the Create New Album Or Album Category button () at the top of the left panel, making sure you click the button, not the small arrow beside it. In the Add New Album panel at the right of the workspace, type **Highlands Hike** as the name for the new album; then, click OK in the Task bar below the panel.

Your new album appears in the Local Albums list in the left panel, and the selected photos are now marked with green album badges. You've just used the Places view to filter your catalog by location to help find the photos for this album.

8 Click Events in the view picker. Shift-click to select the Event stacks NY Marathon 2010 and NY Marathon 2011; then, click the Create New Album Or Album Category button () at the top of the left panel.

9 In the Add New Album panel, type **Running New York** as the name for the new album. Ctrl-click / Command-click in the Content pane to select three or four images that you'd like to exclude from the album, and then click the trash-can icon at the bottom of the panel to remove them. Click OK in the Task bar.

The new Running New York album appears in the Local Albums list in the left panel, grouping the marathon photos that you located by filtering for Events tags.

10 Click Media in the view picker. In the Media view, click each of the albums Double Trouble, Highlands Hike, and Running New York. If you wish, you can rearrange the order of the thumbnails in the grid for each of your newly created albums.

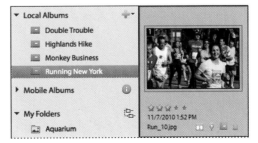

Tip: If you're unable to re-order the photos in an album, check the Sort By setting at the left of the bar above the thumbnails grid. For albums, the default sorting order should be Album Order.

11 When you're done, click the All Media button (All Media) in the actions bar to see the unfiltered contents of your catalog in the Media Browser.

Access your photos anywhere with Mobile Albums

With more and more people using smart phones and tablets to capture and view photos and videos, it's likely that you already have lots of images and movies on at least one mobile device, as well as your desktop computer. Keeping track of what's where and manually moving your media from mobile devices to your desktop—and vice versa—can be difficult and time-consuming but, from Photoshop Elements 12, the new Mobile Albums feature makes it easy to have the latest versions of all your photos and videos with you all the time, wherever you go.

Mobile Albums link your Photoshop Elements catalog to Adobe Revel, where you can access the latest versions of your media from your smart phone or tablet, or from any web browser.

Setting up Elements Organizer to work with Revel

There are no lesson images provided for this exercise; in order to keep your complimentary Revel account uncluttered and stay within the upload limits, you'll use your own photos instead.

1   Choose File > Manage Catalogs. If you've already established a separate catalog for your own photos, select it in the Catalogs list and click Open. If you have not yet started building a personal catalog, click New; then, enter a name for the new catalog and click OK to load it.

2   Import a selection of your own photos to your personal catalog and group a few of your favorites into several small Local Albums; if necessary, refer to the preceding exercises on creating Albums.

3   In the Organizer, click the blue info icon ( ) to the right of the Mobile Albums category in the left panel to sign into Revel.

Note: If you already have a Revel account with the same Adobe ID that you used to register Photoshop Elements, you may not see the blue icon. If you see an orange icon instead, sign in to Revel by choosing File > Sign In To Adobe Revel. If you see only the green plus sign icon ( ), you're already signed in and your catalog is already linked to Revel.

4   In the Elements Mobile Albums sign-in screen, enter your Adobe ID and password; then, click Sign In.

5   On the screen that follows, you can specify whether you want to upload all of the media in your Photoshop Elements catalog, or just those files you select. For now, choose the second option. Click Next; then, click Done to dismiss the final setup screen.

6   Your new Revel library is listed under Mobile Albums in the left panel. Click the arrow beside the green plus sign icon (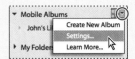) to the right of the Mobile Albums header and choose Settings to open the Adobe Revel tab in Elements Organizer Preferences.

7   Inspect the settings and options in the Adobe Revel preferences pane; you can sign out of Revel, choose a Revel library from the Libraries list, specify a folder for downloads, set Revel to access your entire catalog, and upgrade your Revel account status from Complimentary to Premium. You can also disable or reactivate the Revel Agent, or set it to upload video only when your system is idle. Click Cancel to leave the settings unchanged.

Note: Your complimentary Revel account entitles you to unlimited uploads for the first month, and then 50 photos per month thereafter. For unlimited uploads, upgrade to a Revel Premium account.

Uploading photos to Revel from the Organizer

1   In the Organizer, drag an Album from the Local Albums category onto the listing for your new Mobile Albums library.

2   Repeat step 1 for another of your Local Albums. Wait a minute or two for your upload to be completed; then, launch your web browser and go to adoberevel.com. Sign in with your Adobe ID.

3   At the top of the Revel page in your web browser, click between Photos and Albums. On the Albums page, select an album to see the contents. Click an image to see it enlarged; then, click the album name at the upper left to exit the single-image view.

4   In the actions bar just below the header, click Select Photos; then, select one of the images in your album. Click Delete in the actions bar, and then click OK to confirm the action. Return to the Elements Organizer and click the Mobile Album from which you deleted the photo; the image has been removed from the selected album.

5   Select the other Mobile Album in the left panel. Right-click / Control-click one of the photos in the Media Browser and choose Edit With Photoshop Elements Editor. In the Editor, choose Enhance > Convert To Black And White; then, click OK to accept the default conversion. Choose File > Close, and then click Save. Accept the default name for the edited file and make sure that the options Include In The Elements Organizer and Save In Version Set With Original are both activated. Click Save, and then click OK to accept the JPEG options.

6   Wait a minute or so; then, return to your web browser and click Albums in the header of your Revel page. Choose the album containing the photo you just edited; the edited version appears beside the original in your Revel album. Click the cog icon at the right of the header and choose Sign Out; then, return to the Organizer.

7   Choose File > Manage Catalogs; then select your CIB catalog from the list and click Open.

As you've seen, the link between Adobe Revel and Photoshop Elements works both ways; you can add photos to a Mobile Album from your smartphone and they'll automatically appear in the Organizer. For more detailed information on working with Mobile Albums, please refer to Elements Organizer Help and adoberevel.com, where you can also download the free Revel app for your mobile devices. We'll look at sharing photos and videos from Revel in Lesson 10.

Filtering and finding photos

In this lesson, you've begun to take advantage of the Organizer's search and filter capabilities—even while you've been concentrating on using it to mark and manage your images. Most of the search and filter tools are so well integrated into the Elements Organizer workspace that you're barely aware of using them.

▶ **Tip:** This is what's referred to as an "And" search: "Show me items that are in the Import 1 folder *and* have a rating of three stars or higher."

At the start of this lesson you learned how to apply ratings to your photos. By the time you reached step 5, you had already performed a two-term search—with just two clicks. You filtered your catalog so that you could look at the images in a single folder (by choosing from the list in the left panel), and then refined the search to show only the photos with the highest ratings (by clicking a star in the actions bar).

▶ **Tip:** This is referred to as an "Or" search: "Show me any item that is tagged with this keyword *or* that one … *or* any of these five."

In the next exercise, you tidied up your keywords list by dragging keyword tags into a hierarchy of categories and subcategories. This simple housekeeping task made it possible to find the images for the exercises that followed by running a *seven*-term search—this time with just one click! A single click on the Animals category filtered your catalog for all the images of birds, bison, elephants, giraffes, monkeys, seals, and siamangs—retrieving photos found in seven separate folders.

Finding people, places, and events

The first time you visited the Places, People, and Events views, you were learning how to sort and tag your photos. During the last exercise you discovered that each of these workspaces also serves as a filter, capable of presenting your images in a variety of different arrangements to help you locate the photos you're looking for. In this section, you'll take another look at finding people, places, and events.

Looking for somebody?

1 Click People in the view picker. If you don't see the heading "All People" in the center of the actions bar above the thumbnails, the People view is either displaying images of just one of the people in your catalog, or whatever people it can find in just a selected part of your catalog. To see all of the people in the whole of your catalog, click the Back button or the All People button at the left.

2 If the switch at the left of the actions bar is set to Group, click it to shift to the default People view; you'll look at the Group view a little later.

3 To quickly skim through all the photos in any of your People stacks, move the pointer slowly across the stack thumbnail. Stop moving the pointer, and then right-click / Control-click whichever image is currently visible to see the commands that can be applied to the stack. Skim through each People stack.

Even the All People view is a search result—the stacks displayed are the answer to the question "What people are in my catalog?"

4   Click to select Double Trouble from the Albums list in the left panel. The question is now "What people are in the Dynamic Duo album?" The answer: Pauline and Sophie. To see exactly *which* pictures of Pauline and Sophie are in this album, move the pointer slowly across each of the stack thumbnails.

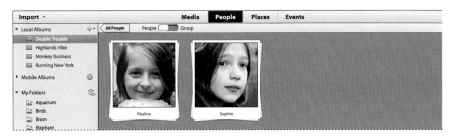

Note: When you skim the contents of a People stack with a single album or folder selected as the image source, rather than the entire catalog, remember that the photo that you set as the profile picture (the image you see at the top of the People stack) may not be present in that album or folder.

5   Click each of the other albums to see who's inside, and then work your way down the My Folders list. You can skip the folders with animal names; the girls do appear here and there, but there are no People tags attached to these images. When you're done, click the All People button at the left of the actions bar.

6   Double-click the Lilly stack to show all the images in the catalog that are tagged with Lilly's People tag. Toggle the switch in the actions bar to shift between the Faces and Photos views. Leave the view set to display the full photos featuring Lilly, rather than the cropped thumbnails of her face.

Tip: In the People view, you can see an image in the enlarged single-image view, just as you can in the Media view, by double-clicking the image. If you do this with one of the thumbnails in Faces mode, you'll find that the view has changed to People mode when you return to the grid.

Your catalog is still small, so there are not so many pictures of any of the people you've tagged, but as your photo library grows, you may see hundreds of photos of a given person in this view. Scanning these thumbnails may be better than looking through every photo in your catalog, but it can still be daunting. You can effectively filter the view by selecting individual albums or folders as the image source.

7   Lilly is not tagged in any of your albums, but click through the four Import folders to see which photos of Lilly appear where. Leaving the Import 4 folder selected, click Back in the actions bar to see all the people in that folder; then, click the All People button to deselect the Import 4 folder as the image source.

Note: In the Groups view, people that are not included in any group will appear under an Ungrouped header.

8 Click the switch in the actions bar to shift from the standard People view to the Group view. If necessary, click the Groups button (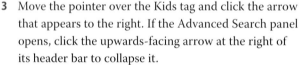) in the Task bar to see the Groups list; then, expand the Family > Kids group. Click back and forth between the Family and Twins listings to shift the focus of the Groups view.

Depending on the size of your screen, you may not see anything happen when you click the different group listings. Make the Organizer window smaller, so that not all the groups are visible, and then repeat the last action. This feature will come in handy when you have more groups in your catalog.

To move a person from one group to another; simply drag her People stack to a different entry in the Groups list. To remove someone from a group, right-click / Control-click his stack and choose Move To Ungrouped from the context menu.

9 Switch the People view back from Group mode to the default view; then, click Media in the view picker to return to a view of your entire catalog.

Finding people from the Media view

You can also work with your People tags in the Media view, making it quick and easy to leverage all that tagging and grouping to find the photos you want.

1 If necessary, click the Tags/Info button at the far right of the Task bar to open the right panel group.

2 In the Tags panel, expand the People Tags category; then, expand the Family group, and the two groups nested inside it.

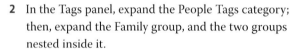

3 Move the pointer over the Kids tag and click the arrow that appears to the right. If the Advanced Search panel opens, click the upwards-facing arrow at the right of its header bar to collapse it.

Depending on the accuracy of your face tagging, this search should return 19 photos. The search results bar above the thumbnails lists the Kids tag as the single search term.

4 Click the Clear button at the right of the search results bar to clear the filter. The Advanced Search panel expands. If necessary, click the Tags/Info button in the Task bar to re-open the right panels.

5 In the People Tags list, click the arrow to the right of the Emma tag. The Media Browser should display nine photos. Click the arrow beside the Sophie tag. The thumbnails in the grid are reduced to those images with both People tags. Click the arrow beside the Pauline tag; the search results bar lists the Emma, Sophie, and Pauline tags as search terms.

The search returns only five images including all four girls; in other words, there are no photos of Emma together with the Sophie and Pauline, but without Lilly.

6 Expand the Events Tags list and click the arrow beside the Annie's Wedding tag. The grid displays only two photos of all four girls taken on that occasion. Annie's Wedding has been added to the terms listed in the search results bar.

7 Click the Clear button in the search results bar to clear the filter and close the Advanced Search pane, if necessary, by clicking the X at the right of its header.

Searching every place

Now you'll revisit the Places view to look at several search and filter features that you've not yet explored.

1 Click Places in the view picker. Press Ctrl+Shift+A / Command+Shift+A to make sure no images are selected. If you see the All Places button in the Actions bar, click it. If you don't see the map, or the map is too small, set up the Places workspace as you did earlier in this lesson, or refer to the exercise "A short trip to the Places view" in Lesson 2. When you're done, choose View > Refresh.

2 In the left panel, click the Highlands Hike album in the Albums list. The map shows two red pins marking locations in Scotland, UK. The thumbnails grid displays the photos in the selected album—a subset of the images from the Scottish Road Trip event that you created in Lesson 2.

3 Click each pin in turn to see which images are placed at each location, and then reverse the process; click photos in the grid to activate their pins.

This search asks the question "Which photos in the Highlands Hike album were shot in Edinburgh?"

4   Click the Running New York album and select any of the images. The map jumps your the pin on Manhattan, New York. Zoom in by two or three clicks.

5   Select the Import 1 folder in the My Folders list, and then select any image; the view jumps back to Scotland. This time, the map is focused on just one of the Scottish locations: the remote and rugged site of the Rua Reidh lighthouse. Select the Import 2 folder and click any image to focus on the city of Edinburgh. Click away from the pin to deselect the selected image from the Import 2 folder.

6   Click the All Places button in the Task bar above the thumbnails to clear the Import 2 filter and display all of the photos in your catalog that have map locations and Places tags. Use the Zoom slider in the Task bar to reduce the size of the thumbnails so that you can see them all.

The image count in the lower left corner of the workspace indicates that there are 55 items associated with marked locations on the Places view map.

7   Zoom the map out so that you can see both of the pins in Scotland; then, watch the thumbnail grid as you click the check box at the lower left of the Map panel to activate the Show Only Media Visible On Map option.

The New York photos are no longer visible in the grid; the number of thumbnails displayed has dropped to 36.

8   Drag the map to the right so that only one of the two pins is visible. When you release the mouse button, the thumbnails grid displays only the 18 items on the northern pin. Drag the map left until only the southern pin is visible, and then release the mouse button; the thumbnail grid displays the 18 photos captured in Edinburgh.

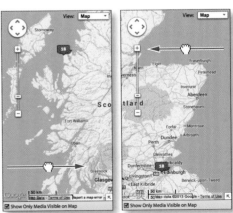

Looking for the right occasion

Lets see what you're missing in the Events view.

1   Click Events in the view picker. In the Events view, choose Edit > Deselect to make sure that you have no Events selected. If you see the All Events button in the Actions bar, click it. If the Events view is set to Smart Events mode, click the switch in the actions bar to shift to the default Events view. The grid displays an Event stack for each of the five Events you created in Lesson 2.

2   If you don't see the calendar, click the Calendar button (▦) at the right of the Task bar. The calendar's header currently reads "All Years," indicating that the Events view is displaying all the Events in your catalog, regardless of their dates.

3   Click the All Years heading; the drop-down menu shows that your catalog contains Events from 2010, 2011, 2012 and 2013. Choose 2010 from the menu. The Events view is now filtered to show only two Events: Annie's Wedding and NY Marathon 2010.

4   The months June and November are high-lighted on the 2010 calendar, indicating that one of the Events on view occurred in each of those months. Click on the month June; the page for this month shows just one Event on the 26th. Click June 26 on the calendar to select the Event listed for that day. Choose 2011, 2012, and then 2013 from the Year menu to filter the view for events falling within those years, then click Clear above the calendar to see the Events view unfiltered. Click the Calendar button in the Task bar to hide the Calendar panel.

5   Use the switch in the actions bar to shift to Smart Events mode. In default mode, Smart Events suggests likely Event stacks amongst the photos in your catalog (or in a selected folder) on the basis of single capture dates. In this mode, the grid shows fourteen suggested events—fourteen dates that account for all the images in your catalog—four of which contain only one photo.

6   Smart Events has divided the Scottish Road Trip photos into the five stacks according to their capture dates. Ctrl-click / Command-click to select the stacks dated 5/21/2013 and 5/22/2013; then, right-click / Control-click either stack and choose Name Event(s). Name the Event **Touring the Highlands**, then, click OK.

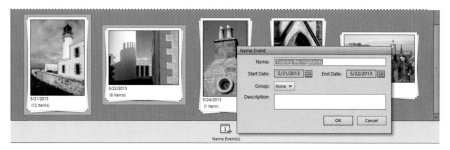

The five-day Scottish Road Trip has not been split up; Smart Events has merely detected the date-based groupings among the photos that make up that Event, and allowed you to name a subset of the whole as an Event in its own right.

7   Name the stack dated 6/1/2011 **A trip to the zoo**.

8   Change the grouping mode from Date to Time in the bar just above the suggested stacks. The number of suggested Events drops to three; Smart Events has now grouped the images in your catalog on the basis of *clusters* of capture dates. Skim the images in the last of the suggested stacks, which contains all of the photos in your catalog other than two single images captured earlier than 2010.

9   Move the grouping slider slowly to the right, increasing the number of suggested Events by narrowing the range of dates in each cluster. Drag the slider all the way to the right, and then look through the ten suggested Events. In the last stack but one, Smart Events has successfully grouped the 36 photos from our road trip in Scotland, which were captured over five days.

10 Switch back from Smart Events mode to the default Events view to see your new Event stacks. When you're done, click Media in the view picker.

Locating files in the folder list

Most of us have our own strategies for organizing and searching for files among the folders on our hard disks. In the folders list you can do everything you're used to doing in the familiar Windows Explorer or the Mac OS Finder—the important difference is that your actions in the folders list are tracked by the Organizer, so that you'll never need to locate and reconnect files that are no longer recognized by the catalog, having been moved or renamed outside Photoshop Elements.

1 If necessary, clear any active filters and deselect any album or folder selected in the left panel by clicking click the Back button and/or the All Media button in the actions bar, and then click the small triangle to expand the My Folders list.

The My Folders list is the default folders view, listing only your *managed folders*: folders containing media files that have already been imported to your catalog.

2 Click the Show Folder Hierarchy button (⊞) at the right of the My Folders list. The Folders list reveals the folder structure on your hard disk. By default, only those branches of the hierarchy that lead to managed folders are expanded. Click the plus sign (+) or minus sign (-) (Windows) or arrow (Mac OS) beside any folder to expand or collapse it. Right-click / Control-click the PSE12CIB > Lessons folder and choose Show All Subfolders from the context menu to see those subfolders not yet managed by Photoshop Elements.

▶ **Tip:** You can identify a managed folder in the hierarchy, (a folder that contains media files that are already part of your catalog) by the picture icon on the folder (⊡). Watched folders (on Windows only) display a binoculars icon (⊟).

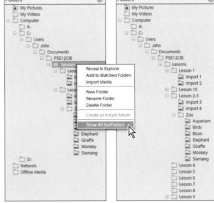

3 Select any managed folder in the Folders list filter the thumbnails grid so that you see only the contents of that folder. Right-click / Control-click the folder from to see the options available in the context menu. Click the All Media button in the actions bar to see all the images in your catalog once more.

4 Right-click / Control-click any image in the Media Browser, and then choose Go To Folder from the context menu. The folder in which that photo is stored is selected in the folders list and the Media Browser display only the managed files inside it. Click the All Media button to see all the images in your catalog. Click the Show Folder List button at the upper right of the Folders hierarchy.

Using the Timeline to refine a search

The Timeline is an effective search tool in its own right, but you can also use it in combination with any of the other search and filter tools to help you to refine a search or to navigate the results. You might search for photos with a particular keyword tag, and then use the Timeline to narrow the search to the files from a particular import batch, or images captured within a specific date range.

Note: The height of the bars indicates the relative number of files captured in each month.

1 Make sure that the Sort By option in the actions bar is set to Oldest; then, choose View > Timeline to show the timeline above the Media Browser. The Timeline breaks your catalog down by import date; you can see that your catalog contains images captured in six different years over a ten-year span, from the oldest entry in September 2003, to the most recent in August 2013.

2 Click any of the bars in the Timeline, or drag the sliding frame; the thumbnails grid scrolls, if necessary, to show you the first image in the grid with a capture date that falls within that month.

3 Drag the markers at the ends of the timeline inwards to define a range of six or eight months. The grid now displays only the images captured in that period.

4 In the actions bar, set the Sort By option to Import Batch. The bars in the Timeline now represent import batches arranged in chronological order.

5 Click a bar in the Timeline; the view scrolls to show you the first image imported in that batch. In the thumbnail grid, the photos are grouped under batch headers. You can select all the images in a batch by clicking the header. Choose View > Timeline to hide the Timeline, and then reset the sorting order to display the oldest images first.

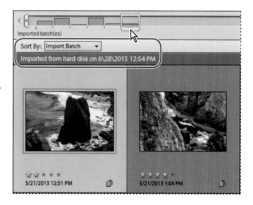

Finding photos by searching for keywords

There are several ways to locate photos that are tagged with a particular keyword, or with a given combination of keywords. We'll start with a basic text search.

1 Press Ctrl+Shift+A / Command+Shift+A to make sure you have no files selected, and then choose View > Expand All Stacks.

2 Click in the text search box at the top of the workspace and type the letter "**A**." A drop-down menu offers shortcuts drawn not only from the keywords in your catalog, but also from any People, Places, and Events tags that match the letters you type. Press Backspace / Delete, and then type the letter "**B**." This time, the menu shows only keywords: one tag from the default Smart Tags, and two that you created earlier. Add the letter "**i**." The choice is narrowed to Birds and Bison and the thumbnail grid is already filtered to show all of your images of birds and bison. Click a menu shortcut, or finish typing whichever keyword you prefer.

▶ **Tip:** Though they will not appear in the shortcut suggestions, a text search will also find matches in file names, album names, captions, notes, dates, and other text embedded in your photos' metadata.

3 Click the Back button in the actions bar above the thumbnail grid to clear the text search. Try typing **Birds and Bison**; are there any images tagged with both of these keywords? Click Back, and then try **Birds or Bison**; how many photos are tagged with at least one of these keywords? Try **walk not lighthouse**. When you're done, clear the keyword search by clicking the Back button.

▶ **Tip:** For a list of supported operators (and, or, not, etc.) for text searches, please refer to Photoshop Elements Help.

4 Now you'll run a keyword search from the Tags panel. If necessary, click the Tags / Info button at the far right of the Task Bar to see the right panel and expand the Other keywords category. Move the pointer over the Lighthouse tag and click the arrow that appears to the right. The Media Browser displays six photos with this tag and the Advanced Search panel appears (expand it, if necessary), with the Lighthouse keyword activated in the first column.

▶ **Tip:** You can refine a keywords search by choosing a folder or album from the left panel to limit the search to that source, or by defining a date range in the Timeline.

5 In the Actions bar, click the second star in the Ratings filter to refine the search.

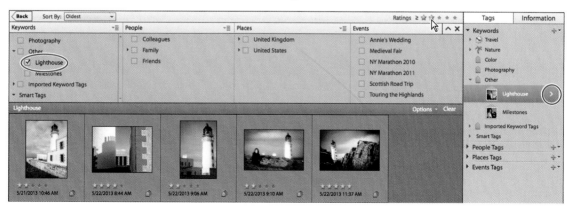

Working with the Advanced Search panel

Don't be intimidated by the name; the Advanced Search panel is actually a very quick and easy way to run a detailed, multiple-criteria search.

1 Click Clear in the search results bar above the thumbnails; then, click the second star in the Ratings filter to disable it. In the Advanced Search panel, scroll down in the Keywords column and expand the Imported Keyword Tags category. Activate the Lesson 02-03 tag as a filter by clicking its checkbox.

2 In the People column of the Advanced Search panel, expand the Family category and activate the Kids tag; the number of files found by this search has dropped from 128 to just 20 (depending on your face tagging). Activate the United Kingdom tag in the Places column; the image count is further reduced to five photos.

Searches set up in the Advanced Search panel are "and" searches; you're asking to see items marked with the Kids tag *and* the Lesson 02-03 keyword *and* the United Kingdom tag. Each term you add to an "and" search further filters the results, returning less items. The search results bar above the thumbnails grid now lists all three search terms.

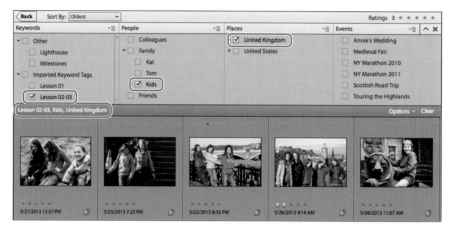

3 In the Events column, choose Touring The Highlands. The thumbnails grid now displays only one photo (if your face tagging was accurate).

▶ **Tip:** You can narrow an advanced search even further by selecting a folder or album in the left panel, defining a date range in the Timeline, setting up a ratings filter in the actions bar, and typing search terms in the text search box.

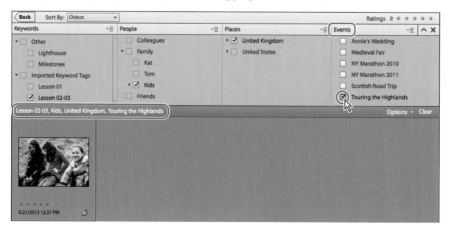

Saving complex searches

It's unlikely that the results of the search you've set up will ever change, no matter how many photos you add to your library; the Scotland vacation and the walk in the Highlands are done. However, when you set up search with more generalized criteria, it can return more images each time new matches are added to the catalog.

1   Disable the criteria in the Keywords and Events columns of the Advanced Search panel; then, set up the search you see in the illustration below. The search will find any photos tagged with the Family Trips keyword (from the Travel category) that feature people in the Kids group, as long as they have Places tags in the United States, and ratings of three stars or higher.

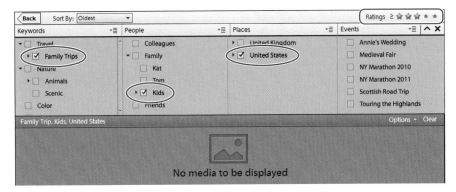

There are no photos in your catalog that match these criteria—but that may well change after the next school break. You can save this search and run it periodically to find the best shots to add to your happiest family album.

2   Click the Options button at the right of the search result bar below the Advanced Search panel and choose Save Search Criteria As Saved Search. In the Create Saved Search dialog box, type in the text box to name the saved search **Best of Kids US Vacations**, and then click OK.

3   Click the Back button in the actions bar to clear the search; then, click the magnifying-glass icon at the left of the text search box at the top of the workspace and choose Saved Searches from the menu.

4   Select your saved search in the Saved searches dialog box, and then click Open. The search results bar lists your saved search criteria. Click clear in the search results bar; then, choose Find > Using Advanced Search to open the Advanced Search panel, ready for the next exercise.

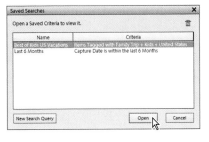

▶ **Tip:** To modify the criteria that define a saved search, and even change it from an "and" search to an "or" search, select the search in the Saved searches dialog box, and then click New Search Query.

Finding photos by visual similarity

In Lesson 2, you used the People Recognition feature and saw how easy it makes the task of tagging the faces in large numbers of photos. In this section you'll look at another set of tools that harness the power of Photoshop Elements' automatic image analysis software.

Note: Clicking the X button in the header of the Advanced Search panel will clear the search and close the panel completely.

1   Use the Advanced Search panel to isolate all the photos with the Animals keyword tag; then, click the upwards facing arrow at the right of the Advanced Search panel's header to collapse the panel without clearing the filter.

2   Click the magnifying-glass icon beside the text search box and choose Visual Similarity Search from the menu.

3   Choose Edit > Deselect, and then drag the image DSC_0609.jpg to the Find bar.

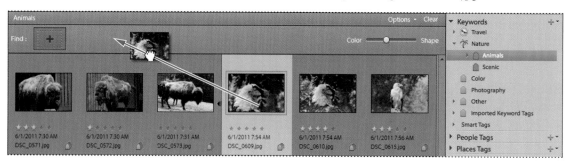

Note: The search results you see on screen may vary from those illustrated here, depending on your operating system.

The search returns images displayed in the Media Browser in descending order of visual similarity to the photo you dragged to the Find bar. A marker displaying the calculated percentage of visual similarity for each image appears in the bottom left corner of its thumbnail, and a slider appears at the Find bar for tweaking the search results. The optimum position for the slider will vary for each image searched.

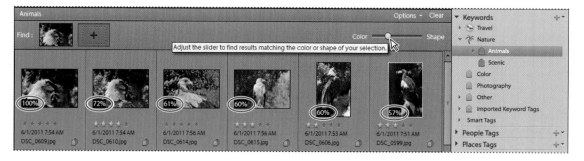

4   Experiment with the Color / Shape slider. A move to the left weights the analysis towards similarities in color, texture, and pattern; moving the slider to the right returns images that share more in terms of shape, proportion, and composition.

5   Right-click / Control-click the thumbnail in the Find bar and choose Remove From Search. Make another image the object of a new search. Experiment with the Color–Shape slider, then repeat the process for several more images.

In some cases it may be helpful to add a second reference photo to your visual search. You can either drag a second image to the find bar, or click the plus sign (+) to the right of the first reference photo in the Find bar and select a second image from the Media Browser. The search will look for a combination of visual attributes.

6   Click Clear at the right of the actions bar; then, repeat step 1.

Finding objects in photos

You can search your photo library for a specific object.

1   In the Media Browser, select the image DSC_0472.jpg, a photo of a Siamang.

2   Choose Find > By Visual Searches > Objects Appearing In Photos.

3   In the enlarged view, drag the bounding box to the ape's head. Use the handles at the corners of the bounding box to fit it neatly around the shape, and then click Search Object.

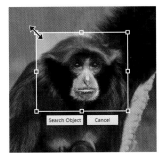

Once again, the results are ranked by similarity to the reference object. As for all visual searches, you can refine the search results by tweaking the Color–Shape slider.

4   When you're done, click the Back button at the left of the actions bar.

Finding and removing duplicate photos

The last of the visual search options finds and groups duplicated, or very similar images, and then gives you the opportunity to either stack them or delete them from your catalog—great for housekeeping as your image library gets bigger.

The process is very similar to the automated stacking workflow (see "Stacking photos automatically" earlier in this lesson). You'll be presented with groups of similar photos; for each group, you can stack the photos and keep them in the catalog, confirm them for removal, or do nothing.

You can search an individual folder for duplicates, or run the search on a selection of images in the Media Browser. If there is no folder or album selected as the image source, no filter in operation, and no active selection in the media Browser, Photoshop Elements searches your entire catalog for duplicates.

> **Tip:** The Duplicate Photos search can be particularly helpful for dealing with long series of photos captured with a camera set to the auto-bracketing or multi-burst mode.

Finding photos by searching their metadata

Some of the metadata that may be attached to an image file is generated automatically by the camera; more is added when you spend time organizing your catalog. Searchable metadata includes file attributes, tags, ratings, albums, version sets, captions, notes, capture date, and a range of camera model, lens, and exposure details—to mention just a few!

The Details (Metadata) search lets you leverage all that information to find exactly the files you want; run any search, and then filter for just the shots taken with a wide angle lens.

1   Choose Find > By Details (Metadata). If you've completed the advanced search exercises, you're already familiar with setting up a multiple-criteria search. In fact, any metadata search you define can be saved as a Saved Search by simply activating that option below the search rules. Set up a few search rules of your own and examine the criteria menus to see the many searchable categories.

2   Click Cancel to dismiss the Find > By Details (Metadata) dialog box.

Hiding files

You've already learned how creating stacks and version sets can help reduce clutter and repetition in the Media Browser, effectively reducing the number of images on view by tucking the excess shots away behind a cover photo.

However, all of those stacked images will still appear in search results—distracting you when making selections, and needing to be taken into consideration whenever you apply a command to the top photo. Once you've settled on the best of a stack of similar photos, or of several edits in a version set, it can be more effective to hide all the other images from view (and from the search tools) completely.

Hiding a photo does not delete it from its folder on your hard disk, remove it from your catalog, or even from an album—you can un-hide it at any time if you start a new project where it might be useful or if you find that you could make use of a differently edited version.

You'll find the commands for marking an image as hidden, and for showing or hiding images marked as hidden, in the Edit > Visibility menu.

Congratulations—you've reached the end of Lesson 3! In this lesson, you've explored advanced options for importing photos from your camera and learned how to acquire images from a PDF file. You've created version sets, stacks, and albums, and discovered more techniques for finding and managing your files.

Before you move on, take a moment to review what you've learned, and test your command of the concepts and techniques presented in this lesson by working through the following questions and answers.

Review questions

1 Do you need to be in the Media view to add keyword tags to an image?

2 What are Version Sets and Stacks?

3 What is the main difference between grouping files using shared keyword tags and grouping them in an album?

4 Once you've activated your complimentary Adobe Revel account, how do you upload images to Revel?

5 Why would you save search criteria from an Advanced Search as a Saved Search?

Review answers

1 Though the Tags panel in the Media view offers the most keyword tagging options, you can add keywords to your photos in any of the other three Organizer views by typing in the text box in the Image Tags panel. To show the Image Tags panel in the People and Events views, you'll first need to expand a stack, and then click the Info button at the right of the Task bar. In the Places view, the Info button is available at all times.

2 A version set automatically groups an original photo and its edited versions. Stacks can be created manually or automatically to group similar or related photos. A version set can be nested inside a stack: if you edit a photo that's in a stack, the photo and its edited copy are put in a version set nested inside the stack. Both Version Sets and Stacks make it easier to locate photos by reducing the clutter in the thumbnails grid.

3 The main difference between grouping files in an album, rather than with a shared keyword tag, is that in an album you can rearrange the order of the files.

4 To upload an album to Adobe Revel, drag it from the Local Albums category in the Organizer's left panel to the listing for your Revel library under Mobile Albums. You can upload a photo or a selection of photos from the Media Browser in the same way.

5 For many searches, you can easily "save" the results—or in other words, preserve the grouping of images that match the search criteria—by creating an Album or by tagging all the photos returned by the search with the same keyword, Place, or Event tag. Once established, these groupings are static; their content will not change over time unless you manually add or remove photos or tags. A Saved Search, on the other hand, can be more versatile; you can run the same complex search again and again, returning more images that match the search criteria each time you add photos to your catalog.

4 IMAGE EDITING BASICS

Lesson overview

Photoshop Elements offers a comprehensive suite of easy-to-use tools and a choice of three editing modes, so it's easy to achieve impressive results, whatever your experience level. Guided edit mode helps novices to learn as they work, Quick edit presents an array of one-touch controls for correcting common image problems, and Expert mode delivers all the power and sophistication experienced users expect.

This lesson begins with an overview of the core concepts behind image correction, and then introduces a range of quick and easy techniques to help you get more from your photos in just a few clicks:

- Making quick and easy edits in the Organizer
- Batch-processing photos and using automatic fixes
- Understanding the histogram, levels, and white balance
- Making Quick Fix adjustments
- Working in Guided edit mode
- Applying editing presets selectively with the Smart Brush
- Correcting an image using Smart Fix
- Working with camera raw images

 You'll probably need between one and two hours to complete this lesson. If you haven't already done so, download the Lesson 4 work files from the Lesson & Update Files tab of your Account page at www.peachpit.com.

Explore the many powerful and versatile editing tools that make it easy to get more from your photos in Photoshop Elements—even if you're a beginner. Start with a few of the easy-to-use, one-step image correction features, and then experiment with some more advanced techniques, such as layering preset adjustments with the Smart Brush.

Note: Before you start this lesson, make sure that you've set up a folder for your lesson files and downloaded the Lesson 4 folder from your Account page at www.peachpit.com, as detailed in "Accessing the Classroom in a Book files" in the chapter "Getting Started" at the beginning of this book. You should also have created a new work catalog (see "Creating a catalog for working with this book" in Lesson 1).

Getting started

You'll start by importing the sample images for this lesson to your CIB Catalog.

1   Start Photoshop Elements and click Organizer in the Welcome Screen. Check the lower right corner of the Organizer workspace to make sure the CIB Catalog is loaded—if not, choose File > Manage Catalogs and select it from the list.

2   Click the Import button at the upper left of the Organizer workspace and choose From Files And Folders from the drop-down menu. In the Get Photos And Videos From Files And Folders dialog box, locate and select your Lesson 4 folder. Disable the automatic processing options; then, click Get Media.

3   In the Import Attached Keyword Tags dialog box, click Select All; then, click OK.

Editing photos in the Organizer

You can fix a range of common image problems without even leaving the Organizer.

Note: The most recent version always appears at the left in an expanded version set, and becomes the image displayed on top of the collapsed version set.

1   In the Media Browser, select the image DSCN0532.jpg. Click the Instant Fix button (⚲) at the right of the Task bar to open the Photo Fix Options panel; then, click the Contrast button (▮). The edited file is grouped with the original in a Version Set. In the Media Browser, the edited version appears as the top image in the collapsed (or closed) Version Set. Click the arrow at the right of the image frame to expand the Version Set.

2   In the expanded Version Set, select the un-edited original, DSCN0532.jpg. Click the Color button (☰). Making sure that you select the original image each time, repeat the process for Levels (🏔), and then for Smart Fix (🖼).

Tip: Each of the Instant Fix adjustments can be used in combination with others. Some combinations will produce different results when the order of the automatic adjustments is varied.

3   Double-click the original image to see it in the single image view. Use the left arrow key on your keyboard to compare the un-edited photo with the results of your single-click adjustments. Double-click the enlarged image to return to the thumbnail view. Select all four edited versions; then, right-click / Control-click any of the selected thumbnails and choose Delete Selected Items From Catalog.

4 In the Confirm Deletion From Catalog dialog box, click to activate the option Also Delete Selected Item(s) From The Hard Disk; then, click OK. You'll work more with this photo later in the lesson.

Editing in Full Screen mode

In the Organizer's Full Screen mode, you'll find the same Instant Fix buttons in the Quick Edit panel, enabling you to make substantial improvements to an image with just a click or two and assess the results at a conveniently high zoom level.

1 In the Media Browser, select DSC_0006.jpg; then, choose View > Full Screen.

2 Hold the Ctrl / Command key and press the Plus key (+) on your keyboard to zoom in. Drag the magnified photo to view a different part of the image. Double-click the photo to fit it to the screen.

3 Move the pointer to the upper left edge of the screen to show the Quick Edit panel; then, click the Pin button at the upper right of the panel (circled in the illustration at the right), so that the Quick Edit panel stays open while you work.

4 In the Quick Edit panel, hold the pointer over each instant fix button in turn to see a tooltip describing the effect it will have on the image. Click the Color button (⟲), and then click the Contrast button (▮).

5 Click to disable the Pin button at the upper right of the Quick Edit panel, and then move the pointer away; the Quick Edit panel closes after a second or so.

You've improved this photo dramatically with just two clicks in the Quick Edit panel, without even leaving the Organizer.

6 Press the Esc key, or click the Close button (X) in the control bar to exit the Full Screen mode. In the Media Browser, expand the new Version Set; then, right-click / Command-click the edited image, DSC_0006_edited-1.jpg, and choose Delete From Catalog. In the Confirm Deletion From Catalog dialog box, activate the option Also Delete Selected Item(s) From The Hard Disk. Click OK. You'll work more with this photo in the next exercise.

▶ **Tip:** You can use the Quick Edit panel to correct image problems even while reviewing your photos as a full-screen slideshow.

Recognizing what your photo needs

For some photos, applying one-click fixes in the Organizer will be enough, but when you want more control—and access to the full power of Photoshop Elements editing, adjustment and correction tools—you'll work in the Editor.

Before you explore the Editor's three working modes, we'll look at some of the basic concepts behind image adjustment and correction.

Recognizing and understanding a photo's problems and deficiencies makes the task of correcting and enhancing the image much faster and easier—even when you're simply choosing from automatic fixes as you did in the full screen view.

1   Ctrl-click / Command-click to select both of the photos that you've already worked with in this lesson; then add the image DSC_0212.jpg to the selection. Click the Editor button (not the arrow beside it) in the Task bar.

2   If you are not already in Expert edit mode, click Expert in the mode picker at the top of the Editor workspace; then, choose Window > Reset panels.

3   Click the arrow beside the More button (⊞) at the right of the Task bar and choose Histogram from the panels menu.

4   If necessary, change the Channel setting in the Histogram panel from the default Colors to RGB; then, click the triangular alert icon (⚠) at the upper right of the black and white Histogram curve to refresh the histogram graph with un-cached information.

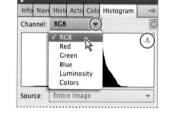

Understanding the histogram

A histogram is a graph that maps the distribution of tonal values in an image, from the shadows at the left end of the curve, through the midtones, to the highlights at the right of the curve.

A peak in the curve shows that the corresponding part of the tonal range is well represented—in other words, the image contains plenty of detail in that area. Inversely, a trough in the histogram curve can indicate a deficiency of image detail.

You can use the histogram both as a "diagnostic" tool that can help you to recognize where corrections need to be made, and also as a source of dynamic feedback that enables you to assess how effective an adjustment will be, even as you set it up.

Note: The first time you launch the Editor, it opens in Quick edit mode; after that, it will reopen to whichever edit mode was active when you last exited the application.

Note: The triangular alert icon will reappear on the histogram each time you change an image; click the icon to refresh the graph.

1 If you don't see the Photo Bin at the bottom of the Editor workspace, click the
   Photo Bin button () in the Task bar.

2 Watch the curve in the Histogram panel as you double-click each of the thumbnails in the Photo Bin in turn to bring that image to the front in the Edit pane.

▶ **Tip:** Refresh the histogram for each image
as it becomes active.

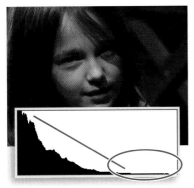

This histogram is heavily weighted towards the left and deficient in the midtones and highlights; the image is overly dark and lacks tonal depth and definition in the girl's face.

With plenty of information at the ends of the curve, the overall contrast is good, but the central trough indicates a lack of midtone detail that gives the shaded skin a dull, underexposed look.

The histogram for this photo shows almost no information at either end and a somewhat lopsided spread of midtones. The image lacks contrast; it appears flat and slightly overexposed.

3 For each of the photos that you've already worked with, double-click the thumbnail in the Photo Bin to bring the image window to the front; then, choose
   Enhance > Adjust Smart Fix. Watch the image and its histogram change as you
   drag the Fix Amount slider to set a value of 60% (for Auto Smart Fix, the value
   is 40%). Click OK to close the Adjust Smart Fix dialog box.

The changes in the images are reflected in their histograms (shown here with the original curves overlaid in gray for comparison). In both cases there is more information in the midtone range, boost-ing detail and definition in skin tones, and a bet-ter spread of tones from dark to light, improving the overall contrast.

Tip: If you can't find the My CIB Work folder, refer to "Creating a work folder" in the Getting Started chapter at the beginning of this book.

4 Bring the image DSC_0006.jpg to the front and choose File > Save As. Name the new file DSC_0006_**AutoSmart.jpg**, to be saved to the My CIB Work folder and included in the Organizer, but not in a Version Set. Click Save; then, click OK to accept the JPEG quality setting and close the file. Repeat the process for the image DSCN0532.jpg, making sure to add _**AutoSmart** to the file name.

Adjusting levels

Once you're familiar with the histogram, the Levels dialog box provides a very direct way to adjust the distribution curve in order to improve an image's tonal range.

1 You should still have the photo DSC_0212.jpg open from the previous exercise. Choose Enhance > Adjust Lighting > Levels. In the Levels dialog box, make sure that the Preview option is activated.

In the Levels dialog box, you can use the shadows, midtones, and highlights sliders below the Input Levels histogram graph (left, middle, and right respectively), or the Set Black Point, Set Gray Point, and Set White Point eyedroppers at the right, to redefine the end points of the curve and adjust the distribution of image information along its length.

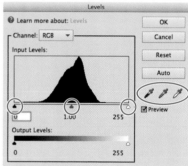

Although the midtones range is most in need of adjustment in this image, it's important to get the shadows and highlights right first.

2 Select the Set Black Point Eyedropper tool; then, watch the histogram as you click the dark area in the lower left corner of the image. The white line and gray area in the histogram indicate the shape of the curve prior to this adjustment.

The black point eyedropper has not worked well on our lesson photo; it should ideally be used to sample a black area, rather than a colored shadow. The deeper shadows have been "clipped" to black and the color has become much cooler as the warm hues have been removed to produce a pure black at the sampled point.

3 In the Levels dialog box, click Reset and we'll try another method for adjusting the shadows. Hold down the Alt / Option key as you drag the shadows slider to the right to set a value of 70: just inside the left-hand end of the tonal curve. The clipping preview shows you where the darkest parts of the image are.

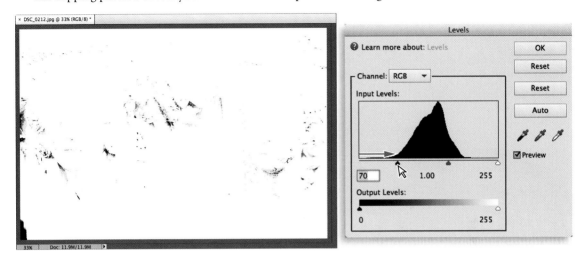

4 Watch the histogram as you release first the Alt / Option key, and then the mouse button. The histogram curve shifts to the left—possibly a little too much. You can see that the left end of the curve has become truncated. In the Levels dialog box, use the shadows slider to reduce the value to 45. The curve in the histogram is adjusted so that there is minimal truncation (clipping).

5 Hold down the Alt / Option key; then, drag the highlights slider to 185. The clipping preview begins to show significant clipping of image detail in the brighter parts of the photo. Drag the highlights slider back to 195, where the clipping is minimal; then release the Alt / Option key and the mouse button.

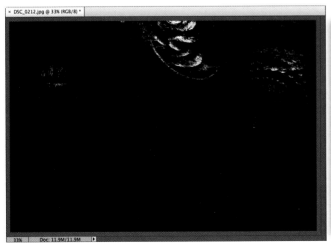
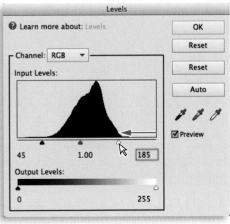

6 In the Levels controls, drag the midtone slider (the gray triangle below the center of the graph) to the right to set the midtone value to 0.8.

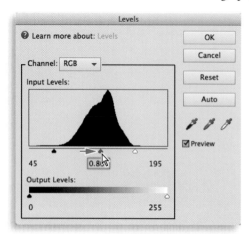

7 In the Histogram panel, click the yellow alert icon to refresh the display.

Tip: Your edits have caused some gaps and spikes in the histogram curve. Where possible, avoid adjustments that create large gaps; even if the image still looks good on screen, gaps indicate a loss of image data that may be apparent as color banding when printed.

8 Compare the original histogram (the red overlay) to the adjusted curve. Information has spread outwards, widening the midtone range as well as filling out both the highlights and shadows.

9 Click OK to close the Levels dialog box. Select Edit > Undo Levels, or press Ctrl+Z / Command+Z to see how the image looked before editing. Choose Edit > Redo Levels, or Press Ctrl+Y / Command+Y to reinstate your corrections.

10 Choose File > Save As. Name the new file **DSC_0212_Levels.jpg** and set your Lessons / My CIB Work folder as the destination. Activate the option Include In The Elements Organizer and disable Save In Version Set With Original. Click Save; then click OK to accept the JPEG settings. Choose File > Close.

Assessing a photo's color balance

Artificial light, unusual shooting conditions, and incorrect camera settings can all result in unwelcome color casts in an image. Unless your camera is properly set up to compensate for current weather conditions, photos shot on an overcast day may have a flat, bluish cast due to a deficiency in the warmer colors, while the "golden" light of late-afternoon sunshine can produce an overly warm appearance. Fluorescent lighting is notorious for producing a dull, greenish tint.

In this exercise, you'll work with an image that has the opposite problem: a warm yellow-red cast commonly seen in indoor shots captured under tungsten lighting. We'll start with a look at the Balance controls in the Quick edit mode.

1 To switch to Quick edit mode, click Quick in the mode above the editing pane. In Quick edit mode, choose Window > Reset panels.

2 Choose File > Open. Navigate to your Lesson 4 folder; then, select the image DSC_0378.jpg and click Open.

3 In the Adjustments panel at the right of the Quick edit workspace, expand the Balance panel. Color imbalances are defined in terms of an image's *temperature* and *tint*; the Balance panel has a separate control pane for adjusting each of these attributes. For now, make sure that the Temperature tab is selected just below the panel's header.

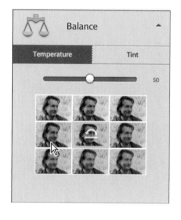

The grid of preview thumbnails shows the full range of variation possible with this control. Clicking the central thumbnail resets an image to its original state—a blue frame highlights the currently selected setting.

4 Move the pointer over each preview thumbnail in the grid in turn to see that level of adjustment applied temporarily to the image in the work area. A white frame highlights the setting currently previewed.

▷ **Tip:** You can preview and apply incremental settings between the levels represented by the preview thumbnails by dragging the slider left or right.

5 Click the Tint tab above the slider control and explore the variations.

The color temperature of an image accounts for casts ranging from cool blue to hot orange-red; "tint" refers to casts ranging from yellow-green to magenta-pink.

Working with the Temperature and Tint settings

If you're new to color correction, the preview thumbnails provide a useful visual reference for understanding what's behind an unwanted color cast. Before we take a closer look at the issue in the Expert edit mode, you can correct this photo using the Balance controls and save the results for comparison to other techniques.

1   In the Temperature pane, click the preview to the left of the central thumbnail.

2   Switch to the Tint pane. Move the pointer over the preview to the left of the central thumbnail. For the Tint controls, moving by one preview in this direction reduces the value by an increment of 25—a little too far for our lesson photo. Instead, drag the slider to set a value of -10.

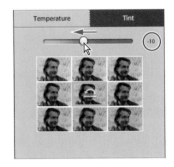

3   Choose File > Save As. Activate the option Save As A Copy. Name the copy **DSC_0378_QuickBalance.jpg**, to be saved to your My CIB Work folder, and included in the Organizer, but not in a version set; then, click Save. Click OK to accept the default JPEG quality settings.

4   In the Adjustments panel header, click the Reset Image button to reset all the controls, reverting the image to its original state.

Consulting the color histogram

Let's see what the histogram has to say about this photo.

1   Click Expert in the mode picker at the top of the Editor workspace.

2   If the Histogram panel is not already open, choose Window > Histogram. If necessary, set the Channel menu at the top of the Histogram panel to Colors.

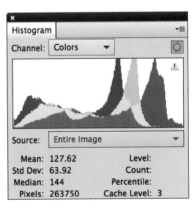

The histogram corroborates the visual evidence: this photo has a serious imbalance in the spread of color information. Rather than a largely unified curve, there is a very marked separation of colors; reds and yellows are over-represented in the upper midtones and highlights, while greens and blues are lacking.

In the next exercise, you'll learn how to correct a color cast by adjusting the photo's *white balance*—or redefining the *white point*, to re-calibrate the image's color.

Adjusting the white balance

A color cast has the appearance of a tinted transparency overlaid on all the colors in your photograph. For example, the blue-green tint commonly associated with fluorescent lighting will be visible even on objects that should appear white, and even white paper photographed under tungsten lighting will have a yellow-red cast, as can be clearly seen in our lesson image.

To adjust the white point, or white balance, you need to identify what should be a neutral tone in your photo—either a white object, or an area of gray that should appear neither noticeably cool nor warm. Photoshop Elements will then recalculate the color values across the entire image in relation to whatever pixels you've defined as the new, color-neutral benchmark.

1 Choose Enhance > Adjust Color > Remove Color Cast. The Remove Color Cast dialog box appears, and the pointer becomes an eye-dropper cursor ( ).

2 Click with the eyedropper to sample the gray stripe in the uphol-stery just behind the collar of the man's jacket. If this introduces too much blue, click the Reset button in the Remove Color Cast dialog box and try again. Try targeting a slightly lighter or darker tone. When you're satisfied with the results, click OK to close the Remove Color Cast dialog box.

3 Examine the color histogram. The histogram curve is much more balanced, though the photo could still be improved. For now, save the corrected image as **DSC_0378_WhiteBalance.jpg**, with all the usual settings; then, close the file.

Although blue and cyan are still predominant in the shadows, the histogram curve is now more unified, without the dramatic separation of colors you saw earlier.

Making easy color and lighting adjustments

In this section, we'll begin our exploration of the Editor, taking a closer look at the tools and techniques that will enable you to get the best from your photos. Now that you've soaked up a little theory, you'll find it easier to understand the processes, whether you're using one-click fixes, or making detailed selective edits.

Whether the problem is inadequate exposure, a lack of contrast, or an unsightly color cast, you can make fast fixes using the simple controls in Quick Edit mode, let the Guided Edit mode step you through a wide range of editing tasks, make detailed adjustments in Full Edit mode—or even arrange for Photoshop Elements to batch-process your photos, applying your choice of automatic corrections.

Fixing photos automatically in batches

In this exercise, you'll batch process all of the image files used in this lesson, saving the auto-adjusted photos as copies so that you can compare the results of the automatic processing to the edits you make using other techniques.

1   If the Editor is not still in Expert mode, click Expert in the mode picker. Choose File > Process Multiple Files. In the Quick Fix options, at the upper right of the Process Multiple Files dialog box, click the check boxes to activate all four auto-fix options: Auto Levels, Auto Contrast, Auto Color, and Sharpen.

2   At the upper left of the dialog box, choose Folder from the Process Files From menu. Under Source, click the Browse button. Locate and select the Lesson 4 folder as the source folder for the images to be processed. Click OK / Choose. Under Destination, click Browse to set the My CIB Work folder as the destination for the processed copies.

3   Under File Naming, activate the Rename Files option. Choose Document Name from the menu on the left, and then type _**AutoFix** in the second field. This will add the appendix "_AutoFix" to the existing document names as the processed copies are saved.

4   Review the settings in the dialog box. Make sure that the resizing and file conversion options under Image Size and File Type are disabled, and then click OK.

> ● **Note:** For Windows users: ignore any alert warning that files could not be processed. This is caused by a hidden system file and will have no impact on the success of your project.

Photoshop Elements opens, processes, and closes the images. The newly created copies are automatically tagged with the same keywords as the source files.

Adding the auto-corrected files to your catalog

When you modify an image in the Editor, the Include In Organizer option in the Save and Save As dialog boxes is activated by default. However, when you batch-edit files with the Process Multiple Files command, this option isn't part of the process—you must add the automatically edited copies to the Organizer manually.

1   Switch to the Organizer by clicking the Organizer button () in the Task bar; then, click the Import button at the upper left of the Organizer workspace and choose From Files And Folders from the drop-down menu.

2   In the Get Photos And Videos From Files And Folders dialog box, locate and open your My CIB Work folder. Ctrl-click / Command-click or marquee-select all the files with the suffix "_AutoFix." Disable any automatic processing option that is currently active; then, click Get Media.

3   In the Import Attached Keyword Tags dialog box, click Select All; then, click OK. The files are imported to your CIB Catalog and displayed in the Media Browser. Click the Back button (< **Back** >) to display all the images in your catalog.

Correcting photos in Quick Edit mode

In Quick Edit mode, Photoshop Elements conveniently groups easy-to-use controls for the most common basic image correction operations in the Adjustments panel.

Earlier in this lesson, you tried some one-click fixes in the Organizer's Instant Fix panel. Later, you applied a combination of the same automatic fixes while batch-processing files. The Adjustments panel presents similar automatic adjustment options, but also gives you the opportunity to preview and fine-tune the settings.

1   You should still be in the Organizer from the last exercise. If you don't see the right panel group, click the Tags/Info button at the far right of the Task bar. If you don't see the list of keywords, click the Tags tab at the top of the right panel. Expand the Imported Keyword Tags category; then, move the pointer over the Lesson 04 tag and click the arrow at the right.

Note: In this illustration, the Lesson 04 tag icon has been customized: you may see a different thumbnail.

2   Select the original photo of the colored perfume bottles, DSC_2474.jpg, making sure not to confuse the un-edited file with the AutoFix copy; then, click the Editor button ()—not the arrow beside it—in the Task bar.

3   Use the mode picker to switch the Editor to Quick mode. If you don't see the Adjustments panel at the right, click the Adjustments button in the Task bar.

Applying quick fixes

All of the Quick Edit adjustments have manual controls. Automatic fixes are available for Smart Fix, Levels, Color, and Sharpen, but not for Exposure or Balance.

Note: Smart Fix is a combination of several adjustments; it corrects overall color balance and improves shadow and highlight detail.

1   Choose Before & After - Horizontal from the View menu above the Edit pane. In the Adjustments panel, expand the Smart Fix pane and click the Auto button. Notice the immediate effect on the image in the After view.

2 Expand the Levels pane, and then click both Auto Levels and Auto Contrast, noting the effects of the adjustments in the After view.

3 Expand the Color pane and click the Auto button.

Smart Fix: Auto   + Levels and Contrast: Auto   + Color: Auto   + Exposure: 0.7

4 Choose File > Save As. In the Save As dialog box, type **DSC_2474_QuickFix** as the name of the new file, to be saved to your My CIB Work folder in JPEG format and included in the Organizer but not as part of a Version Set. Click Save. In the JPEG Options dialog box, accept the default quality and click OK.

▶ **Tip:** Click a thumb-nail in the preview grid to apply that level of adjustment; then, use the slider to fine tune the effect. The preview grids not only provide an intuitive editing inter-face, but also serve as a great way to learn the effects of the various adjustment controls as you work with them.

5 Expand the Color pane once again and click the Saturation tab. A grid of preview thumbnails shows the range of variation possible with the Saturation slider. A blue frame highlights the central thumbnail, which represents the image in its current state. Move the pointer slowly over each thumbnail in the grid to preview your image with that level of saturation in the work area.

6 Repeat the process for the Color pane's Hue and Vibrance controls.

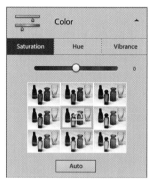

Saturation: -100   Saturation: +100   Vibrance: -100   Vibrance: +100

7 Return to the Levels panel and explore the Shadows, Midtones and Highlights panes in the same way. To reset a control, click the thumbnail with the Reset icon (not always the central preview).

8 To discard any changes you've made and revert the image to its last saved state, click the Reset Image button in the header of the Adjustments pane.

9 Choose File > Close.

Adding quick effects, textures and frames

New in Quick edit mode from Photoshop Elements 12, the Effects, Textures, and Frames panels present a range of one-click choices that make it easy to add a creative touch to your photos. You can access these three new panels by choosing from the buttons at the right of the Task bar.

The Effects (fx) panel offers ten instant photo effects, from Summer Day, Toy Camera, and Light Leak, which simulate nostalgic camera and film effects, to photo processing styles and the Pencil Sketch and Lithograph treatments, which can turn even a snapshot into a work of art. The previews in the Effects panel are "live," so you can see how the effect will look on your photo before you apply it.

Choose from the Textures panel to give the surface of your photo the look of a peeling paint, soft canvas, or pitted chrome. Other textures are applied with a colored pattern overlay. Add a frame to make your image really stand out. The Frames panel presents choices from simple graphic photo-print borders to the 3D, photographic look of the Aged, Scrapbook, and Flowers And Buttons frames.

You can scale, rotate, or move a photo inside its frame without leaving Quick edit mode. If you prefer to have more control over the way the effects and textures are applied to your image, you can take it into Expert mode, where each effect and texture has its own layer and layer mask. You can modify the opacity and blending mode for each layer, or edit its layer mask to create areas in the photo where the effect or texture is reduced or removed entirely.

Working with Auto Smart Tone

Note: The Enhance > Auto Smart Tone command is available in both Quick and Expert modes in the Editor.

From Photoshop Elements 12, the Auto Smart Tone feature provides a new, highly intuitive way to make the most of your photos with just a few clicks. Even if you begin with no clear idea of what adjustments an image needs, the Auto Smart Tone dialog box provides visual clues and simple controls that make the process easy.

Called "smart" for a good reason, the Auto Smart Tone feature uses "intelligent" algorithms to analyze and correct an image automatically—and then actually learns from whatever adjustments you make.

Auto Smart Tone begins by comparing your image to a database drawn from hundreds of images of all types; then references information about how those images were corrected by different photographic professionals in order to calculate an automatic adjustment that is uniquely suited to the particular photo you're editing. Auto Smart Tone adjustments combine corrections to different aspects of both tone and color, depending on the deficiencies of the image at hand.

1 In the Organizer, isolate the photos for this lesson, if necessary, by clicking the Lesson 4 folder in the list at the left, or the white arrow beside the Lesson 04 tag in the Tags panel. Select the un-edited images DSC_0006.jpg, DSC_0212.jpg, DSC_0378.jpg, and DSCN0532.jpg; then, click the Editor button in the Task bar.

2 In the Editor, click Expert in the mode picker at the top of the workspace to switch to Expert edit mode; then bring the image DSC_0378.jpg to the front by clicking its name tab at the top of the Edit window. Choose Auto Smart Tone from the Enhance menu to open the Auto Smart Tone dialog box.

The Auto Smart Tone dialog box opens with the automatic adjustment pre-applied. In the center is a "joystick" control that can be dragged in any direction: a preview in each corner shows what to expect from dragging in that direction. For this photo, the upper left preview is dark, low-contrast, and saturated; the thumbnail at the lower left is also dark, but has more contrast and less saturated color. At the right, the upper preview is brighter, with more neutral colors; the lower is even brighter, with more contrast.

3 Toggle the Before / After switch at the lower left of the dialog box to see the photo with and without the pre-applied automatic adjustment.

4 Click the upper-right preview—the closest to a technically balanced solution; the joystick control moves to the limit of its range in that direction. Click and hold the control; a reference grid appears. Drag the control downwards by two grid divisions to increase saturation, and one square left to deepen the shadows. As you drag, the display defaults to the After view to reflect your changes.

5 Click OK, and then repeat the process from step 2 for each of the other three open images. If you're unsure, drag the joystick left to right and top to bottom to become accustomed to the effects; then, refer to the illustrations below as a rough guide. Start from the points indicated, and then season to taste. Leave the last photo open in the Auto Smart Tone dialog box and read on.

  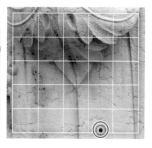

As you tweak the automatic adjustment, Auto Smart Tone learns from your actions. Each time you use the feature, your adjustments are recorded, and then taken into consideration when Smart Tone is calculating a solution for the next photo. Over time, Auto Smart Tone remembers whether you tend to favor a high-contrast, color-saturated look or dreamy, high-key treatments and begins to tailor it's automatic adjustments accordingly for similar images.

6 Click the small menu icon (▼≡) at the lower left of the Auto Smart Tone dialog box to see the options available. For now, leave both options activated. Click OK to confirm your adjustment and return to the Editor.

Tip: Once you're comfortable with Auto Smart Tone, you can hide the corner thumbnails for a clear view of your photo. You can also disable learning for the current image.

If you feel that Auto Smart Tone may be picking up your beginner's bad habits, you can reset the learning feature on the General tab in Preferences.

7 For each of the four images, choose Save As; then add the suffix **_SmartTone** to the filename and save a JPEG file to your work folder, to be included in the Organizer, but not in a Version Set. When you're done, choose File > Close All.

Adjusting images in Guided Edit mode

● **Note:** As you try more advanced tasks in Photoshop Elements, you may find that you need more information to solve any problems you encounter. For help with some common problems you might have while working through the lessons in this book, see the section "Why won't Photoshop Elements do what I tell it to do?" in Lesson 5.

If you're a newcomer to digital image editing, the Guided Edit mode is a great place to start. By letting Photoshop Elements step you through the process of improving your photos you'll not only achieve impressive results quickly, but also learn a lot about image problems and solutions as you work. Even experienced users will enjoy the ease of working in Guided Edit mode—and may just pick up some new tricks.

For this exercise, you'll work once again with the image of the old perfume bottles, which has an obvious color cast as a result of inadequate artificial lighting.

1   Switch to the Organizer by clicking the Organizer button (▦) in the Task bar. If necessary, click the arrow to the right of the Lesson 04 tag in the Keyword Tags panel to isolate the Lesson 4 images in the Media Browser.

2   Locate the photo of the perfume bottles, DSC_2474.jpg, making sure not to confuse the original with the edited copies. Right-click / Control-click the image and choose Edit With Photoshop Elements Editor from the context menu.

3   In the Editor, click Guided in the mode picker at the top of the Editor work-space to switch to Guided edit mode. Choose the Before & After - Horizontal view from the View menu at the left of the bar above the Edit pane. If the Photo Bin is open below the Edit pane, click the Photo Bin button (▦) at the far left of the Task bar to hide it.

In the Guided edit mode, the Zoom and Hand tools are the only items in the tool-bar; everything you'll need for a long list of image editing tasks—including the long list itself—can be found in the Guided Edits panel at the right.

4 Scroll down in the Guided Edits panel, expanding the Touchups, Photo Effects, and Photo Play categories, if necessary, to see the all of the procedures and projects for which the Guided edit mode offers step-by-step assistance.

In the Touchups category, you'll find a comprehensive menu of all the most common image correction tasks, some of which involve several separate operations. The Photo Effects and Photo Play categories host an array of stylish photographic treatments and eye-catching special effects that will help you to introduce a little variety and creative flair in your image library, and to add atmosphere and sophisticated high-notes to your photo albums, prints, projects, and presentations.

5 Click a few of the editing tasks listed in each of the three categories in the Guided Edits panel to see easy to follow steps and instructions and informative tips, presented together with any tools and controls that you'll need for the procedure. Click cancel to exit each guided task and return to the list.

In the exercises to follow, we'll concentrate on the Guided Touchups category; you'll have some fun with the Photo Effects and Photo Play edits in Lesson 7.

Guided color and lighting corrections

You're already familiar with the process of correcting a color cast by adjusting the white balance, so rather than looking at the Remove A Color Cast guided edit in the Touchups list, we'll explore some other ways to manipulate a photo's colors.

1 Choose Enhance Colors from the Touchups category. Click *twice* on the Auto Fix button to correct the color and contrast; the photo improves dramatically. For photos with less extreme problems, a single click produces satisfactory results.

Note: As is often the case with poorly exposed photos, this photo has more than just one problem. If you had applied the Remove A Color Cast adjustment, you would still need to correct the lighting, as the image is dull and underexposed. The automatic Enhance Color fix takes care of both problems.

2   In the Enhance Colors pane, drag the Hue slider to the left to set a value of **-33**.

All the colors in the image are shifted along the spectrum: the red bottle becomes purple, the blue-green glass is warmed to yellow-green, the orange bottle turns red, and the violet-blue reflections in the clear glass are shifted to cyan.

3   Set the Saturation value to **40**, and the Lightness to **10**. Click Done at the bottom of the Guided Edits panel. The new colors become more vibrant, but the overall contrast is still inadequate.

4   Still in the Touchups category, click Lighten And Darken. Drag the Shadows slider to **33** to retrieve detail in the dark bottle caps and bases; then set the Midtones to **100** to increase contrast by shifting the tonal spread. Click Done.

5   Choose Save As. Name the file **DSC_2474_EC-LD** (for Enhance Colors, Lighten And Darken) and save it to the My CIB Work folder with all the usual settings. In the JPEG Options, set the Quality to 10; then, click OK. Choose File > Close.

More guided solutions

Let's try a few more of the guided touchups on a different image.

1   In the Organizer, select the image DSC_0347.jpg; then, click the Editor button.

Fluorescent back-lighting behind the translucent surface on which the bottles are standing has caused a combination of problems in this photo. The image not only has a dull, yellow-green color cast, but like many back-lit photos, it's also underexposed—in auto-exposure mode, the camera has reduced the exposure in order to compensate for the brightness of the background.

2   In the Guided Edits panel, choose the Remove A Color Cast adjustment from the Touchups category. Move the eyedropper cursor over the image and click on the translucent background between the bottles to reset the white point; then, click Done.

3   Choose the Brightness And Contrast guided touchup in the Guided Edits panel. Click the Brightness And Contrast Auto Fix button, and then click Done.

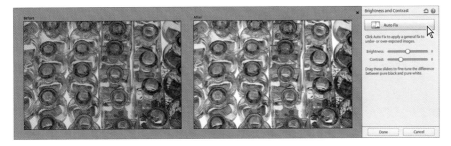

4   Click the Sharpen edit in the Touchups list. Drag the Zoom slider to 100%, or choose View > Actual Pixels; working at 1:1 zoom level will help you to avoid the image artifacts that can result from over-sharpening. Click the Auto Fix button in the Sharpen Photo pane. Click Done; then, choose Save As. Save the new file as **DSC_0347_CC-BC.jpg**, with all the usual settings, and then close it.

Selective editing with the Smart Brush

Tip: For images with a subject that is back-lit, like our lesson photo, overall adjustments will never suit both the shaded subject *and* the brightly lit background. In such cases, using the Smart Brush to adjust differently lit areas in the image separately is the perfect solution.

Sometimes the best way to enhance a photo is to modify just part of the image, or to treat separate areas—such as background and foreground elements—differently, rather than applying an adjustment to the photo overall.

The quickest and easiest way to do this is to paint your adjustments directly onto the image with the Smart Brush tool. The Smart Brush is both a selection tool and an image adjustment tool—as you paint, it creates a selection based on similarities in color and texture, through which your choice of editing preset is applied.

1   Isolate the Lesson 4 images in the Media Browser. Select the un-edited image DSCN0532.jpg, and then click the Editor button (🖼) in the Task bar.

2   In the Editor, click Expert in the mode picker, if necessary. In Expert mode, choose Window > Reset Panels. Click the Photo Bin button (🖼) at the left of the Task bar to hide the Photo Bin; then, choose View > Fit On Screen.

3   Select the Smart Brush (✒) from the toolbox. If the tool options pane doesn't open automatically at the bottom of the workspace, click the Tool Options button (✒) in the Task bar.

Tip: You'll use the tool options pane several times in this exercise. If you prefer, you can hide it as you work, and then show it again as needed by clicking the Tool Options button in the Task bar.

4   In the tool options pane, use the slider to set a brush size of 25 px (pixels); then, click the colored thumbnail to open the Smart Brush presets picker. Choose the Nature category from the Presets menu at the top of the pup-up menu, and then select the Make Dull Skies Blue preset.

Tip: Press the left bracket key ([ ) to decrease the brush size, and the right bracket key ( ]) to increase it. While you're fine-tuning the selection, use a small brush and make slow, short strokes.

5   Press the Esc key on your key-board to close the preset picker. Starting above and to the left of the taller girl's head, drag across the sky. If your selection expands too far, subtract areas such as the distant shoreline from the selection by holding down the Alt / Option key and painting carefully back over them. When you're happy with the adjustment area, Choose Select > Deselect, so that a new stroke will create a new adjustment, rather than add to the current one.

6   Starting at the left, drag to select the water. As long as the adjustment remains active, your strokes will add to the current adjustment area. Hold Alt / Option if you need to paint out submerged legs and the highlights on the girls' arms.

7   If you don't see tabs for the Layers, Effects, Graphics and Favorites panels at the top of the Panel Bin, click the arrow beside the More button (▣) at the right of the Task bar and choose Custom Workspace. Drag the Layers panel out of the Panel Bin by its name tab, and then hide the Panel bin by un-checking its name in the Window menu.

Two new layers have been created for the adjustments; each displays a colored icon representing the gradient used for the Blue Skies effect and a black and white thumbnail representing the layer mask through which the adjustment has been applied. Colored markers—Smart Brush adjustment *pins*—mark the points in the photo where you started dragging with the Smart Brush for each adjustment.

Each Smart Brush edit occupies its own layer, where it remains active and separate from the image itself—so you can add to or subtract from the selection, tweak the effect, or even change which preset is applied, without permanently affecting your original photo. The adjustment pins will be visible whenever the Smart Brush is active.

8   Deselect the Blue Skies 2 adjustment by clicking the Background layer in the Layers panel. Open the Smart Brush presets picker by clicking the Blue Skies thumbnail in the tool options pane. Select the Lighten Skin Tones preset from the Portrait category. Press Esc to close the Smart Brush presets picker.

9   Drag over the two girls, including their hair and swimsuits. If your selection expands to include areas of water; hold Alt / Option as you paint out the unwanted areas. Make sure the selection includes hands, elbows, and at least a little of the base of some of the windswept wisps of hair. You won't see a dramatic effect in the selected areas yet; you'll tweak the adjustment a little later.

A new adjustment pin appears on the image; in the Layers panel, a new adjustment layer is added for the Lighten Skin Tones effect. To the left of its layer mask thumbnail, the new adjustment layer displays a different icon from the Blue Skies effect, indicating that it applies a different type of adjustment through the painted mask.

10 Right-click / Control-click the new adjustment layer (not its black-and-white layer mask icon) and choose Duplicate Layer. Type **Lighten Skin Tones 2** to name the new layer; then, click OK.

11 Hold down the Alt / Option key as you carefully paint the girl on the right out of the selection completely; then, drag the new Smart Brush adjustment pin aside a little to see the marker for your original Lighten Skin Tones adjustment.

Tweaking Smart Brush adjustments

Each Smart Brush adjustment has its own set of controls that let you customize the effect—even in a later editing session, as long you've saved the file with its layers.

Note: You can use the Smart Brush on the same area in an image as many times as you wish. If you re-apply the same preset, the effects are usually cumulative; if you apply more than one effect to the same image area, their effects are combined. Adjustment layers affect all lower layers in the Layers panel; rearranging the order of different adjustments applied to the same area can alter the combined effect.

1 In the Layers panel, double-click the gradient icon () on the Blue Skies 1 layer. In the Gradient Fill dialog box, you can modify the gradient's colors, angle, and fade rate. Watch the sky as you choose Reflected from the gradient Style menu; then, click OK.

2 Use the Opacity slider at the top of the Layers panel to decrease the opacity of the Blue Skies 1 layer from 75% to 30%. You can use the adjacent menu to change the blending mode, but for now, leave it set to Color Burn.

3 Select the layer Blue Skies 2—the adjustment for the sea. Double-click the gradient icon ( ) for Blue Skies 2; then, disable the Reverse option. Click OK. Reduce the opacity of the Blue Skies 2 layer from 75% to 40%.

4 Double-click the Brightness/Contrast icon ( ) on the Lighten Skin Tones 1 to open the Adjustments panel in Brightness/Contrast mode. Set a Brightness value of +60 and increase the Contrast to +25. Repeat the process for the layer Lighten Skin Tones 2, at the top of the layers list. Set both the Brightness and Contrast to a value of 15; then, close the Brightness/Contrast controls.

5 Click the Hand tool to disable the Smart Brush and hide the pins. In the Layers panel, toggle the eye icon (,) beside each adjustment layer's name to show and hide its effect so that you can assess just how the image has changed.

6 Choose File > Save As. Name the file **DSCN0532_SmartBrush** and set up the usual save options. This time, choose the Photoshop file format and activate the Layers option so that you can edit your adjustment layers later. Close the file.

Working with camera raw images

Raw images are high-quality image files that record the maximum amount of image data possible, in a relatively small file size. Though larger than compressed formats such as JPEG, raw images contains more data than TIFF files and use less space.

Many common file formats involve in-camera processing of the incoming image data that can effectively degrade the quality of the image. In creating a compressed file, data deemed superfluous is discarded; in mapping the spread of captured data to a defined color space, the range of the color information can be narrowed. In contrast, raw images retain all of the data captured for each and every pixel.

Capturing your photos in raw format gives you more flexibility and control when it comes to editing your images. Raw files do incorporate camera settings such as exposure, white balance and sharpening, but this information is stored separately from the image data. When you open a raw image in Photoshop Elements, these recorded settings effectively become "live;" the Camera Raw plug-in enables you to adjust them to get more from the raw image data. With 12 bits of data per pixel, it's possible to retrieve shadow and highlight detail from a raw image that would have been lost in the 8 bits/channel JPEG or TIFF formats.

In the following exercises, you'll work with a raw image in Nikon's NEF format as you explore the Camera Raw window> This section will also serve as a review of the image editing concepts and terminology that you learned earlier.

Note: Although not all digital cameras can capture raw images, the newer and more advanced models do offer this option. To see an up-to-date list of the camera models and proprietary raw file formats currently supported by Photoshop Elements, visit the Adobe website.

1 In the Organizer, isolate the Lesson 4 images in the Media Browser, if necessary, by clicking the arrow beside the Lesson 04 keyword tag in the Tags panel. In the thumbnail grid, locate the camera raw image DSC_5683.NEF. Right-click / Control-click the thumbnail and choose Edit With Photoshop Elements Editor from the context menu. Photoshop Elements opens the image in the Camera Raw window.

The moment you open a camera raw file for the first time, the Camera Raw plug-in creates what is sometimes referred to as a *sidecar file* in the same folder as the raw image file. The sidecar file takes the name of the raw file, with the extension ".xmp." Any modification that you make to the raw photograph is written to the XMP (Extensible Metadata Platform) file, rather than to the image file itself, which means that the original image data remains intact, while the XMP file records every edit.

Note: The Camera Raw plug-in, used by Photoshop Elements to open raw files, is updated as new cameras are added to the list of those supported. Check for updates and download the latest version of the plug-in at www.adobe.com.

2 Use the Windows System Tray or Notification Area, or the Dock on Mac OS, to switch back to the Elements Organizer. In the My Folders list in the left panel, right-click / Control-click the Lesson 4 folder and choose Reveal In Finder from the menu. A Windows Explorer or Mac OS Finder window opens to show your Lesson 4 folder. Click the folder, if necessary, to see the contents; the newly created XMP sidecar file, DSC_5683.xmp, is listed beside the NEF image file.

3 Return to the Editor—and the Camera Raw window—in Photoshop Elements.

Getting to know the Camera Raw window

▶ **Tip:** Click the Detail tab to access controls for sharpening image detail and reducing the grainy digital artefacts known as noise.

On the right side of the Camera Raw window is a control panel headed by three tabs: Basic, Detail, and Camera Calibration. For this set of exercises you'll work with the Basic tab—the default—which presents controls for making adjustments that are not possible with the standard editing tools in Photoshop Elements.

1 Make sure that the Preview checkbox above the image window is activated.

2 Hold the pointer over each tool in the toolbar to see a tooltip with the name of the tool and the respective keyboard shortcut. Click the Toggle Full Screen Mode button (⬌) at the right of the tool bar to switch to full screen mode.

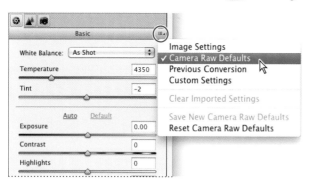

3 Click the menu icon at the right of the Basic tab's header bar to see the choices available from the control panel Options menu. You can apply the same settings you used for the last image you worked with, have Photoshop Elements revert to the default Camera Raw profile for your camera by choosing Reset Camera Raw Defaults, or save your own custom settings as the new default for the camera that captured this image.

Adjusting the white balance

The white balance presets can help you to rectify a color cast caused by lighting conditions. You could correct the white balance of a photo shot on an overcast day, for example, by choosing the Cloudy preset. Other presets compensate for artificial lighting. The As Shot preset uses the settings recorded by your camera, while the Auto setting recalculates the white balance based on an analysis of the image data.

Note: Incandescent lighting typically causes an orange-yellow color cast, while fluorescent lighting is notorious for a dull green tint.

1 Switch between the presets in the White Balance menu, comparing the effects to the default As Shot setting. In the following pages you'll discover why setting the appropriate white balance is so important to the overall look of the image.

Auto preset

Daylight preset

Fluorescent preset

2 For now, choose As Shot from the White Balance presets menu.

For many photos, the right preset will produce satisfactory results or at least serve as a basis for manual adjustment. When none of the presets takes your image in the right direction, you can use the White Balance tool (🖉) to sample a neutral color in the photo, in relation to which Camera Raw will recalculate the white balance. The ideal target is a light to medium gray that is neither discernibly warm or cool. In our sample photo, the weathered wood is a potential reference, but we can probably be more certain that the steel fencing wire in the background is a neutral gray.

Tip: In some images it can be difficult to identify a neutral tone; in the absence of a definitive visual reference you may at times rely on what you know about the photo: that it was taken on a cloudy day, for example, or under fluorescent lighting. It may help to look for references such as white paper, clothing, or paint, and then sample a shaded area.

3 Zoom into the image by choosing 100% from the Zoom Level menu in the lower left corner of the image window, or by double-clicking the zoom tool. Select the Hand tool (✋) and drag the image downwards and to the right so that you can see the thick wire to the left of the girl's hat.

4 Select the White Balance tool (🖉), right beside the Hand tool in the tool bar. Sample a medium gray from the center of the wire where it crosses a relatively dark area. If you see little effect, click a slightly different point.

5 Zoom out by choosing Fit In View from the Zoom Level menu in the lower left corner of the preview window.

The White Balance is now set to Custom and the image has become cooler. The weathered wood in the background is a more neutral gray and the skin tones are rosier. The eyes also look clearer, having lost the original yellow-orange cast.

● **Note:** Depending on where you clicked to set the white balance, you may see different values from those illustrated.

6 Use the White Balance menu to alternate between your custom settings and the As Shot preset, noting the change in the preview window, as well as the differences in the Temperature and Tint settings.

Working with the Temperature and Tint settings

▶ **Tip:** There are no hard and fast rules in color correction; there might be times when you choose to retain a slight color cast for aesthetic purposes. For example, although *technically* in need of correction, you might prefer the original, too-warm cast of our lesson image (caused by late afternoon sunlight) for its evocative, summery look. Although most often used for fine color correction, the white balance settings can also be applied creatively to achieve surprising and dramatic atmospheric effects.

The White Balance tool can accurately remove any color cast or tint from an image but you may still want to tweak the Temperature and Tint settings. In this case, the color tint seems fine, but the skin tones still have a slightly orange look that can be corrected by fine-tuning the blue/yellow balance using the Temperature control.

1 Use the Zoom tool or the Zoom Level menu in the lower left corner of the preview window to focus closely on the woman's face.

2 Test the Temperature slider by dragging it from one end of its range to the other. You'll see that the colors of the image become cooler or warmer as you move the slider. Reset the Temperature control a little below the edited value of 3700 (your value may differ, depending on where you clicked to set the white balance) either by dragging the slider or typing the value **3400** into the text box.

3 Double-click the Hand tool or by choose Fit In View from the Zoom Level menu. Now that the temperature has been adjusted towards blue, the automatically corrected tint of the image appears just a little pink.

4 Decrease the Tint setting to -5 with the slider or type **-5** in the Tint text box. Press Ctrl+Z / Command+Z to toggle between the new Tint setting and the value set with the White Balance tool, comparing the effect.

At the left, the skin tones produced by the White Balance tool still look a little too orange. On the right, the skin tones look more natural once the Temperature and Tint values have been reduced manually.

Using the tone controls on a raw image

Below the White Balance sliders on the Basic tab are sliders for improving a photo's tonal range and *presence*, or image definition.

Exposure adjusts the overall lightness or darkness of an image. Its effect is most apparent through the middle of the histogram; an increased Exposure setting will move the body of the curve to the right, compressing the highlights if possible, rather than shifting them off the end of the curve. Tweak the Exposure to brighten a dull, underexposed photo or correct the flat, faded look of an overexposed image.

Contrast is the amount of difference between the lightest and darkest areas of an image. The Contrast control has the most effect at the ends of the histogram; an increased setting moves information outwards from the center of the curve. Adjust Contrast to add definition to a flat image, or to soften one that is too harsh or stark.

Highlights recovers detail from overexposed highlights and improves midtone definition by shifting image information from the far right of the curve inwards.

Shadows recovers details from shadowed areas—something close to the inverse of the action of the Highlights control—and adds depth to the midtone range.

Whites specifies which input levels are mapped to pure white in the final image. Lowering the Whites value decreases clipping at the right end of the histogram. Clipping occurs when a pixel's color values are higher or lower than the range that can be represented in the image; over-bright values are clipped to output white, and over-dark values are clipped to output black.

Blacks specifies which input levels will be mapped to black in the final image. Raising the Blacks value decreases clipping at the left end of the histogram.

Clarity increases the *local* contrast between adjacent light and dark areas, sharpening detail without producing halo effects, and enhancing the midtone contrast.

Vibrance boosts color saturation selectively, having most effect on the muted colors in an image, while avoiding over-saturation of bolder colors and skin tones.

Saturation is the purity, or strength, of a color. Increasing the Saturation reduces the amount of black or white mixed with the color, making it more vivid. Reducing the Saturation increases the amount of black or white, making it more muted.

First you'll adjust the overall exposure and contrast; then, set the white and black points to avoid clipping at the ends of the histogram before tweaking the highlights and shadows to bring out as much image detail as you can.

1 Press the letter O on your keyboard to activate the white clipping warning; then, keep an eye on the histogram as you drag the Exposure slider slowly all the way to the right. The red areas that appear in the preview warn you which parts of the image are being clipped to white.

● **Note:** The values at which clipping appears may differ slightly for you , depending on where you clicked with the White Balance tool.

2 Drag the slider to the left until all the red areas disappear—even from the woman's head-band;. The Exposure control doesn't cause white clipping until the setting is extreme; for now, set the Exposure value to +0.5.

3 Watch the histogram as you drag the Contrast slider through its full range, before setting it to a value of +50.

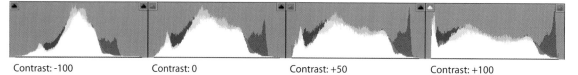

Contrast: -100   Contrast: 0   Contrast: +50   Contrast: +100

4 Put the Whites slider through its paces. White clipping is already beginning to appear when the setting reaches +15. Return the Whites to a zero setting.

5 Press U on your keyboard to activate the black clipping warning, and then play with the Blacks slider. Set the Blacks to -10—the point below which the blue clipping warning appears in the darkest areas of the image.

6 Move the Highlights slider all the way to the right. Although the effect on the image is quite extreme, there is no clipping now that you've set the white point. Watch the textural detail reappear in the sunlit wood as you reduce the Highlights setting to -50. Drag the Shadows slider to set a value of +50, watching as detail is retrieved from the darkest areas in the photo. Press the U and O keys on your keyboard to disable the clipping warnings.

7 Choose a magnification level of 100% from the Zoom menu at the lower left of the image window, or double-click the Zoom tool. Use the Hand tool to center your view on the girl's face; then, drag the Clarity slider to +30. Double-click the Hand tool to see the entire image, and then set the Vibrance value to +25.

8 To compare the adjusted photo to the raw image, toggle the Preview check box at the right of the tool bar above the preview.

The photo originally looked somewhat dull, muddy, and indistinct, and a little too dark. It now shows a broader range of detail and is more vivid; the colors are brighter and the tones are more realistic. For the sake of clarity in our demonstration however, some of the adjustments you made were quite extreme. If you wish, you can now tone down the corrections to balance the image to your taste.

Saving the image in the DNG format

Each camera manufacturer has its own proprietary raw format, and not every raw file can be read or edited by software other than that provided with the camera. There is also the possibility that manufacturers might not support every format indefinitely. To help alleviate these problems, Photoshop Elements gives you the option to save raw images in the DNG format, a publicly available archival format for raw images that provides an open standard for files created by different camera models, ensuring that you'll still be able to access your images in the future.

1   To convert and save the image, click the Save Image button at the lower left of the Camera Raw dialog box. Under Destination in the Save Options dialog box, click Select Folder. Navigate to and open your Lessons folder; then, highlight your My CIB Work folder and click Select.

2   Under File Naming, leave Document Name selected in the menu on the left. Click the menu on the right and select 1 Digit Serial Number. This will add the number 1 to the end of the file name.

3   Click Save. The file, together with all your current settings, will be saved in DNG format, which you can reprocess repeatedly without losing the original data.

4   Click the Open Image button in the right lower corner of the Camera Raw dialog box. Your image will open in a regular image window in Photoshop Elements. Choose File > Save. Navigate to your My CIB Work folder, name the file **DSC_5683_Work**, and choose the Photoshop format. Make sure that the new file will be included in the Organizer, but not in a Version Set.

5   Click Save, and then choose File > Close.

Congratulations! You've completed the lesson; take a look in the Media Browser to see how much you've learned.

Before you move on, take a moment to read through the review on the facing page.

Review questions

1 What are the key differences between adjusting images in Expert mode, Quick edit mode and Guided edit mode?

2 Can you apply automatic fixes when you are in Expert mode?

3 What is the purpose of the Photo Bin?

4 What is the Smart Brush tool?

5 What do the terms temperature and tint refer to in image editing?

Review answers

1 Expert mode provides the most flexible and powerful image correction environment, with lighting and color correction commands and tools for fixing image defects, making selections, adding text, and painting on your images. Quick edit provides easy access to a range of basic image editing controls for quickly making common adjustments and corrections. If you're new to digital photography, Guided edit steps you through each procedure to help you get professional-looking results.

2 Yes; the Enhance menu in Expert mode contains commands that are equivalent to the Auto buttons in the Quick Edit Adjustments panel: Auto Smart Fix, Auto Levels, Auto Contrast, Auto Color Correction, as well as Auto Red Eye Fix. The Enhance menu also provides an Adjust Smart Fix command, which opens a dialog box in which you can specify settings for automatic adjustments.

3 The Photo Bin provides easy access to the photos you want to work with, without needing to leave the Editor workspace. You can set the Project Bin to display all the photos that are currently selected in the Media Browser, just those images that are open in the Editor (helpful when some of the open images are hidden behind the front window), or the entire contents of any album in your catalog.

4 The Smart Brush is both a selection tool and an image adjustment tool—it creates a selection based on similarities in color and texture, through which your choice of editing preset is applied. You can choose from close to seventy Smart Brush presets, each of which can be customized, applied repeatedly for a cumulative effect, or layered with other adjustment presets to produce an almost infinite variety of results.

5 If an image's color temperature is too warm or too cool, it will have either a orange-red or blue color cast. A yellow-green or magenta color cast is referred to as a tint.

5 WORKING WITH COLOR

Lesson overview

Photoshop Elements delivers a broad selection of tools and controls for correcting, adjusting, and getting creative with color.

Whether you want to make corrections to compensate for inadequate lighting conditions, brighten a smile, or paint the town red, you'll find a range of solutions, from one-click Auto Fixes to customizable tools that give you precise control of the adjustments you apply.

This lesson introduces you to a variety of tools and techniques for fixing color problems in your photos:

- Using automatic options to correct color
- Tweaking automatic color adjustments
- Adjusting skin tones
- Whitening yellowed teeth
- Removing red eye and "pet-eye" effects
- Making, saving, and loading selections
- Changing the color of a pictured object
- Replacing a color throughout an image
- Working with color management

 You'll probably need between one and two hours to complete this lesson. If you haven't already done so, download the Lesson 5 work files from the Lesson & Update Files tab of your Account page at www.peachpit.com.

From one-step fixes to more specialized features and techniques, you'll find that all of the powerful and versatile color tools in Photoshop Elements are easy to master, giving you all the control you need to quickly correct the color balance across an entire image, or adjust just one area selectively.

Getting started

Note: Before you start this lesson, make sure that you've set up a folder for your lesson files and downloaded the Lesson 5 folder from your Account page at www.peachpit.com, as detailed in "Accessing the Classroom in a Book files" in the chapter "Getting Started" at the beginning of this book. You should also have created a new work catalog (see "Creating a catalog for working with this book" in Lesson 1).

You'll begin by importing the sample images for this lesson to the CIB Catalog that you created at the beginning of Lesson 1.

1   Click the Import button at the upper left of the Organizer workspace and choose From Files And Folders. In the Get Photos And Videos From Files And Folders dialog box, navigate to and select your PSE12CIB / Lessons / Lesson 5 folder. Disable any automatic processing options that are active; then, click Get Media.

2   In the Import Attached Keyword Tags dialog box, click Select All; then, click OK.

Batch-processing the lesson files

Before you start working with the Lesson 5 images, you can batch-process them as you did in Lesson 4. At the end of each exercise in this lesson, you can compare the combined auto-fixes to the results that you achieve using various other techniques.

1   Click the Editor button (📷) in the Task bar to switch to the Editor. If necessary, click Expert in the mode picker to switch the Editor to Expert mode.

2   Choose File > Process Multiple Files. In the Process Multiple Files dialog box, click the check boxes to activate all four Quick Fix options. Browse to locate and select the Lessons / Lesson 5 folder as the source for the images to be processed and your My CIB Work folder as the destination for the processed copies.

```
┌─ Quick Fix ──────
│  ☑ Auto Levels
│  ☑ Auto Contrast
│  ☑ Auto Color
│  ☑ Sharpen
└──────────────────
```

3   Activate Rename Files and set the options to add the appendix "_AutoFix" to the existing document names. If necessary, disable the resizing and file conversion options under Image Size and File Type are disabled, and then click OK.

4   Click the Organizer button (▦) in the Task bar. In the Organizer, click the Import button; then, navigate to and open your Lessons / My CIB Work folder. Select all the files with names that begin with "05," and then click Get Media.

5   In the Import Attached Keyword Tags dialog box, click Select All; then, click OK.

Correcting color problems

Tip: Even when a photo is technically perfect, you may still wish to adjust the color—either across the entire image, or just for a particular area or object—in order to create an effect.

Artificial lighting, weather conditions, and incorrect camera settings can result in one of the most common image problems: a color cast that affects the entire image.

For some images your color problem may be more localized, such as red eyes in a photo taken with a flash, or a portrait spoiled by yellow-looking teeth.

You'll begin this lesson by revisiting and comparing some of the tools for making quick and easy, image-wide adjustments in the Quick and Guided edit modes. Later, you'll explore methods for fixing red eyes and yellow teeth, and learn how to use the selection tools—an essential skill for making localized edits in Expert mode.

Comparing methods of fixing color

The automatic correction features in Photoshop Elements do an excellent job of bringing out the best in most photographs, but each image—and each image problem—is unique; some photographs require a more hands-on approach.

Photoshop Elements offers a variety of tools and controls for adjusting color; the more techniques you master, the more likely it is that you'll be able to meet any challenge presented by a difficult photograph.

1   If you don't see the Lesson 5 images already isolated in the Media Browser, click the arrow beside the imported Lesson 05 keyword tag.

2   Select the image 05_01.jpg in the Media Browser; then, click the Editor button (⬛) in the Task bar.

This photo exhibits the overly warm, yellow-orange cast common to many images taken in standard tungsten—or incandescent—lighting.

In the exercises in this section, you'll compare three different techniques for correcting the same color problem, so you'll create three copies of the original photo.

3   Click Quick in the mode picker to switch the Editor to Quick mode. Choose Window > Reset Panels. In the action bar above the Edit pane, make sure that the View is set to After Only, and then choose View > Fit On Screen. If the Adjustments panel is not open at the right of the Quick edit workspace, click the Adjustments button (⬛) at the right of the Task bar

4   Show the Photo Bin, if necessary. Right-click / Control-click the image in the Photo Bin and choose Duplicate from the context menu. In the Duplicate Image dialog box, click OK to accept the default name 05_01 copy.jpg. Repeat the process to create two more duplicates, 05_01 copy 2.jpg and 05_01 copy 3.jpg.

While you're in Quick edit or Guided edit mode, you won't see image window tabs displayed at the top of the Edit pane; in both these modes you can view only one image at a time in the work area. To see which photos are open in the Editor, and which of them is currently active, and also to switch between them, you'll use the Photo Bin. The name of each image appears as a tooltip when you hold the pointer over its thumbnail in the Photo Bin. Alternatively, right-click / Control-click anywhere inside the Photo Bin and choose Show File Names from the context menu.

In the Photo Bin, a blue frame highlights the active image; that is, the photo that you see in the After Only view in the Edit pane.

Correcting color automatically

For the batch processing at the start of this lesson, you applied all four automatic Quick Fix options together. In this exercise, you'll apply the automatic color adjustment on its own, so that you can assess the result unaffected by other settings.

1 In the Photo Bin, double-click the second photo, 05_01 copy.jpg to make it active; then, choose Before & After - Vertical from the View menu in the action bar above the Edit pane. Use the Hand and Zoom tools to focus on the faces.

2 If the tool options pane replaces the Photo Bin when you select the Hand tool or the Zoom tool in the toolbar, click the small menu icon (▼≡) at the upper right of the tool options pane and disable Auto Show Tool Options; then, click the Photo Bin button (⬚) in the Task bar to show the Photo Bin.

3 In the Adjustments panel, expand the Color pane and click the Auto button. Compare the Before and After views. There is a marked improvement; the Auto Color fix has corrected the worst of the orange color cast. Skin tones are slightly cooler, clothing colors a little brighter, but the tonal range is still somewhat flat.

▶ **Tip:** If you can't find the My CIB Work folder, refer to "Creating a work folder" on page 3.

4 Choose File > Save. Name the file **05_01_AutoColor**, to be saved in JPEG format to your My CIB Work folder and included in the Organizer, but not as part of a version set. Click Save; then, click OK in the JPEG Options dialog box.

Adjusting the results of an automatic fix manually

An automatic fix can serve as a good starting point for some manual fine-tuning.

1 In the Photo Bin, double-click the third photo, 05_01 copy 2.jpg to make it the active image; then, expand the Color pane and click the Auto button.

2 Click the Saturation tab at the top of the Color pane; then, reduce the setting to -**25** to give the color a more natural look. Click the Hue tab and reduce the value to -**5** to shift the color away from yellow-green. Increase the Vibrance to a setting of **20** to re-saturate the color a little, without affecting the skin tones.

▶ **Tip:** To type a new value for any setting, first click to select the number to the right of the adjustment slider.

Original image   Auto color adjustment   Saturation reduced   Hue and Vibrance adjusted

3 Expand the Balance pane and click the Temperature tab. Reduce the Temperature setting to **40** and increase the Tint value to **15** to further reduce the color cast.

4 Expand the Exposure pane, and then increase the Exposure setting to **0.8**. In the Levels pane, set the Midtones value to **15**.

Temperature reduced   Tint increased   Exposure boosted   Midtones adjusted

The contrast has improved, the colors are brighter, and the skin tones have lost the "fake tan" look common in photos captured without a flash in tungsten lighting.

5 Choose File > Save. Name the file **05_01_AutoColorPlus**, to be saved in JPEG format to your My CIB Work folder and included in the Organizer, but not as part of a version set. Click Save; then, click OK in the JPEG Options dialog box.

Tweaking an automatic fix using Color Curves

The five commands following Auto Smart Tone in the Enhance menu apply the same adjustments as the Auto buttons in the Adjustments panel and are available from the Enhance menu in both Quick and Expert modes, but not in Guided edit mode.

Both the Quick and Expert edit modes also offer other methods of enhancing color that give you finer control over the results. These are the commands in the lower half of the Enhance menu. In this exercise, you'll use one of these options to tweak the adjustments applied by the Auto Color fix button.

1 In the Photo Bin, double-click the image 05_01 copy 3.jpg to make it active.

2 In the Color pane, click the Auto button to apply the automatic Quick Fix correction; then, choose Enhance > Adjust Color > Adjust Color Curves to open the Color Variations dialog box.

3   In the Select A Style menu at the lower left of the Adjust Color Curves dialog box, click each color curve preset in turn, noting the effect on the curve in the graph at the right as well as the After image above it. Select Increase Midtones.

4   Drag the Adjust Highlights slider to a point about a third of the distance from the default central position to its limit at the right. Drag the Midtone Brightness and Midtone Contrast sliders about half as far to the right; then, click OK.

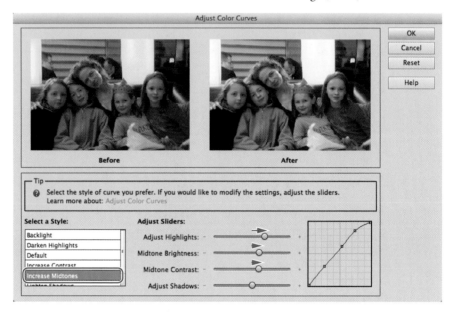

5   Choose File > Save. Name the file **05_01_ColorCurves**, and set up the usual work file settings. Click Save; then, click OK in the JPEG Options dialog box.

Comparing results

A glance at the Photo Bin will tell you that all three of your saved work files are still open in the Editor. Let's compare them to the batch-processed AutoFix file.

1   Right-click / Control-click the image at the left of the Photo Bin—the original photo—and choose Close from the context menu.

2   Choose File > Open. Locate and open your My CIB Work folder; then, select the file 05_01_AutoFix and click Open. Click Expert at the top of the workspace to switch to Expert mode.

3   Choose Preferences > General from the Edit / Photoshop Elements Editor menu. Activate the option Allow Floating Documents In Expert Mode; then, click OK.

Floating document windows are now the default for Expert mode. Throughout the rest of this book however, it will be assumed that you are working with image windows that are docked (consolidated) in the Edit pane. At the end of this exercise you'll disable floating windows so that you can follow the exercises as written.

4   Hide the Photo Bin, if necessary, by clicking the Photo Bin button (). Choose Window > Images > Float All In Windows, and then choose Window > Images > Tile. To synchronize the view across all four image windows, choose Match Zoom, and then Match Location, from the Window > Images menu.

5   Click the Zoom tool (Q) in the toolbar; then, click the Tool Options button (✏) in the Task bar. In the tool options pane, activate the Zoom All Windows option below the Zoom slider. Click the Hand tool (✋) and activate Scroll All Windows; then, click the Tool Options button to hide the tool options pane. Use the Zoom and Hand tools to focus on the faces in any of the image windows.

6   Drag your favorite version out of the tiled arrangement by its header bar and float the image window in the center of the work area; then, double-click the Hand tool to fit it to the screen. Press Ctrl-Tab or Ctrl-Shift-Tab to cycle through all the open image windows, bringing each to the front in turn.

7   Choose Preferences > General from the Edit / Photoshop Elements Editor menu and disable floating documents; then, click OK. Choose File > Close All.

Note: Only one image window is active at any given time. The file name and image details are dimmed in the title bars of all but the currently active image window.

Adjusting skin tones

When your primary concern is the people in your photo, you can correct a color cast across the entire image by concentrate on achieving natural, good-looking skin tones. Photoshop Elements offers tools to do just that in all three Edit modes.

1   In the Organizer, select the image 05_01.jpg in the Media Browser, and then click the Editor button (🖼) in the Task bar. Use the Zoom and Hand tools to focus on the faces of the mother and the two daughters sitting closest to her.

2 Choose Enhance > Adjust Color > Adjust Color For Skin Tone. In the Adjust Color For Skin Tone dialog box, make sure the Preview option is activated.

3 As you move the pointer over the image, the cursor changes to an eyedropper tool. With the eyedropper tool, click the lightly shaded area of skin to the right of center on the youngest sister's forehead. The color balance of the entire photo is adjusted using the sampled skin tone as a reference.

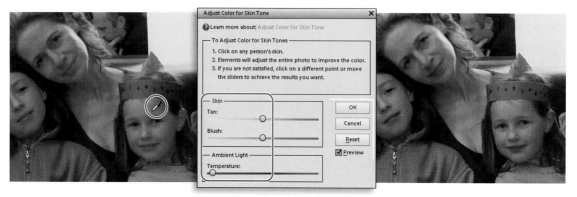

4 Move the Tan, Blush, and Temperature sliders to achieve the skin tones you want, and then click OK. Choose File > Save As. Name the file **05_01_Skin** and save it to your My CIB Work folder with the usual options. Choose File > Close.

Removing a color cast with one click

As you learned in Lesson 4, the Color Cast Eyedropper tool provides yet another solution to difficult color balance problems. If you wish to try the Color Cast Eyedropper on the photo you've been working with, you can do so in any of the three edit modes. In Quick edit and Expert modes, choose Remove Color Cast from the Enhance > Adjust Color menu. In Guided edit mode, select Remove A Color Cast.

Use the Color Cast Eyedropper to define a color that should appear temperature-neutral—neither warm nor cool—and the color balance is re-calculated around it. The best choice is a mid gray, though black or white can also work. Choosing the right color can take a little practice. In our sample photo, for example, the zippered sweater that appears to be a neutral gray in the before image actually contains a lot of cool blue; instead, try sampling the brightest point on the lily in the foreground.

Working with red eye

As you learned in Lesson 2, Photoshop Elements can apply an automatic red eye fix during import, so that your images are corrected before they reach the Organizer. However, the automatic solution is not effective for every photo; in this exercise, we'll look at the manual techniques you can use to deal with those difficult cases.

Note: The red eye effect happens when the camera's flash is reflected off the retina at the back of the eye, causing the pupil at the center to appear bright red instead of black.

Using the automatic Red Eye Fix

1 If necessary, use the Tags panel or the My Folders list to isolate the Lesson 5 images. Select the images 05_02a.jpg and 05_02b.jpg, and then click the Editor button (🖼) in the Task bar. Switch the Editor to Expert mode.

2 At the top of the work area, click the name tab for the image 05_02a.jpg to bring that photo to the front. Use the Zoom and Hand tools to focus as closely as possible on both of the girls' faces; then, choose Enhance > Auto Red Eye Fix.

As you can see, the auto correction does a great job with two of the four red eyes. Unfortunately, they're not even on the same face! The Red Eye Removal tool may fail to identify a pupil if your photo is out-of-focus, poorly exposed, or has a color cast; if possible, try correcting those problems first.

3 Press Ctrl+Z / Command+Z to undo the Auto Red Eye Fix. Keep the file open.

Using the Red Eye Removal tool

For stubborn red eye problems, you can use the Red Eye Removal tool (⁺👁), which you'll find in the toolbar in both Quick edit and Expert modes.

1 Zoom and drag the photo to focus the view on the eyes of the girl at the left.

2 Select the Red Eye Removal tool (⁺👁); then, click the Tool Options button (🖌) in the Task bar to open the Tool Options pane. Choose Reset Tool from the options menu on the menu icon (▼≣) at the far right. Click once in each eye, close to center of the pupil.

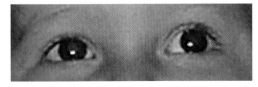

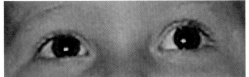

For this example, The Red Eye Removal tool works perfectly. If you ever find that the red eye correction is over-extended, blackening portions of the iris or spilling onto the skin around the eye, try clicking at a different point.

3 Zoom and drag the photo to focus the view on the eyes of the girl at the right.

▶ **Tip:** Once again, the Red Eye Removal tool produces a good result easily. For difficult cases that don't improve, no matter where you click or drag, undo and adjust the Pupil Size and Darken sliders in the Tool Options pane before you try clicking or dragging again.

4 This time, drag a marquee rectangle with the Red Eye Removal tool around each eye in turn. Experiment with the size and placement of the rectangle to get the best results. If you're not satisfied, undo and try again. Hold the Alt / Option key to draw the rectangle from its center.

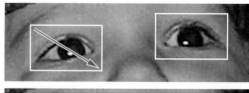

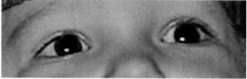

5 Choose File > Save As. Name the new file **05_02_RedEye**, to be saved to your My CIB Work folder in JPEG format and included in the Organizer, but not in a Version Set. Click Save. Accept the JPEG settings and choose File > Close.

Eye treatments for furry friends

As every pet owner knows, animals' eyes also reflect light from a camera flash. Though the reflection from pets' eyes is sometimes red, it's more often blue, green, yellow, or white and will not respond well to the automatic red eye fix. From Photoshop Elements 12, you can switch the Red Eye Removal tool to Pet Eye mode.

1 You should still have the image 05_02b.jpg open in Expert mode in the Editor. Select the Red Eye Removal tool (⊕); then, click the check box in the Tool Options pane to switch the tool to Pet Eye mode.

2 Try both of the techniques you practiced in the previous exercise in turn, undoing after each attempt. Experiment with the full range of the Pupil Size and Darken sliders in the Tool Options pane until you're happy with the result.

3 Choose File > Save As. Name the new file **05_02_PetEye** and save it to your My CIB Work folder with all the usual settings; then, choose File > Close.

Brightening a smile

Sometimes a photo can be spoiled by a color problem as simple as yellow-looking teeth. As with the red eye effect, Photoshop Elements offers an easy solution that's available in all three Edit modes.

Located in the toolbar in Quick edit mode and as part of the Perfect Portrait procedure in Guided edit mode, the Whiten Teeth tool is a preset variant of the Expert mode's Smart Brush, which functions as both a selection tool and an image adjustment tool. You can use the Whiten Teeth tool (or the Smart Brush with the Whiten Teeth preset loaded) to select the yellowed teeth, exactly as you would with the Quick Selection tool, and the preset whitening adjustment is applied inside the selection.

The Whiten Teeth selection and adjustment is made on a new layer separate from the original image in the background layer. The edit remains active on its own adjustment layer—so you can return to alter the selection area or the way the adjustment is applied at any time. You can use the tool more than once on the same area, building up multiple layers that you can then blend for a natural effect.

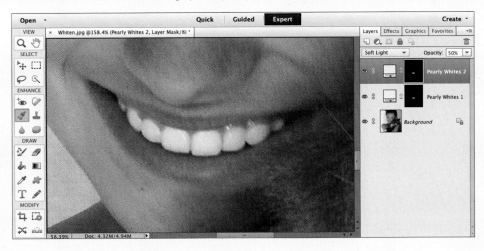

Making selections

By default, the entire area of an image is active—any adjustments you make are applied across the whole photo. If you wish to edit a specific area or object within the image, you first need to select it. Once you've made a selection it becomes the only active area of the image; the rest of the photo is protected.

Typically, the boundaries of a selection are indicated by a selection marquee: a flashing border of black and white dashes, sometimes likened to marching ants. Selections can be geometric in shape or free form, with crisp borders or soft edges. They can be created manually with the pointer, or calculated automatically by Photoshop Elements, based on similarity in color and texture within the image.

You can save a selection; then, re-use it or edit it later, saving you time when you're creating a complicated selection, or when you need to isolate the same area again.

Perhaps the simplest, most effective way to create a selection is to "paint" it onto your image. This exercise focuses on the use of two selection tools in Photoshop Elements that let you do just that: the Selection Brush and the Quick Selection tool.

Note: The lesson image has been saved in Photoshop file format rather than as a JPEG file. The Photoshop file format can store extra information together with the image data, including layers and saved selections.

1   In the Organizer, use the Lesson 05 tag to locate the photo 05_03.psd. Select the image in the Media Browser, taking care not to confuse the original file with the AutoFix copy; then, click the Editor button (⊞) in the Task bar.

2   If necessary, click Expert in the mode picker to switch to Expert edit mode. Hide the Panel Bin by un-checking its name in the Window menu; then, hide the Photo Bin by clicking the Photo Bin button (⊞) in the Task bar. Double-click the Hand tool or choose View > Fit On Screen.

3   Choose Select > Load Selection. In the Load Selection dialog box, choose the saved selection "Bees" from the Source menu; then, click OK.

The saved selection is loaded. The four bees and the central crown of the water lily flower are now surrounded by a flashing selection marquee. The area inside the flashing border has become the active portion of the image; the rest of the photo is protected from the effects of any edits you execute.

In the exercise to follow, you'll select the whole flower, together with the bees, and then use the pre-saved selection to help you isolate the petals.

4   Choose Select > Deselect to clear the current selection.

Using the Selection Brush

The Selection Brush tool has two modes: the default Selection mode, where you paint over the area you want to select for editing, and Mask mode, which lets you brush a semi-opaque overlay onto the areas you want to protect from editing. The Selection Brush (✐) is grouped with the Quick Selection tool (✎) and the Magic Wand tool (✴) in the Select category in the toolbar.

1   Select the Quick Selection tool—or whichever of its variants is currently visible at the right the Lasso tool in the toolbar—then, click the Tool Options button (✐) in the Task bar to open the tool options pane at the bottom of the Edit window.

2   In the tool options pane, click the Selection Brush tool to activate it. In the Selection Brush tool options, make sure that the Add To Selection button at the left is activated (*see below*); then, choose Selection from the Mode menu, set the brush Size to 35 px (pixels), and set the brush Hardness value to 100%. Click the Tool Options button (✐) in the Task bar to hide the Tool Options pane.

3   Drag with the Selection Brush to paint a live selection over four or five of the petals at the lower left. Don't try to paint all the way to the edges; you'll do that in the next step. You can paint over the bees to include them in the selection.

▶ **Tip:** While you paint your selection onto the image, release the mouse button every second or two so that you don't have to repeat too much work if you need to undo a stroke.

Now you need to reduce the brush size to paint around the edges of the petals, adding to your selection. You could open the tool options to change the brush size, but while you're working it's far more convenient to press the open bracket key ([) to reduce the brush size in increments and the close bracket key (]) to enlarge it.

Note: The bracket keys change the brush size in five pixel increments while the brush is larger than ten pixels; when the brush is set smaller than that, the increments are reduced to one pixel.

4   Press the left bracket key ([) five times to reduce the Selection Brush size to ten pixels, and then paint your selection to the edges of the petals. If you go too far, simply hold down the Alt / Option key to switch the Selection Brush to Subtract From Selection mode, and paint out your mistakes. Use the bracket keys to change the brush size as needed, until the selection outline completely surrounds the petals in the lower left quadrant of the flower.

Using the Quick Selection tool

With the Quick Selection tool, all you need to do is click or "scribble" in the area that you wish to select and Photoshop Elements will do most of the work. You don't need to be precise; the quick selection border automatically expands to find the edges of the area you're selecting by identifying similarities in color and texture.

1   Click the Selection Brush tool in the toolbar; then, open the Tool Options pane.

2   In the Tool Options pane at the bottom of the workspace, click the Quick Selection tool ( ); then, make sure the Add To Selection mode is activated. You can set the brush size with the slider, and adjust other brush attributes by clicking Brush Settings. For the purposes of this exercise, you can use the default brush—with a diameter of 30 px (pixels) and the Hardness set to 100%. Click the Tool Options button in the Task bar to hide the Tool Options pane.

3   Starting from inside your active selection, scribble slowly inside the outline of the flower, making sure to draw through areas of different color and brightness—including the bees and the central stamens. Release the mouse button once or twice to see the result. As you draw, Photoshop Elements automatically expands the selection to any area adjacent to your stroke that has similarities in color and texture.

Selecting the flower directly was simple enough, but objects with more complex shapes and a lot of internal detail can sometimes be more difficult. In those cases, it can be more effective to use the Quick Selection tool to select everything *but* the object, and then invert the selection.

4   Press Ctrl+Shift+A / Command+Shift+A to deactivate the current selection; then, drag around the outside of the flower to select the leafy background. Once more, be sure to draw through areas of different brightness.

5   To turn the selection inside out choose Select > Inverse. Check the tips of the petals and the angles where they meet; if you're missing a petal tip, paint it in with the Selection Brush tool. If fragments of background are selected between the petals, hold down the Alt / Option key and paint out the extraneous areas.

The background is now masked, and the water lily flower is selected—together with its furry friends—ready for the next exercise.

Working with saved selections

In this exercise you'll save your live selection, and then modify it by loading the selection that was previously saved with the image file.

1   With your selection still active, choose Select > Save Selection.

2   In the Save Selection dialog box, name the selection **Flower**.

By default, the Selection menu is set to New: the selection will be saved in its own channel. At this setting the alternative Operation options are unavailable; you'll look at those a little later.

3   Click OK to close the Save Selection dialog box.

4   Without deactivating the selection, choose Select > Load Selection. In the Load Selection dialog box, click the Source Selection menu to see your Flower selection listed. Choose the saved selection Bees as the selection to be loaded.

5   Under Operation, activate Subtract From Selection. This will deselect any areas where the selection you're loading and the currently active selection overlap. Click OK.

6   Choose Select > Save Selection. In the Save Selection dialog box, name the new selection **Petals**. Make sure that the Selection menu is set to New to save the selection in its own channel, rather than replacing one of the existing selections.

7   Click OK to close the Save Selection dialog box.

Next, you'll apply adjustments to the image through your new saved selections.

Note: "Add To Selection" combines the saved and current selections. "Intersect With Selection" selects the areas where the two selections overlap.

Editing through selections

Now that you've saved different selections from the image, you can use them to do some selective editing, applying different treatments to separate areas of the photo.

1. Choose Select > Load Selection. In the Load selection dialog box, choose the Flower selection from the Source Selection menu.

2. Click the check box to activate the Invert option; this will select the leafy back-ground—in other words, everything *but* the flower. Make sure that the Operation option is set to New Selection; then, click OK.

3. Choose Enhance > Adjust Lighting > Brightness/Contrast. Reduce the Brightness value to **-100**, increase the contrast to **20**, and then click OK.

The adjustment to the lighting in the background has lifted the flower from its surroundings and effectively put it in the spotlight, even though the pixels within the flower's outline remain completely unchanged. As well as focusing our attention on the flower, the change in lighting has also given the photo a different feel, shifting it from mid-day to morning, and perhaps deeper into the forest.

4. Choose Select > Load Selection. This time, choose the saved Petals selection from the Source Selection menu in the Load selection dialog box. Make sure that the Operation option is set to New Selection; then, click OK.

This is the selection that you created by isolating the background with the Quick Select tool, inverting the selection, and then subtracting the saved selection Bees.

The petals of the flower look a little flat and washed out—underexposed in some areas, and burned-out in others as a result of the dappled sunlight. Let's try to bring out some midtone detail and recover some color.

5   From the Enhance > Adjust Lighting menu, choose Shadows/Highlights. Reduce the default Lighten Shadows value to zero. Increase the Darken Highlights setting to **10**% and the Midtone Contrast to **20**%, and then click OK.

The petals now have much more color detail, and an improved tonal spread that helps to increase texture and definition.

6   Choose the Adjust Hue/Saturation command from the Enhance > Adjust Color menu.

7   In the Hue/Saturation dialog box, decrease the Hue value to -**50**. Leave the Saturation and Lightness values unchanged. Click OK.

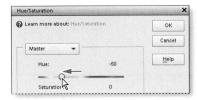

Changing the color of the petals serves to narrow the focus further to the bees and their business at the center of the flower. As a finishing touch, we'll use the last of our saved selections to boost that effect.

8   Choose Select > Load Selection. In the Load selection dialog box, choose the selection Bees from the Source Selection menu. Make sure that the Operation option is set to New Selection, and then, click OK. Choose Levels from the Enhance > Adjust Lighting menu. Drag the highlights slider at the right of the histogram to the left to set a new value of 225; then, click OK.

Once again, the levels of adjustment used in this demonstration are quite extreme.

9   Choose File > Save As. Name the file **05_03_SavedSelections**, to be saved in Photoshop format, with all the usual settings. Click Save, and then close the file.

Why won't Photoshop Elements do what I tell it to do?

In some situations, the changes you try to apply to an image may not seem to work. You may hear a beep, indicating that you're trying to do something that's not allowed. The following list offers explanations and solutions for common issues that might be blocking your progress.

Commit is required

Several tools, including the Type tool require you to click the green check-mark Commit button before you can move on to another task. The same is true when you crop with the Crop tool or resize a layer or selection with the Move tool.

Cancel is required

The Undo command isn't available while you have uncommitted changes made with certain tools: for example, the Type tool, Move tool, and Crop tool. If you want to undo these edits, click the Cancel button instead of using the Undo command or shortcut.

In Quick edit and Guided edit modes, and also in any of the Photomerge workspaces, you'll need to use the Cancel button at the bottom of the right panel to dismiss the task-specific tools and instructions and return the right panel to its default state.

Edits are restricted by an active selection

When you create a selection (using a marquee tool, the Quick Selection tool, or the Selection Brush tool, for example), you limit the active area of the image. Any edits you make will apply only within the selected area. If you try to make changes to an area outside the selection, nothing happens. Edits are restricted by an active selection. If you want to deactivate a selection, choose Select > Deselect, and then you can work on any area of the image.

Move tool is required

When you drag a selection, the selection marquee moves, not the image within the selection marquee. If you want to move a selected part of the image or an entire layer, use the Move tool.

Background layer is selected

Many changes cannot be applied to the Background layer. For example, you can't erase, delete, change the opacity, or drag the Background layer to a higher level in the layer stack. If you need to apply changes to the Background layer, double-click it and rename it (or accept the default name, Layer 0).

Active layer is hidden

In most cases, the edits you make apply to only the currently selected layer—the one highlighted in the Layers palette. If an eye icon with a red bar appears beside that layer in the Layers palette, the layer is hidden and you cannot edit it.

Another possibility is that the image on the selected layer is not visible because it is blocked by an opaque area on an upper layer; if that is the case, you will actually be changing that layer, but you won't see the changes in the image window.

The active layer is hidden, the view is blocked by opacity on an upper layer, or the active layer is locked.

Active layer is locked

If you lock a layer by selecting the layer and then clicking the Lock in the Layers palette, the lock prevents the layer from changing. To unlock a layer, select the layer, and then click the Lock at the bottom of the Layers palette to remove the Lock.

Wrong layer is selected (for editing text)

If you want to make changes to a text layer, be sure that layer is selected in the Layers palette before you start. If a non-text layer is selected when you click the Type tool in the image window, Photoshop Elements creates a new text layer instead of placing the cursor in the existing text layer.

Replacing the color of a pictured object

▶ **Tip:** The color
replacement technique
that will be most effec-
tive depends on the
characteristics of the
photo that you're work-
ing with and the extent
of the changes that you
wish to make.

Photoshop Elements offers two very different methods for switching a specific color in an image: the Color Replacement tool and the Replace Color dialog box.

Using the Color Replacement tool

The Color Replacement tool enables you to replace a targeted color in an image by painting over it with another; it's equally effective for making localized color corrections, or used as a "magic brush" to enhance a photo creatively.

The cursor for the Color Replacement tool consists of cross-hairs at the center of a circle that indicates the brush size. When you drag in the image, the color pin-pointed by the cross-hairs is sampled as the target color and the new color is then applied to any pixel inside the cursor circle that matches the targeted color, within the tolerance range set in the tool options bar.

What this means is that you can be quite relaxed as you paint; as long as you keep the cross-hairs inside the area of color that you wish to replace, the circle can over-lap the neighboring area without changing the color, making it easy to paint right up to the edge. The only pixels affected are those inside the cursor circle that match the targeted color under the cross-hairs.

1   Use the Lesson 05 keyword tag, if necessary, to isolate the lesson 5 images. Select the image 05_04.jpg; then, click the Editor button (⬚) in the Task bar.

2   If necessary, switch the Editor to Expert mode. Hide the Panel Bin by un-checking its name in the Window menu; then, hide the Photo Bin by clicking the Photo Bin button (⬚) in the Task bar. Choose View > Fit On Screen.

3   Click the foreground color swatch below the toolbar to open the Color Picker. Type in the text boxes to set the Hue (H), Saturation (S), and Brightness (B) to values of **200**, **80**, and **100** respectively. Click OK to close the Color Picker.

4   Select the Brush tool (✏) (grouped in the toolbar with the Impressionist Brush and the Color Replacement tool); then, click the Tool Options button (✏) in the Task bar, if necessary, to access the tool settings. In the Tool Options pane, select the Color Replacement tool at the lower left; then, click the small menu icon (▾≡) at the far right and choose Reset Tool. Set the brush size to **200** px. Leave the rest of the settings unchanged and hide the Tool Options pane.

You'll use the new foreground color to repaint the boat behind the Rhea (WK7).

5   Click in the upper left corner of the red paint at the boat's bow; then drag around the edges of the area bounded by the white paint at the top, the ropes to the right, and the stone wall at the left. Work carefully into the edges, always keeping the cross-hairs within the outlines of the red paint. Reduce the brush size by pressing the left bracket key ([ ) and magnify the view as needed as you move towards the back of the boat, painting over all the red areas. Release the mouse button frequently so you can undo any over-painting without losing too much work.

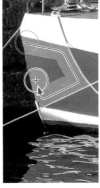

So far, so easy; the Color Replacement tool automatically adapts the new color for both lit and shaded areas. Now you need to deal with the reflections on the water. Obviously, it won't be possible to "keep inside the lines" to protect the areas reflecting white, so you'll change the way the Color Replacement tool operates.

6   In the Tool Options pane, switch the sampling mode from Continuous to Once, increase the Tolerance setting to **40**%, and set the brush size to **100** pixels.

7   Zoom in so that you see only the area where the reflections are to be re-colored. Click inside one of the darker red patches close to the blue boat; then, without releasing the mouse button, "scrub" over all the reflections that should now be blue. Take your time, paying attention to any small areas still showing red.

8   Choose File > Save. Name the file **05_04_BlueBoat**, to be saved as a JPEG file to your My CIB Work folder, and included in the Organizer, but not in a version set. Click Save; then, click OK in the JPEG Options dialog box. Close the file.

Replacing a color throughout an image

Using the Replace Color dialog box can be faster than painting with the Color Replacement tool, but it can be difficult to control—especially when the color of the object you want to change is also present in other parts of the photo. Even with difficult images, you can achieve a good result by using the Replace Color dialog box in conjunction with a selection.

In the following exercises, you'll switch the colors of two pictured objects, making your changes on a duplicate of the Background layer, so that you can easily compare the finished project to the original picture. First, you'll work on the entire image, which will give you an indication of just where—and how much—the color change will affect the rest of the photo. In the second stage, you'll use a selection to constrain the changes.

1   In the Organizer, use the Lesson 05 keyword tag, if necessary, to isolate the lesson 5 images. In the Media Browser, right-click / Control-click the image 05_05.jpg, and then click the Editor button () in the Task bar.

2   In the Editor, choose Window > Reset Panels. Hide the Photo Bin, if necessary, by clicking the Photo Bin button ( ) in the Task bar; then, double-click the Hand tool or choose View > Fit On Screen. If you don't see the Layers panel at the right of the workspace, click the Layers button ( ) in the Task bar.

3   The layers panel shows that this image has only one layer, which is active (selected) by default. Choose Layer > Duplicate Layer and accept the default name. Alternatively, drag the Background layer to the New Layer button ( ) at the upper left of the Layers panel. With a duplicate layer, you'll have an original to fall back on should you need it.

4   With the new Background copy layer selected in the Layers panel, choose Enhance > Adjust Color > Replace Color.

5   In the Replace Color dialog box, make sure that the left-most of the three eyedropper buttons is activated—as in the illustration at the right—and that Fuzziness is set to the default value of 40. Make sure that Preview is activated, and switch the selection preview thumbnail to the Image view option.

6   Move the pointer over the thumbnail preview in the Replace Color dialog box and click once with the eyedropper on the yellow taxi. Change the selection preview from Image to Selection, so that you can see the extent of the color selection you just made highlighted in white on a black background.

7 Below the selection preview, either use the sliders or type in the text boxes to set the Hue, Saturation, and Lightness values to **90**, **100**, and **0** respectively; a bright green that will be very easily seen wherever it appears in the image.

8 To adjust the area of selected color—or color-application area—start by clicking the second of the three eyedropper buttons to switch the Eyedropper tool to Add To Sample mode, as illustrated at the right, below; then, click in the main image window in a few areas where the paint on the car still appears yellow.

9 Use the Add To Sample eyedropper again, if necessary, and then drag the Fuzziness slider left and right and until you have full coverage on the car. In both the Edit pane and the black and white selection preview, you can see that it's not possible to change the color of the car using this technique without affecting the woman's skin and hair, as well as various parts of the background. Click Cancel to close the Replace Color dialog box.

Replacing a color in a limited area of an image

In this exercise you'll limit the color change to a selected area of the photograph.

1 Make sure the layer Background copy is still selected in the Layers panel. In the toolbar, switch to the Quick Selection tool (⟨⟩). Press the left and right bracket keys ([,]) to set a workable brush size.

2 Use the Quick Selection tool to select all the yellow areas of the car. As much as possible, try to include the reddish halo that surrounds the yellow areas (clearly visible on the roof, at the front of the taxi, and around the wheel arches and signage). If you go too far and need to trim the selection, simply hold down the Alt / Option key as you work to switch the Quick Selection tool temporarily to Subtract From Selection mode.

3   Choose Enhance > Adjust Color > Replace Color. Repeat steps 5, 6, and 7 from the previous exercise on page 154. Be sure to follow the steps in order; you need to sample the original yellow before setting hue, saturation, and brightness to define the replacement color. This time, set the Hue, Saturation, and Lightness values to **-85**, **-30**, and **0** respectively; a color that will match the woman's scarf.

4   When you're satisfied with the results, click OK to close the Replace Color dialog box; then choose Select > Deselect, or press Ctrl+D / Command+D.

5   Repeat the process for the scarf. First, select it with the Quick Selection tool, taking particular care with the shaded areas in the deeper folds, and the areas adjacent to the woman's hair and under her chin. Then, choose Enhance > Adjust Color > Replace Color, sample the scarf thoroughly, and set the Hue, Saturation, and Lightness values to **70**, **60**, and **0**; a color that would have once matched the taxi.

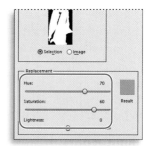

6   To compare the edited image to the original, toggle the visibility of the Background copy layer by clicking the eye icon beside the layer thumbnail. Make the new layer visible again, and then Right-click / Control-click the Background copy layer and choose Flatten Image from the menu. The image is flattened to a single layer; the layer you edited replaces the original background layer.

7   Choose File > Save. Name the file **05_05_ColorSwitch**, to be saved to your My CIB Work folder, and included in the Organizer, but not in a version set. Click Save; then, click OK in the JPEG Options dialog box. Close the file.

About printing color pictures

Color problems in your photos can result from a variety of causes, such as incorrect exposure, the quality of the camera, artificial lighting, or even weather conditions. If an image is flawed, you can usually improve it by editing it with Photoshop Elements, as you did with the images in this lesson. Sometimes, however, pictures that look great on your computer don't turn out so well when you print them; fortunately, there are things you can do to make sure that what you get from the printer is as close as possible to what you see on screen.

Firstly, it's important that you calibrate your monitor regularly, so that it's set to display the range of color in your photographs accurately. However, even with a correctly calibrated display, your prints may still look disappointing if your printer interprets color information differently from your computer. You can correct this problem by activating the appropriate type of color management.

Working with color management

Moving a photo from your camera to your monitor and from there to a printer can cause an apparent shift in the colors in the image. This shift occurs because every device has a different *color gamut* or *color space*—the range of colors that the device is capable of interpreting and reproducing.

To achieve consistent color between digital cameras, scanners, computer monitors, and printers, you need to use color management. Color management software acts as an interpreter, translating colors so that each device can reproduce them in the same way. This software knows how each device and program understands color, and adjusts colors so that what you see on screen is similar to the colors in your printed image. It should be noted, however, that not all colors may match exactly.

Color management software calls on device-specific color profiles: mathematical descriptions of each device's color space. If these profiles are compliant with the standards of the ICC (International Color Consortium), they will help you maintain consistent color. When you save a file, activate Embed Color Profile in the Save As dialog box. In Photoshop Elements, you can access the color management controls from the Edit menu in both the Organizer and the Editor.

Setting up color management

1   Choose Edit > Color Settings; then, select one of these color management options in the Color Settings dialog box:

- **No Color Management** uses your monitor profile as the working color space. This setting removes any embedded profiles when opening images, and does not apply a profile when saving.

- **Always Optimize Colors For Computer Screens** uses sRGB as the working color space, preserves embedded profiles, and assigns sRGB when opening untagged files. Computer screens are capable of reproducing all of the colors in the sRGB range, so this setting will ensure an accurate display for any device that supports the sRGB color space.

- **Always Optimize For Printing** uses Adobe RGB as the working color space, preserves embedded profiles, and assigns Adobe RGB when opening untagged files. This setting will display your photos based on the colors within the AdobeRGB color space, commonly used for printing images.

- **Allow Me To Choose** lets you choose whether to assign sRGB (the default) or Adobe RGB when opening a file that has an unsupported color profile, or no embedded profile at all.

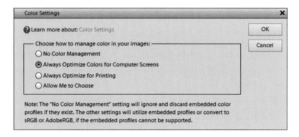

2   Click OK to close the Color Settings dialog box.

Further information on color management, including monitor calibration, can be found in a series of topics in Photoshop Elements Help.

Congratulations, you've completed another exercise. You've learned a wide variety of techniques for working with color in your photos—from tweaking automatic corrections to switching the color of a pictured object. You've gained a lot of experience in all three Edit modes and honed your selection skills—essential for many sophisticated and creative color edits. Now, take a minute to refresh your knowledge by reading through the review questions and answers on the following page.

Review questions

1 What makes selections so important for adjusting color?

2 Name at least two selection tools and describe how they work.

3 How does the Color Replacement tool work?

4 What is the difference between the Continuous and Once sampling modes for the Color Replacement tool, and how are they used?

Review answers

1 A selection defines an area as the only part of a layer that can be altered. The areas outside the selection are protected from change for as long as the selection is active. This enables you make adjustments selectively, targeting specific areas or objects.

2 The first selection tool you used in this lesson is the Selection Brush tool, which works like a paintbrush. The Quick Selection tool is similar, but is in most cases a faster, more flexible option. There are more selection tools than are discussed in this lesson: The Magic Wand tool selects areas with the same color as that on which you click. The Rectangular Marquee tool and the Elliptical Marquee tool make selections of a fixed geometric shape. The Lasso tool lets you draw free-form selections, and the Magnetic Lasso tool helps to draw complicated selections around even irregular object edges. The Polygonal Lasso tool is the tool of choice for selecting straight-sided objects.

3 The Color Replacement tool samples the color under the pointer and replaces it with any color that you choose. The cursor for the Color Replacement tool consists of cross-hairs at the center of a circle indicating the brush size. When you drag in the image, the color under the cross-hairs is sampled and the foreground color is applied to any pixel inside the circle that matches the sampled color, within the tolerance value specified in the tool options bar. As long as you keep the cross-hairs inside the area of color that you wish to replace, you can overlap the adjacent area without changing the color, making it easy to paint right up to the edge.

4 In Continuous sampling mode, the Color Replacement tool continuously samples the pixels under the cursor cross-hairs, updating the target color as you drag across the image. This is useful for re-coloring an area that has varied tones, without increasing the tolerance. In the Once sampling mode, the target color is set with the first click. Use this mode for detailed areas where it's not easy to keep the cross-hairs inside the lines.

6 FIXING EXPOSURE PROBLEMS

Lesson overview

Photoshop Elements makes it easy to fix images that are too dark or too light and rescue photos that are dull, flat, or simply fading away.

Start with Quick Fix and Guided edits and work up to Expert mode as you learn how to make the most of poorly exposed images, retrieve detail from photos that are too dark or pale and faded, and liven up images that look flat and washed-out. Photoshop elements delivers powerful, easy-to-use tools for correcting exposure and lighting problems in all three Edit modes.

In this lesson you'll be introduced to a variety of techniques for dealing with a range of common exposure problems:

- Brightening underexposed photographs
- Correcting parts of an image selectively
- Saving selection shapes to reuse in later sessions
- Working with adjustment layers and layer masks
- Using layer blending modes and opacity settings
- Adjusting lighting controls manually
- Enhancing overexposed and faded photographs

 You'll probably need between one and two hours to complete this lesson. If you haven't already done so, download the Lesson 6 work files from the Lesson & Update Files tab of your Account page at www.peachpit.com.

Learn how to make the most of images that were
captured in unusual lighting conditions, retrieving
detail from overly dark photos and putting the spark
back into images that look dull or washed-out.
Find out how Photoshop Elements can help you save
those faded memories—no matter what your level
of experience—with a suite of powerful, easy-to-use
tools and the versatility of three Edit modes.

Getting started

● **Note:** Before you start this lesson, make sure that you've set up a folder for your lesson files and downloaded the Lesson 6 folder from your Account page at www.peachpit.com, as detailed in "Accessing the Classroom in a Book files" in the chapter "Getting Started" at the beginning of this book. You should also have created a new work catalog (see "Creating a catalog for working with this book" in Lesson 1).

To start, you'll import the sample images for this lesson to the CIB Catalog that you created at the beginning of Lesson 1.

1   Start Photoshop Elements and click Organizer in the Welcome Screen.

2   In the Organizer, check the lower right corner of the workspace to make sure the CIB Catalog is loaded—if not, choose File > Manage Catalogs and select it from the list.

3   Click the Import button at the upper left of the Organizer workspace and choose From Files And Folders from the drop-down menu. In the Get Photos And Videos From Files And Folders dialog box, locate and select your Lesson 6 folder. Disable the automatic processing options; then, click Get Media.

4   In the Import Attached Keyword Tags dialog box, click Select All; then, click OK.

Batch-processing the lesson files

As you've already seen, the batch-processing command lets you apply automatic adjustments to an entire folder of image files at once.

1   you start this lesson, you can set up automatic processing for the lesson 6 images by following the steps in the exercise "Batch-processing the lesson files" at the beginning of Lesson 5.

2   At the end of each exercise in this lesson, compare the automatic fixes to the results that you achieve using various other techniques.

Adjusting images for tonal balance

Most image problems fall into two basic categories: color or exposure. In some photos, the two issues can be inter-related, and there is also some overlap in the tools and techniques you'll use to correct them.

In the previous lesson, you gained experience recognizing and dealing with color deficiencies in your photos. This lesson will focus on exposure and lighting: issues that effect the *tonal balance* of your image.

Ideally, an image should have a good spread of tonal values from dark to light; any imbalance can result in a photo that is too dark or too light, has too little contrast or too much, or is lacking detail in the shadows, the mid-tones, or the highlights.

As with color correction, Photoshop Elements offers a range of tools for adjusting exposure that are available in all three Edit modes. In the exercises to follow, you'll look at a variety of ways to get the best from poorly exposed images, retrieve detail from photos that are too dark, and liven up images that look flat and washed-out.

Brightening an underexposed image

Underexposed photographs look too dark or dull and flat, often across the entire image, but sometimes in just part of it. While the lighting auto-fixes do a good job with many photos, this exercise will teach you techniques to give you more control for adjusting the exposure in problem images.

Applying Quick Fix lighting adjustments

Let's start by combining Exposure and Levels adjustments in Quick edit mode.

1   If necessary, click the arrow beside the Lesson 06 tag to isolate the lesson images. Select the file TooDark.jpg; then, click the Editor button () in the Task bar. In the Editor, click Quick in the mode picker to switch to Quick edit mode.

2   Expand the Exposure pane and increase the Exposure setting to **1.3**.

3   Expand the Levels pane and click the Shadows tab. Set the (lighten) Shadows value to **10**. Increase the Midtones setting to **15**, and (darken) Highlights to **25**. Watch the detail in the water and reflections as you darken the highlights.

▶ **Tip:** Use the View menu above the Edit pane to switch between the After Only view and the Before & After views to help you assess the results of your adjustments as you work.

You've improved the image substantially with just a few clicks. However, though the skin tones have been lightened and have more definition, they are still a little cool.

4 Expand the Color pane. Click the Saturation tab and reduce the value to **-25**. Expand the Balance pane. Set the Temperature value to **53** and the Tint to **3**.

| Original image | Adjust Exposure and Levels | Correct Temperature and Tint |

▶ **Tip:** In order to clearly demonstrate the effects of the various tonal controls on our lesson photo, some of the settings suggested in these exercises are quite extreme. If you wish, you can undo your steps, and then tweak the settings to your own taste before saving the results of each procedure.

5 Choose File > Save. Make sure that Include In The Elements Organizer is activated and disable Save In Version Set With Original. Name the new file **TooDark_QuickEdit**, to be saved to your My CIB Work folder in JPEG format. Click Save. In the JPEG Options dialog box, use the slider to set the Quality to 9, and then click OK. Choose File > Close.

Adjusting exposure in Guided Edit mode

When you're not sure exactly what adjustments a poorly exposed image needs, the Guided edit mode offers three procedures for correcting lighting and exposure: Brightness And Contrast, Levels, and Lighten And Darken—each with easy-to-follow prompts and instructions that make it simple for even a novice to get great results. You can improve your photos quickly, at the same time as learning image correction concepts and techniques that you can apply even in Expert mode.

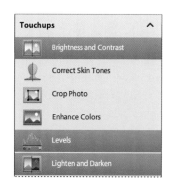

● **Note:** In the guided edit panel, numerical values for the settings are displayed in tooltips when you click or move the slider controls.

1 In the Organizer, select the image TooDark.jpg in the Media Browser; then, click the Editor button (⬚) in the Task bar. Click Guided in the mode picker to switch the Editor to Guided edit mode. In the guided tasks menu, expand the Touchups category, if necessary; then, click Brightness And Contrast. Drag the sliders to increase the Brightness setting to **60** and the Contrast to **20**; then, click Done at the bottom of the guided edit panel.

2   Click the Levels guided edit in the Touchups list; then, click the Create Levels Adjustment button at the top of the guided edit panel. Click OK in the New Layer dialog box to accept the default name for the new adjustment layer. Drag the gray midtones stop (below the center of the histogram curve) to the left to brighten the photo by setting the midtones value to **1.2**. Click OK; then, click Done at the bottom of the guided edit panel.

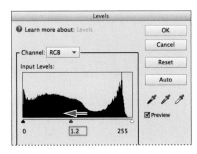

3   Choose Lighten And Darken in the guided Touchups list. Set the Shadows, Highlights, and Midtones to **5**, **15**, and **15** respectively, and then click Done.

4   Choose File > Save As. Make sure that the new file will be saved to your work folder and included in the Organizer, but not in a version set. Change the file format from Photoshop to JPEG; then, name the new file **TooDark_Guided**. Click Save; then, click OK to close the JPEG Options dialog box. Choose File > Close , and then click No to avoid saving the changes to the original file.

Once again, the adjusted image looks considerably better than the original; however, it would be ideal if we could treat the three girls in the foreground separately from the brighter background, so that it doesn't become over-exposed.

Fixing exposure in Full Edit mode

If your photo is a difficult case, more elaborate methods than those you've used in the Quick and Guided edit modes might be necessary to achieve the best results. In Full Edit mode you can work with multiple layers and blending modes, and also make selections to isolate specific parts of an image for special treatment.

Using blending modes

In a multiple-layered image file, each layer has its own blending mode that defines the way it will interact with any layer below it in the stacking order. By default, a newly created layer uses the Normal blending mode: it will not blend with the layers below it except where it contains transparency or when the master opacity for the layer is set to less than 100%. A layer with the blending mode set to Darken or Lighten will blend with the layers below it only where the result will darken or lighten the lower layers. Other blending modes produce more complex results.

If a photo is too dark, applying the Screen blending mode to an overlaid duplicate of the background layer may correct the problem. If your photo is overexposed, an overlaid duplicate with the Multiply blending mode can be a solution. You can adjust the master opacity of the overlaid layer to control the intensity of the effect.

1   In the Media Browser, right-click / Control-click the image TooDark.jpg and choose Edit With Photoshop Elements Editor from the context menu, taking care not to confuse the original file with the edited copies.

Note: Strong lighting behind a foreground subject is a classic cause of exposure problems; a setting that achieves an adequate exposure level across the entire frame will often leave the subject underexposed. In our example, the bright reflections on the lake behind our subjects may contribute to the problem in this way; the water is quite well lit, while the lighting on the girls' faces is low and indirect.

Tip: For information on the effects produced by the different layer blending modes, please refer to Photoshop Elements Help.

2 Switch to Expert mode by clicking Expert in the mode picker at the top of the Editor workspace. Choose Window > Reset Panels, and then hide the Photo Bin by clicking the Photo Bin button () at the left of the Task bar (twice, if necessary). Choose View > Fit On Screen.

▶ **Tip:** You can also duplicate a selected layer by choosing Duplicate Layer from the Layer menu or by right-clicking / Control-clicking the layer and choosing from the layer's context menu.

3 In the Layers panel you can see that the image has only one layer: the Background. Duplicate the Background layer by dragging it onto the New Layer button (⬒) at the left of the Layers panel's header.

In the Layers panel, the new Background copy layer is highlighted to indicate that it is the currently selected—or active—layer.

▶ **Tip:** If the layer blending mode menu is disabled, make sure that you have the copy layer—not the original Background—selected in the Layers panel.

4 With the Background copy layer selected, choose Screen from the blending mode menu at the top of the Layers panel. The image becomes much brighter overall, but the skin tones still look flat. Reduce the opacity of the Background Copy layer to **75**%, then duplicate it by dragging it onto the New Layer button. At the top of the Layers panel, set the second duplicate layer's blending mode to Color Dodge and its opacity to **25**%.

5 Choose File > Save. Name the new file **TooDark_Blend**, to be saved to your My CIB Work folder and included in the Organizer, but not as part of a version set. To preserve the layers you created, save the image in the Photoshop (PSD) file format and make sure the Layers option is activated, and then click Save.

6 To quickly compare the adjusted image to the original, toggle the visibility of the Background Copy layers by clicking the eye icon (👁, ✎) beside each layer's thumbnail. When you're done, close the file without saving.

In this exercise you've seen how you can use blending modes to brighten a dull image. For many photos, however—including our lesson image—applying blending modes over the entire image can adversely affect areas that were OK to begin with.

In our example, the reflected sky in the background is now overly bright and has lost almost all color and midtone detail. The resultant high-contrast glare of the blended background seems to dominate the less well-lit subjects in the foreground.

About adjustment layers

An adjustment layer affects the underlying layers like an overlay or lens filter, perhaps darkening the photo, perhaps making it appear pale and faded or intensifying its hues—but remaining separate from the image itself. Effects applied on an adjustment layer can be easily revised, or even removed, because the pixels of the image layers are not permanently modified. You can even copy an adjustment layer from one photo and paste it on top of the image layers in another—a real time-saver when you wish to apply the same treatment to several similar images.

● **Note:** A new adjustment layer is always created immediately above the currently selected layer. For a one-layer image, the Background is active (selected) by default.

Using adjustment layers to correct lighting

In this exercise you'll try some different techniques to correct and enhance the same underexposed photo that you used for the last series of exercises.

1   In the Organizer, select the image TooDark.jpg in the Media Browser; then, click the Editor button ( ) in the Task bar.

2   Click the Create New Fill Or Adjustment Layer button ( ) in the header of the Layers panel and choose Brightness/Contrast from the menu. In the Brightness/Contrast panel, drag the sliders or type in the text boxes to set Brightness and Contrast values of **75** and **20** respectively.

3   Click the Create New Fill Or Adjustment Layer button again, this time choosing Levels from the menu. Notice the new Levels 1 adjustment layer in the Layers panel. The Adjustments panel is updated to present the Levels controls.

4   Select the middle of the three eyedropper tools at the right of the Levels controls and sample a neutral gray in the area of ruffled water above the head of the girl at the right. The gray point eyedropper makes the color warmer, adding some life to the skin tones. Lighten the midtones by dragging the gray midtones stop under the center of the graph to the left to set a new value of **1.15**.

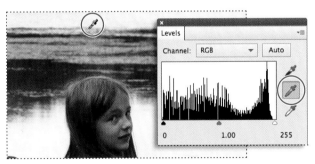

5 Choose File > Save. Name the new file **TooDark_AdjustLayers**, to be saved to your My CIB Work folder and included in the Organizer, but not as part of a version set. To preserve the layers, save the image in the Photoshop (PSD) file format and make sure the Layers option is activated, and then click Save.

6 To quickly assess the effect of the adjustment layers, toggle the visibility of each layer by clicking the eye icon beside its thumbnail in the Layers panel. When you're done, close the file without saving.

As long as you save the file in the Photoshop format, preserving the layers, you can return to adjust your settings at any time. Even after closing the file, the adjustment layers retain the values you set, and remain live; if necessary, you could even revert to the original image by either hiding or deleting the adjustment layers.

Correcting parts of an image selectively

Our adjustment layers brought out color and image detail from the overly dark foreground, but the background is now overexposed and lacking in tonal depth. So far in this lesson, all the corrections you've made have been applied to the entire image; in the next set of exercises you'll selectively adjust just part of the photo.

Creating a selection

In this exercise you'll isolate our subjects in the foreground from the watery backdrop so that you can treat these two areas of the image separately. To start, you'll select the combined silhouette of the girls on the grass and save that selection.

You've already explored some of the many ways to make a selection in Lesson 5. We'll start by revisiting the Quick Selection tool, which automatically determines selection borders based on similarity in color and texture.

1 Open the original image file TooDark.jpg once again.

2 In the toolbar, click the Quick Selection tool (🖎), or whichever of its variants is currently visible at the right of the Lasso tool, and then click Tool Options button (🖊) in the Task bar to access the tool settings. In the tool options pane, make sure that the New Selection mode is activated for the Quick Selection tool. Set a brush diameter of around 100 px (pixels) and activate Auto-Enhance.

3 Starting in the lower right corner, drag to the left along the bottom of the photo to select the grass area; then, drag up over each of the girls to create a rough selection surrounding all the foreground elements. With each stroke, the selection automatically expands to include more of the combined silhouette.

Next, you need to refine the selection border to capture the silhouette as closely as possible. You'll need to deselect the small areas of background that are visible between arms and torsos, and pay extra attention around the edges of the hair.

While refining your selection, you can alternate between the Quick Selection tool's Add To Selection and Subtract From Selection modes by holding down either the Shift key or the Alt / Option key. To reduce or increase the brush size as you work, without using the Tool Options pane, press the left and right bracket keys ([,]).

4 Keeping the Quick Selection tool selected, hold the Ctrl / Command key and press the plus sign (+) to zoom in. Hold the spacebar and drag the image to focus on the loose hair to the right of the older girl's face.

5 Press the left bracket key ([ ) on your keyboard repeatedly to reduce the brush size to 10 px. Drag in the unwanted fragment of background, holding down the Alt / Option key to operate the Quick Selection tool in Subtract From Selection mode. The selection contracts to exclude the extraneous area. Reduce the brush size further and alternate between the Alt / Option and Shift keys, using clicks and short strokes to refine the selection border around the deselected area.

6 Without being overly fussy, continue to refine the selection around the subjects' edges. Your work will be much simpler if you use the keyboard shortcuts detailed in steps 4 and 5 to navigate in the image and adjust the tool settings. Unless you have a lot of time on your hands, you can exclude the taller grass at the lake's edge, together with the bright water visible between the stems.

7 To smooth and soften the edges of the selection, choose Select > Refine Edge. Alternatively, you could show the Tool Options pane and click the Refine Edge button. In the Refine Edge dialog box, activate the Smart Radius option for the Edge Detection control and set the Radius to **2** px. Under Adjust Edge, set the Smooth value to **2**. Under Output, make sure the Output To option is set to Selection.

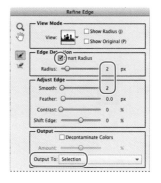

▶ **Tip:** Take a moment to move the pointer over each control in the Refine Edge dialog box in turn to see a description of its action displayed in a tooltip.

8 While you're working on refining your selection, you can preview the results against a variety of backgrounds, each helpful in different circumstances. Under View Mode, click the View button. Move the pointer over each of the seven preview options to see a tooltip description, then click on each in turn to see the result in the Edit window.

9 Click OK to apply your edge refinement settings to the selection; then, choose Select > Save Selection. In the Save Selection dialog box, choose New from the Selection menu, type **Girls** for the selection name, and then click OK. Once a selection is saved, you can always re-use it—after assessing your adjustments you can reload the selection to modify them. Choose Select > Deselect.

Using layer masks to isolate parts of an image

Now that you've created a selection including only the figures in the foreground, you can adjust the exposure and lighting for the subjects and the background independently. You could use your selection (even at a later date, now that you've saved it) to temporarily isolate part of the image for editing. Instead you'll use the saved selection to create separate layer masks for the different areas in the image.

A layer mask can be permanently linked to a particular layer in an image, so that any modification made to that layer will be applied only through the mask. The parts of the layer protected by the layer mask are hidden from view when it's blended with the other layers in your image. Layer masks can be edited by painting and erasing, so you can add to or subtract from a layer mask (and thereby, add to or subtract from the area that will be modified by an editing operation) without affecting the image pixels on the layer to which the mask is attached.

1 Duplicate the Background layer by dragging it onto the New Layer button (⬚) at the left of the Layers panel's header.

2 Click the menu icon (▾≡) at the far right of the Layers panel's header to open the Layers panel Options menu; then, choose Panel Options. In the Layers Panel Options dialog box, select either large or medium thumbnails—seeing the layer thumbnails can help you visualize the layers you're working with. Click OK. If necessary, choose View > Fit On Screen so that you can see the entire image.

3 Choose Select > Load Selection. Choose the saved selection Girls from the Source Selection menu, click the check box to activate the Invert option and choose New Selection under Operation; then click OK.

4 Make sure the layer Background copy is still selected, and then click the Add Layer Mask button (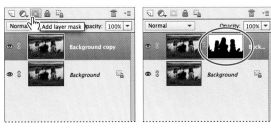) at the top of the Layers panel.

A mask thumbnail appears on the Background copy layer, showing that your active selection in the image window has been converted to a layer mask on that layer. The blue frame around the mask thumbnail indicates that the mask is currently selected—any change you make right now will modify the mask, not the image pixels on this layer.

5 Alt-click / Option-click the layer mask thumbnail to make the mask visible in the Edit window. With the mask selected, as it is now, you can edit it using painting and selection tools—or even the Text tool. Alt-click / Option-click the layer mask thumbnail again to hide the mask.

6 Click the image thumbnail on the masked layer; then click the eye icon beside the image thumbnail on the original Background layer to make the layer temporarily invisible. You can see that the protected areas of the masked layer are actually hidden from view. Make the Background layer visible again.

▶ Tip: Edits made on a masked layer will be applied at full strength through the white parts of the mask; black areas in the mask represent the parts of your image that are completely protected. A gray area will allow a modification to be applied at a strength equivalent to the percentage of white present; a layer mask containing a gradient from white to black can be a great way to fade one image into another.

While this layer mask is active, any change made to the original Background layer will be visible only in the figures in the foreground; any change you make to the masked layer will be applied only the backdrop around them.

7 Make another copy of the original Background layer by dragging it onto the New Layer button ( ) at the left of the Layers panel's header bar. Choose Select > Load Selection. Select your saved selection, Girls, as the Source Selection, but this time, leave the Invert option disabled. Under Operation, choose New Selection; then click OK.

8 Make sure the new layer, Background copy 2 is still selected, and then click the Add Layer Mask button () at the top of the Layers panel. Repeat steps 5 and 6 for the new mask layer.

If you keep the layer masks linked to the Background copy layers as they are now, they will remain editable. For the purposes of this exercise however, we've already refined our selection, and we have no other reason to keep the mask active.

9 Right-click / Control-click each black and white layer mask thumbnail in turn and choose Apply Layer Mask from the context menu.

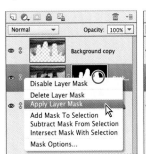

The layer masks can no longer be edited; they have been permanently applied to their respective layers. The layer mask thumbnails have now disappeared and the image thumbnails show areas of transparency indicating protected areas on those layers.

10 You'll find it much easier to deal with layers—especially when you're working with many of them—if you give your layers descriptive names in the Layers panel. Double-click the name text of Background copy 2 and type **Girls** as the new name for the layer. Change the name of Background copy to **Lake**.

Correcting underexposed areas

We can now apply a slightly adjusted version of the most effective brightening technique from the earlier exercises to the subjects of our photo selectively.

1 In the Layers panel, make sure the Background layer is visible; then, select the layer Girls. Choose Screen from the blending menu and set the opacity to **75%**.

2 Duplicate the Girls layer. Set the blending mode for the new layer to Color Dodge and the opacity to **35%**. The figures in the foreground are brighter and clearer, while the lake in the background remains unaffected.

Adding more intensity

Now that the figures in the foreground look so much better, the dimly-lit surface of the lake behind them needs to be adjusted to appear less dull and flat.

With the foreground and background isolated on separate masked layers, you're free to apply whatever modifications you choose. There are no hard-and-fast rules; you might decide to emphasise the figures by making the background bright and pale, or by making it darker and more dramatic. For the purposes of this exercise, we'll boost the colors and textural detail, making the background less "murky," while preserving the soft lighting dynamics of the original image.

1 In the Layers panel, select the layer Lake. Choose Enhance > Adjust Color > Adjust Hue/Saturation. Increase the Saturation setting to **50** and the Lightness to **15**. Click OK. Choose Enhance > Adjust Lighting > Brightness/Contrast; then, set the Brightness to **5** and the Contrast to **15**. Click OK.

With these few adjustments to the separate layers, the photograph now looks far more lively. There are still possibilities for improving the separated areas of the image; for example you could apply a Gaussian blur to the background to create a depth-of-field effect. There's also more you could do with blending modes and layer opacity—you'll learn more of these techniques as you work through this book.

The background looks clearer and more vibrant, while the soft contrast prevents it from over-whelming the figures in the foreground.

2 Choose File > Save. Make sure that Include In The Elements Organizer option is activated and Save In Version Set With Original is disabled. Name the new file **TooDark_LayerMasks** and choose the Photoshop (PSD) format. Make sure the Layers option is activated, and then click Save. If the Format Options dialog box appears, activate Maximize Compatibility and click OK. Close the file.

3 In Lesson 5 you learned how to tile the image windows to best compare the results of different correction methods. Use that technique now to compare the six adjusted and saved versions of this photograph before moving on.

Improving faded or overexposed images

In this section, you'll work with the scan of a family keepsake in need of restoration. This badly faded photo has problems similar to those found in overexposed images, and will respond to the same correction techniques.

The automatic fixes applied to a copy at the beginning of this lesson improved the image markedly, but also removed the characteristic sepia tint, treating it as a color cast. In this project, you'll try to do even better using other correction techniques, while preserving the evocative antique look.

1 In the Organizer, isolate the Lesson 6 images, if necessary. In the Media Browser, select the file TooDark.jpg; then, click the Editor button (🖼) in the Task bar.

2 If the Editor is not already in Expert mode, click Expert in the mode picker.

3 If you don't see the Photo Bin, show it by clicking the Photo Bin button (🖼) at the left of the Task bar. If you don't see the filename beneath the thumbnail in the Photo Bin, right-click / Control-click the thumbnail and choose Show Filenames. Choose Window > Reset Panels, and then View > Fit On Screen.

Creating a set of duplicate files

You'll compare a variety of editing techniques during the course of this project. You can begin by creating a separate file to test each method, named for the technique it will demonstrate.

1 Right-click / Control-click the thumbnail image in the Photo Bin and choose Duplicate from the context menu. In the Duplicate Image dialog box, name the file **TooLight_Shad-High**; then, click OK. Repeat the process to create two more copies, with the names **TooLight_Bright-Cont**, and **TooLight_Levels**.

2 In the Photo Bin, double-click the thumbnail TooLight.jpg to make that image active and bring its image window to the front. If you can't see the whole of a filename under a thumbnail in the Photo Bin, hold the pointer over the thumbnail; the name of the file is displayed as a Tooltip.

3 Choose File > Save As. Select your My CIB Work folder as the destination for the new file, then activate Include In The Elements Organizer and disable the option Save In Version Set With Original. Type **TooLight_Blend-Modes** as the new filename and select Photoshop (PSD) from the Format menu. Click Save. Leave all four images open for the rest of this project.

Using blending modes to fix a faded image

The blending mode applied to a layer can make it interact with the layers beneath it in a variety of ways. The Multiply mode intensifies or darkens pixels in an image. The Overlay mode tends to brighten the image while preserving its tonal range.

1. Make sure that TooLight_Blend-Mode.psd is still the active image. If necessary, double-click its thumbnail in the Photo Bin to make it active. In the Layers panel right-click / Control-click the Background layer and choose Duplicate Layer from the context menu. Click OK in the Duplicate Layer dialog box to accept the default name "Background copy."

2. In the Layers panel, choose Multiply from the layer blending mode menu. Note the effect in the image window. Drag the Background copy layer with its Multiply blend mode onto the New Layer button (⬚) at the top of the Layers panel to create a copy of the Background copy layer.

3. Change the blending mode for the layer Background copy 2 from Multiply to Overlay, watching the effect on the image. Set the layer's Opacity value to **50**%, either by dragging the Opacity slider or by typing the new value in the text field.

Original image　　　+ Second layer: Multiply mode, 100%　　　+ Third layer: Overlay mode, 30%

Adding a layer with the Multiply blending mode made the image bolder, and then the third layer in Overlay mode brightened it considerably and improved definition. Taken together, your changes have made the photo clearer, but the contrast in parts of the image, particularly in the lighter clothing, is still unimpressive.

4. Choose File > Save to save the file in your My CIB Work folder, leaving the image open. If a message appears about maximizing compatibility, click OK to close it, or follow the instructions in the message to prevent it from appearing again.

Adjusting shadows and highlights manually

Although both the Auto-fix and blending modes do a good job of correcting many fading images, some of your own photos may be more challenging. You'll try three more techniques in the exercises to follow. The first involves manually adjusting the Shadows, Highlights, and Midtone Contrast of the image.

1. In the Photo Bin, double-click TooLight_Shad-High to make it the active image.

2. Choose Enhance > Adjust Lighting > Shadows/Highlights. If necessary, move the Shadows/Highlights dialog box so that it doesn't obscure the image window. Make sure that the Preview option is activated.

> **Tip:** If you can't see the whole of the filename in the Project Bin, hold the pointer over the thumbnail; the name of the file is displayed as a Tooltip.

By default, the Lighten Shadows setting is 35%. You can see the effect on the image by toggling the Preview option on and off in the Shadows/Highlights dialog box.

3   In the Shadows/Highlights dialog box, set the Lighten Shadows value to **5%**, the Darken Highlights value to **25%**, and the Midtone Contrast to **+50%**.

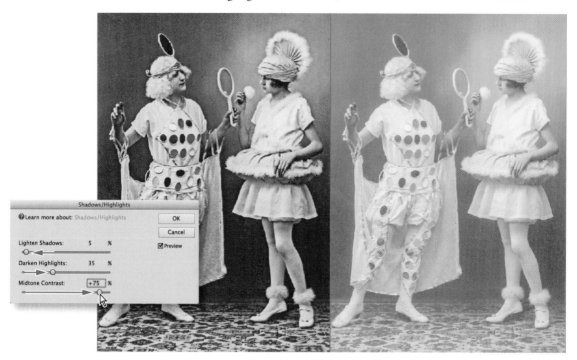

▶ **Tip:** The controls you are using to make the adjustments for this technique are also available in the Lighting panel in Quick Fix mode.

4   Adjust the three settings as needed until you think the image is as good as it can be. When you're done, click OK to close the Shadows/Highlights dialog box.

5   Choose File > Save and save the file to your My CIB Work folder, in JPEG format. Make sure that the image will be included in the Organizer, but not in a Version Set. Click Save, and then click OK in the JPEG Options dialog box and leave the file open.

Adjusting brightness and contrast manually

The next approach you'll take to fixing an exposure problem makes use of another option from the Enhance > Adjust Lighting menu.

1   In the Photo Bin, double-click the image TooLight_Bright-Cont to make it active. If necessary, choose View > Fit On Screen or double-click the Hand tool.

2   Choose Enhance > Adjust Lighting > Brightness/Contrast. If necessary, drag the Brightness/Contrast dialog box to one side so that it doesn't block your view of the image. Make sure that the Preview option is activated so you can see the effects of your adjustments on the photo as you make them.

3 Drag the Brightness slider to –70, or type **–70** in the text field, being careful to include the minus sign when you type. Increase the Contrast to **100**.

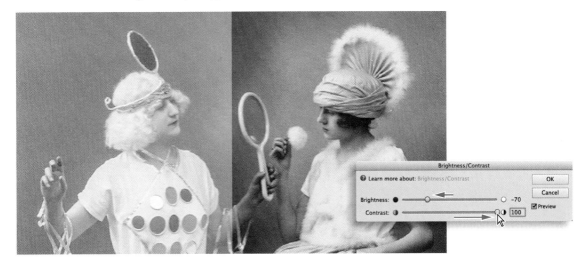

4 Adjust the Brightness and Contrast settings until you are happy with the look of the image. Click OK to close the Brightness/Contrast dialog box.

5 Choose File > Save and save the file to your My CIB Work folder, in JPEG format. Make sure that the image will be included in the Organizer, but not in a Version Set; then, click Save. Click OK in the JPEG Options dialog box, but keep the file open. Choose Window > Images > Tile.

Adjusting levels

The Levels controls affect the distribution of tonal values in an image—the range of tones from dark to light, regardless of color. In this exercise, you'll enhance the image by shifting the reference points that define the spread of those tonal values.

1 In the Photo Bin, double-click the image TooLight_Levels to make it active. Choose Window > Images > Float In Window; then double-click the Hand tool.

2 Choose Enhance > Adjust Lighting > Levels. Activate the Preview option in the Levels dialog box, if it is not already active. If necessary, drag the Levels dialog box aside so that you can also see most of the image window.

The Levels graph represents the distribution of tonal values across all the pixels in the image, from darkest at the left to lightest at the right. A trough (or gap) in the curve indicates that there are few (or no) pixels mapped to that part of the range; a peak shows the opposite.

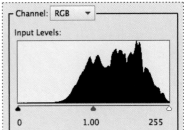

As you can see from the graph, this image has no black pixels, very few tones of less than 40% brightness; most of the image information is clustered at the light end of the scale.

3 In the Levels dialog box, drag the black triangle below the left end of the graph to the right; the value in the first Input Levels box should be approximately 80. Drag the white marker from the right side of the graph until the value in the third Input Levels box is approximately 245. Drag the gray marker to set the mid-tone value to approximately 0.75. Click OK to close the Levels dialog box.

4 Choose File > Save and save the file to your My CIB Work folder in JPEG format as TooLight_Levels. Make sure that the image will be included in the Organizer, but not in a Version Set. Click Save; then, click OK in the JPEG Options dialog box and leave the file open.

Comparing results

You can now compare the six versions of the image: the original file, the four files you edited, and the image that was fixed automatically at the start of this lesson.

1 Choose File > Open. Locate and open the file TooLight_Autofix.jpg from the My CIB Work folder; then repeat the process for the original file from your Lesson 6 folder, TooLight.jpg. The Photo Bin should show six open files.

2 Click the Photo Bin button in the Task bar to hide the Photo Bin; then, hide the Panel Bin by un-checking its name in the Window menu.

3 Choose Window > Images > Tile. Use the Zoom and Hand tools to position the photo in any of the image windows so that you can see enough of the image to enable you to make a comparison of the different treatments; then, choose Window > Images > Match Zoom and Window > Images > Match Location.

4 Choose File > Close All. Save any changes to your CIB Work folder if you're prompted to do so.

Congratulations! You've finished another lesson. Before you move on to the next chapter, take a few moments to review what you've learned by reading through the questions and answers on the next page.

Review questions

1 How can you create an exact copy of an existing layer?

2 Where can you find the controls for adjusting the lighting in a photograph?

3 How can you arrange multiple image windows in the work area automatically?

4 What is an adjustment layer and what are its unique advantages?

Review answers

1 You must be in Expert mode to copy a layer. Select a layer in the Layers panel and choose Layer > Duplicate Layer. You can access the same command in the Layers panel Options menu or by right-clicking / Control-clicking the layer in the Layers panel. Alternatively, drag the layer to the New Layer button. Whichever method you use, you get two layers identical in all but their names, stacked one above the other.

2 You can adjust the lighting for a photo in Expert, Guided edit, and Quick edit mode. In Expert mode, you can use the Enhance > Adjust Lighting menu to open various dialog boxes that contain the controls. Alternatively, you can choose Enhance > Auto Levels, Enhance > Auto Contrast, or Enhance > Adjust Color > Adjust Color Curves. In Guided edit mode, choose the Brightness And Contrast, Levels, or Lighten And Darken operations from the Touchups category. In Quick edit mode, you can use the Exposure and Levels panes in the Quick Fix panel.

3 You cannot rearrange image windows in Quick edit and Guided edit modes, which display only one photograph at a time. In the Expert workspace, there are several ways you can arrange them. Choose Window > Images, and select one of the choices listed there—you can access some of the same options, and several more, by clicking the Layout button in the Task bar. Some of the options require that you enable floating windows in Expert mode, which can be done in the Preferences dialog box.

4 An adjustment layer does not contain an image; instead, it modifies some quality of all the layers below it in the Layer panel. For example, a Brightness/Contrast layer will alter the brightness and contrast of any underlying layers. One advantage of using an adjustment layer instead of adjusting an existing layer directly is that adjustment layers can be easily modified or even removed. Toggle the eye icon for the adjustment layer to remove or restore the edit instantly. You can change a setting in an adjustment layer at any time—even after the file has been saved. An adjustment layer can also be copied and pasted into another image to apply the same settings there.

7 REFRAMING, RETOUCHING, AND RECOMPOSING IMAGES

Lesson overview

For some photos you'll need to deal with image flaws other than color or lighting problems.

A picture that was taken hurriedly might be spoiled by being tilted or poorly composed; even a technically perfect exposure can be let down by an extraneous object that clutters an otherwise striking composition, by dust or water spots on the lens, or by blemishes on a portrait subject's skin.

In this lesson, you'll learn a range of techniques for, cropping, retouching, and rearranging the composition of such flawed images:

- Using the Straighten tool
- Using the Crop tool to reframe an image
- Creating a photo border
- Improving the impact of an image with the Recompose tool
- Enhancing composition by repositioning objects in the frame
- Retouching skin with the Healing Brush tool
- Removing unwanted objects with content-aware healing
- Reinventing an image with creative effects

 You'll probably need between one and two hours to complete this lesson. If you haven't already done so, download the Lesson 7 work files from the Lesson & Update Files tab of your Account page at www.peachpit.com.

Photoshop Elements delivers a range of tools to help you bring out the potential in a photo, despite its flaws. The same tricks and techniques that enable you to remove or reposition an inconveniently placed object, retouch spots and blemishes in a portrait, or restore a treasured keepsake by repairing creases and tears can also be used creatively to manipulate reality in order to produce exactly the image you want.

Getting started

You'll begin by importing the sample images for this lesson to your CIB Catalog.

Note: Before you start this lesson, make sure that you've set up a folder for your lesson files and downloaded the Lesson 7 folder from your Account page at www.peachpit.com, as detailed in "Accessing the Classroom in a Book files" in the chapter "Getting Started" at the beginning of this book. You should also have created a new work catalog (see "Creating a catalog for working with this book" in Lesson 1).

1 Start Photoshop Elements and click Organize in the Welcome Screen.

2 In the Organizer, check the lower right corner of the workspace to make sure that your CIB Catalog is loaded—if not, choose File > Manage Catalogs and select it from the list.

3 Click the Import button at the upper left of the Organizer workspace and choose From Files And Folders from the drop-down menu. In the Get Photos And Videos From Files And Folders dialog box, locate and select your Lesson 7 folder. Disable the automatic processing options; then, click Get Media.

4 In the Import Attached Keyword Tags dialog box, click Select All; then, click OK.

Improving the composition of a photo

When you're hurried, distracted by movement, or shooting in awkward conditions, the result is often a photo that *could* have been great—if only it had been framed better. In the Full Edit mode toolbar, the Crop tool and the Straighten tool will help you turn the shot you got into the photo you *should* have captured.

Sometimes you're just too busy fitting everyone into frame to notice a crooked horizon. The Straighten tool makes it easy to quickly correct a tilted image. The Crop tool can be customized, by choosing from a range of preset aspect ratios and cropping overlays to help you bring out the visual potential of your image.

Using the Straighten tool

You can use the Straighten tool to pick out a feature in your crooked photo that should be either horizontal or vertical; then, Photoshop Elements will rotate the image to straighten it in relation to your reference line.

1 Select the image 07_01.jpg in the Media Browser, and then click the Editor button (🖼)—not the arrow beside it—in the Task bar. Alternately, you could select the file and choose Edit > Edit With Photoshop Elements Editor. If the Editor doesn't open to Expert mode, click Expert in the mode picker.

2 Choose Window > Reset Panels; then, press Shift+Tab to hide the Panel Bin and the Photo Bin or tool options pane—if either is currently open. Choose View > Fit On Screen or double-click the Hand tool to see the entire image at the highest magnification possible. Hold down the Ctrl / Command key and press the minus sign (−) key once to zoom out just enough to see a little of the blank *artboard* (colored gray by default) surrounding the photo in the Edit pane.

3 Select the Straighten tool (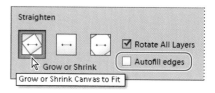) in the toolbar; then, click the Tool Options button (🖉) in the Task bar, if necessary, to open the Tool Options pane. Make sure that the Straighten tool is set to Grow Or Shrink Canvas To Fit mode and the Autofill Edges option is disabled; then, hide the tool options pane.

This photo features a sea horizon—the most reliable of reference levels. In the absence of a natural horizon, you can often use a horizontal architectural feature.

▶ **Tip:** Choose Grow Or Shrink Canvas To Fit when you wish to crop the rotated image manually; the other options will trim it automatically.

4 Drag a long line along the horizon in the right half of the photo (at the left the horizon is hidden by the land in the middle distance). When you release the mouse button, Photoshop Elements straightens the image relative to the line you drew. Note the newly enlarged canvas surrounding the rotated image.

You could crop the straightened image manually to trim away the angled edges, but for the purposes of this exercise, you'll look at a couple of alternative options.

5 Press Ctrl+Z / Command+Z to undo the Straighten tool. Show the Tool Options pane and click the second of the three icons at the left to activate the Remove Background mode; then, use the Straighten tool to trace the horizon again. Photoshop Elements crops the largest area possible within the angled edges. Hide the Tool Options pane to examine the results.

6 Undo the operation; then, reset the Straighten tool to the Grow Or Shrink mode and activate the Autofill Edges option. Trace the horizon, and then inspect the results; rather than trimming the angled edges, Photoshop Elements has used content-aware image analysis to fill the white extended canvas that you saw in step 4 with detail that matches the image.

As you can see in the illustration at the right, this method has preserved all the detail of the original photo—especially important along the bottom, where cropping would affect the composition.

7 Choose Layer > Flatten Image; then, choose File > Save As. Name the new file **07_01_Straight**, to be saved to your My CIB Work folder in JPEG format and included in the Organizer, but not in a Version Set. Click Save; then, click OK to accept the settings in the JPEG Options dialog box. Keep the file open.

8 Staying in the Editor, choose File > Open; then, navigate to and open your Lesson 7 folder, select the file 07_02.jpg, and click Open.

In many photos it's difficult to identify a reliable horizontal reference; in these cases, you can look for a vertical feature such as or a sign-post or any structural element that isn't too obviously affected by perspective or lens distortion.

For this image, where the horizon is not visible and almost every man-made horizontal is pictured in perspective, the tower provides the strongest reference.

9 With the Straighten tool (⊞) selected, open the tool options pane. Click the second of the three icons at the left to activate the Remove Background mode.

● **Note:** By default, the Straighten tool is set for a horizontal reference; to designate a vertical reference you need to use the tool with the Ctrl / Command key.

In Remove Background mode, the Autofill Edges option is disabled; for our lesson photo, Autofill Edges is likely to produce unwanted artifacts in the other modes.

10 Click and hold on the tip of the tower; then, press the Ctrl / Command key and drag a line down through the center of the structure. As the tower is stepped in towards the top and pictured in slight perspective, the bottom of your reference line should pass through the entrance arch somewhat to the right of center. When you're done, release the mouse button, and then the Ctrl / Command key.

▶ **Tip:** In some cases, you can achieve good results by choosing either Straighten Image, or Straighten And Crop Image from the Image > Rotate > menu. Both of these commands perform straightening functions automatically.

11 Choose File > Save As. Name the file **07_02_Straight.jpg**, to be saved to your My CIB Work folder in JPEG format and included in the Organizer, but not in a Version Set. Click Save; then, click OK to accept the settings in the JPEG Options dialog box. Choose File > Close.

Reframing a photo with the Crop tool

Composing your photo well can make the difference between an ordinary snapshot and a striking, memorable image. Unfortunately, in practice there's often just not enough time while you're shooting to frame your photo carefully.

Tip: Remember that you can use cropping not only to trim away portions of an image, but also as a way to re-frame a photo in order to draw the eye to your subject and improve the image's balance.

Framing too much irrelevant detail can diminish the impact of your photo by detracting from your intended focus, and an awkward arrangement of forms within the frame can make your picture appear unbalanced. The Crop tool can be custom-ized to achieve exactly the crop you want, and offers a choice of overlays to guide you in framing a balanced composition.

1 With the image 07_01_Straight.jpg open in the Editor, select the Crop tool (⬚). In the tool options pane, choose Use Photo Ratio from the aspect menu. By default, the Crop Overlay is set to Rule Of Thirds, a guide based on the principle that a composition looks balanced when its elements are aligned with the lines and intersections of a grid that divides the image into three equal parts on both axes. Drag a rectangle so that the horizon lies on the upper horizontal guide and the vertical guide at the right passes between the two girls.

2 Click the Cancel button (⊘) at the lower right of the cropping rectangle. In the tool options pane, activate the Golden Ratio overlay. This guide is based on a for-mula that has been used to create appealing composi-tions in painting and architecture through the ages.

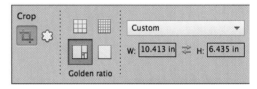

3 Drag a small rectangle anywhere in the image. In the Tool Options bar, click the Flip button (◀ Flip) to flip the Golden Ratio guide horizontally, and then drag the lower right handle of the cropping box upwards and to the left in the image window to turn the rectangle "inside-out," mirroring the new orientation of the guides on both axes.

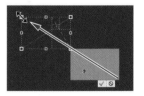

4 Adjust the cropping rectangle to define a pleasing crop, with the focus of the Golden Ratio centered a little below the horizon and between the girls' heads. Click the Commit button (✓) to execute the crop.

5 Choose File > Save As. Make sure that the new file will be included in the Organizer, but not in a Version Set. Name the file **07_01_GoldenCrop.jpg**, to be saved to your My CIB Work folder in JPEG format. Click Save; then, set the highest quality in the JPEG Options dialog box and click OK. Keep the file open.

Working with the image canvas

You can think of the image canvas as the equivalent of the paper on which a photo is printed. While you're working with a digital photo, image data may temporarily lie outside the canvas space, but it will be clipped to the canvas boundary as soon as the image is flattened. To extend our limited analogy just a little further, think of the layer data as the image projected by a photographic enlarger in the darkroom. Although the projected image may be offset or enlarged so that it falls outside the borders of the paper, the data still exists; you can continue to work with it right up until the moment that the photographic paper is exposed.

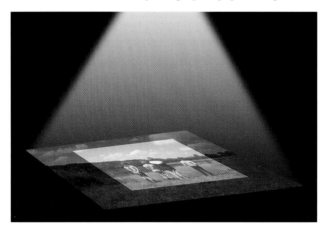

Adding a border to a photo

By default, the canvas is the same size as the image and is therefore not visible. If you increase the size of the image file, the canvas is enlarged automatically; however, you can also choose to enlarge the canvas independently of the image size, effectively adding a border around your photo—just as if you printed a photo on a sheet of paper larger than the image.

By default, the extended canvas, and therefore the border, takes on the Background color as set in the color swatches at the bottom of the toolbar.

1 With the cropped image 07_01_GoldenCrop.jpg still open and the Editor in Expert mode from the previous exercise, double-click the Hand tool (🖑) or choose View > Fit On Screen; then, press Shift+Tab (twice, if necessary) to hide everything but the image and the toolbar.

2 If you don't see a reasonable amount of the blank gray background surrounding the image, hold down the Ctrl / Command key and press the Minus key (-) on your keyboard or choose View > Zoom Out.

3 Choose Image > Resize > Canvas Size. If necessary, move the Canvas Size dialog box aside so that you can see at least the left half of the image.

4 Set the Canvas Size dialog box as shown in the illustration at the right. Activate the Relative option; then, set the units menus to Inches, if necessary, and type a new value of **0.5** for both Width and Height. Leave the Anchor control at the default centered setting. Choose Black from the Canvas Extension Color menu, and then click OK.

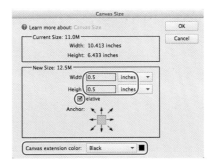

The new black border appears around the photo in the image window. For the purposes of this exercise, we'll take it one step further, and extend the canvas again to turn the border into an asymmetrical frame.

5 Choose Image > Resize > Canvas Size. In the Canvas Size dialog box, confirm that the Relative check box is still activated. Leave the Width value at **0** and set the Height value to **1** inch. In the Anchor control grid diagram, click the central arrow in the top row. With this Anchor setting, the one-inch increase to the height of the canvas will be applied at the bottom edge of the image only. Leave the Canvas Extension Color setting unchanged and click OK.

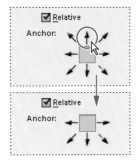

6 If you can't see all of the border framing the image, double-click the Hand tool or choose View > Fit On Screen.

The extended border gives you space to add text to the image, making it an easy and effective way to create a postcard, a stylish cover page for a printed document, or a title screen for a slideshow presentation.

Working with text

Whether you wish to fit an image to a specific purpose, or simply add a message, the Photoshop Elements type tools make it easy to create good-looking text.

▷ **Tip:** You can open the tool options pane by clicking the Tool Options button (📝) in the Task bar, or by double-clicking a tool in the toolbar.

1   In the toolbar, click to select the Horizontal Type tool (T). In the tool options pane, choose Lithos Pro from the Font Family  menu. Set the font style to Regular. Type **57** pt in the Font Size box; then, press Enter / Return. Choose Center Text (≡) from the paragraph alignment options.

2   In the Tool Options bar, click the text color swatch below the font menus. As you move the pointer over the Color Swatches picker, it becomes an eye-dropper cursor. Use the eyedropper cursor to select the white swatch in the top row; then, press the Esc key to close the Color Swatches picker.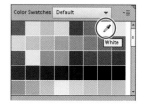

3   With the Type tool, click below the center of the black space beneath the photo and type **GREETINGS FROM GREECE**. Swipe over the text by to select it. Click the foreground color swatch (now white) below the tools in the toolbar to open the Color Picker. Move the pointer over the image window; the cursor becomes an eyedropper.

4   Move the eyedropper over the orange flower near the girl at the left's shoulder. Refer to the illustration at the right; then, sample an ochre-gold and click OK in the Color Picker to close it.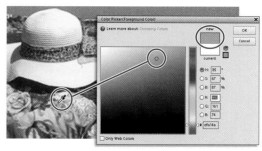

5   Swipe over the word FROM to select it; then, click the foreground color swatch and use the eyedropper to sample a bright turquoise from the background. Click OK in the Color Picker to close it.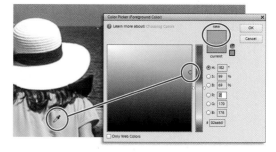

6   Click the green Commit button (✔) at the lower right corner of the new text. Drag the text with the Move tool to center it. Use the handles on the text bounding box to resize it slightly if necessary; then commit the changes.

7 Choose File > Save As. Name the file **07_01_Greece** and save it to your My CIB Work folder in Photoshop format with Layers activated. Activate Include In The Organizer and disable Save In Version Set With Original. Choose File > Close.

Adding a quick border

When precision isn't an issue, you can quickly add a border to an image by using the Crop tool, rather than increasing the size of the canvas.

1 Zoom out far enough so that you can see some of the blank art-board surrounding the image in the edit window.

2 Use the crop tool to drag a cropping rectangle right around the image.

3 Drag the corner handles of the crop marquee outside the image area onto the art-board to define the size and shape of border that you wish to create.

4 When you're satisfied, click the Commit button in the lower right corner of the image. The canvas expands to fill the cropping rectangle, taking on the background color set in the color swatch at the bottom of the toolbar.

Recomposing an image within its frame

Tip: As with the Healing brushes and the Clone Stamp tool that are covered later in this chapter, and the Photomerge tools that you'll use in Lesson 8, the Recompose tool is also a lot of fun to use creatively, enabling you to manipulate reality in order to produce the image you want.

Do you have a group shot where you wish the group had stood closer together? Or a photo where a walk-on extra draws attention away from the stars? With the Recompose tool you can fix these image composition problems in a few easy steps.

Essentially, the Recompose tool enables you to crop your photo from the *inside*, rather than at the edges. Whether you want to bring people closer together, fit a horizontal image to a vertical space, or remove extraneous elements that spoil the composition, the Recompose tool puts image editing magic at your fingertips. In this exercise, you'll use the Recompose tool to tighten the arrangement of a group photo and reframe the landscape format to create a square composition.

1   If you're still in the Editor, click the Organizer button (⊞) in the Task Bar. If necessary, click the arrow beside the Lesson 07 tag in the Tags panel to isolate the images for this lesson; then, right-click / Control-click the image 07_03.jpg and choose Edit With Photoshop Elements Editor.

2   Make sure the Editor is in Expert mode; then, choose Window > Reset Panels. Press Shift+Tab on your keyboard to hide everything but the image window and the toolbar. Double-click the Hand tool, or choose View > Fit On Screen; then, press Ctrl / Command together with the minus sign (–) key to zoom out just enough to see a little empty gray space around the photo in the Edit window.

Tip: You can also open the tool options pane by double-clicking a tool in the toolbar.

3   Click the Recompose tool (🔧) in the toolbar, and then click the Tool Options button (✏️) in the Task bar open the tool options pane.

The image is now surrounded by a live bounding box, with control handles at the corners and at the mid-point of each side. For simple recomposing operations, all you need to do is drag the handles; the Recompose tool makes use of content-aware scaling technology that distinguishes people and other featured objects and attempts to prevent them being distorted as the background is compressed around them. For this exercise, however, we'll use the special Recompose brushes instead. For more complex images, this generally produces better results.

Note: The Threshold control lets you adjust the degree to which content-aware scaling is applied as the image is "squeezed." At 100%, protected areas will be completely free of distortion when the photo is scaled. At a Threshold of 0%, the content-aware feature is turned off; scaling on one axis will "squash" pictured objects.

4   Select the Mark For Protection brush—the brush with a plus sign (+)—at the left of the tool options pane. Either type in the brush size text box or use the slider to increase the brush size to about **300** px. Make sure that the Threshold and aspect ratio are set to the default 100% and No Restriction, respectively.

As its name suggests, you can use the Mark For Protection brush to define those areas in the image that you want shielded from any scaling operation.

5 Click the Tool Options button () in the Task bar to hide the tool options pane.

6 Paint over the girl at the left of the photo. Extend your strokes to the left edge of the image, as shown at the right: the girl is already very to the edge of the frame and unless this area is protected it will be compressed during the recompose operation. If you find you've over-painted, use the eraser with the plus sign, beside the protection brush in the Tool Options pane to modify your strokes. Use the left and right bracket keys ([,]) to reduce or increase the size of the eraser as you work.

Note: The green protection brush over-lay is difficult to see against the grassy field in our lesson photo. For the sake of clarity, the surrounding image has been dimmed in these illustrations.

7 Right-click / Control-click the image and change the brush mode from the default Use Normal Highlight to Use Quick Highlight. In Quick Highlight mode you can mark an area for protection by simply drawing a line around it. Show the Tool Options pane for a moment to set the brush size to **50** px. Draw an outline to surround the three girls at the right, including the space between the group and the right edge of the photo. When you're done, release the mouse button; Photoshop Elements fills the area inside the outline automatically.

8 Right-click / Control-click the image and reset the Recompose tool to the Use Normal Highlight mode. Show the Tool Options pane and select the Mark For Removal brush (the brush with a minus sign). Set the brush size to **100** px. Scribble through the space between the girl at the left and her sisters to mark the area for removal—rather than compression—during the scaling process.

Tip: If necessary, you can modify your Mark For Removal brush strokes with the associated eraser. Use the left and right bracket keys ([,]) to reduce or increase the brush size as you work.

9 Now for the fun part! Move the pointer over the handle on the left side of the bounding box and, when the double-arrow cursor appears, drag the handle slowly in towards the center of the photo. Watch the photo as you drag; some areas of the image are removed while others are compressed and merged with their surroundings. As the proportions of the image become closer to a square, keep an eye on the width (W) and height (H) values in the tool options pane; stop dragging and release the mouse button when the two values are equal.

▶ **Tip:** As this was a rather extreme editing operation, you may find some image artifacts, especially near the seam between areas that were removed or protected. If these are noticeable enough to worry you, a few strokes with the Clone Stamp or the Healing Brush will fix the problem. You'll learn more about those tools later in this lesson. Zoom in to inspect the seam. Try recomposing the image differently, marking a smaller area for removal, limiting your strokes to the patch separating the sisters, rather than the larger vertical strip.

10 Click the green Commit button at the lower right of the recomposed photo or press Enter / Return to accept and render the new composition.

11 Choose Image > Crop. A cropping box appears on the image; drag the handles to crop the file to the new square format, trimming away the transparent area. The edges of the cropping box snap to the edges of the image to make the operation very easy. Click the green Commit button or press Enter / Return.

12 Choose File > Save As. Name the image **07_03_Recomposed**, to be saved to your My CIB Work folder and included in the Organizer, but not as part of a Version Set. Change the file format to JPEG. Click Save; then click OK to accept the JPEG quality settings. The recomposed image is saved as a copy. Choose Edit > Revert to restore the original photo, keeping it open for the next exercise.

The Recompose tool is as easy to use as it is powerful—with creative possibilities that are virtually limitless. Play with as many pictures as you can; you'll learn how content-aware scaling works and what to expect from different types of image as you have fun finding creative new ways to make the most of your photos.

Moving objects to enhance a composition

From Photoshop Elements 12, the Content-Aware Move tool lets you reposition an object within the frame, and then uses content-aware photo magic to cover your tracks, blending the object with its new surroundings and patching the hole it left.

The Content-Aware Move tool is perfect for dealing with objects that are too close to the edge of a photo or separated from the main action, enabling you to improve an unbalanced composition and turn a bystander into a star. In the first part of this exercise, you'll use the Content-Aware Move tool on the image from the previous project—this time, reuniting the sisters without altering the photo's proportions.

1. With the image 07_03.jpg still open in Expert mode in the Editor, double-click the Hand tool, if needed, to see the whole photo as large as possible; then, select the Content-Aware Move tool (✖), beside the Straighten tool in the Toolbar.

2. Open the Tool Options pane and make sure that the tool is set to Move mode, rather than Extend, and the Healing slider is set to the central stop. Draw loosely around the girl at the left. Include some of her surroundings in your selection, but draw the line closer at the right of the girl's form.

3. Click and hold inside the selection; then, hold down the shift key as you drag the girl close to her sisters. The Shift key will constrain the movement horizontally, maintaining the girl's distance from the viewpoint. Release the mouse button, and then release the Shift key; Photoshop Elements blends the girl into her new position and fills the hole she left with detail that matches the surroundings. Click outside the selected area to deselect it.

4. Draw around the reunited group. Include a reasonable amount of the surrounding detail, except at the right where your line should follow the older girl's form quite closely. Click and hold inside the selection; then, hold the Shift key as you drag the sisters to the left to center them horizontally in the frame. Release the mouse button before the Shift key; then deselect the repositioned group.

▶ **Tip:** If the area from which the girls were moved is filled without any flowers at all, undo and vary the shape and size of your selection.

5. Choose File > Save As. Name the new image **07_03_Move-1**, to be saved to your My CIB Work folder with all the usual settings. Activate the option Save > As A Copy; then, click Save. Click OK to accept the JPEG quality settings, and then choose Edit > Revert to restore the original photo, keeping it open for the next part of the exercise.

6 Draw around the girl at the left of the photo with the Content-Aware Move tool, just as you did in step 2, except that this time you can include the same amount of the surrounding area all of the way around her form.

7 Drag the selection on a downwards diagonal to the right. Position the girl about half as far from her sisters and the bottom edge of the photo as her original position.

8 Choose Image > Resize > Scale. Hold down the Alt / Option key as you drag a corner handle to scale the selection up from its center. Watch the width and height values in the Tool Options pane and stop when they are close to 200%. Click the green check-mark to commit the transformation. Click and hold inside the selection; then, hold the shift key as you drag to center the girl below her three sisters. Click outside the selected area to deselect it.

9 Choose Image > Crop. Drag the cropping rectangle into the lower right corner of the photo, where it will snap to the edges. Drag the handle at the upper left corner of the cropping rectangle to produce a balanced, portrait-format crop of the same height as the original image; then, commit the operation.

10 Choose File > Save As. Name the new image **07_03_Move-2**, to be saved with all the usual settings. There is no need to save the image as a copy. Click Save; then, click OK to accept the JPEG settings and choose File > Close.

Experiment on your own photos with the Content-Aware Move tool to get a feel for its capabilities. Switch from Move to Extend mode to copy your selection, rather than merely move it. Tweak the Healing slider to improve a blend that is too obvious or produces artifacts; move the slider to the right to prioritize the selected content in the blend, or to the left to introduce more detail from the surroundings.

Removing wrinkles and spots

Retouching skin to improve a portrait photograph can be a real art, but fortunately Photoshop Elements provides several tools that make it easy to smooth out lines and wrinkles, remove blemishes, and blend skin tones—even for a novice.

1   If you're still in the Editor, click the Organizer button (![icon]) in the Task Bar. If necessary, click the arrow beside the Lesson 07 tag in the Tags panel to isolate the images for this lesson; then, right-click / Control-click the image 07_04.jpg and choose Edit With Photoshop Elements Editor.

2   Make sure that the Editor is in Expert mode. If you don't see tabs for the Layers, Effects, Graphics and Favorites panels at the top of the Panel Bin, click the arrow beside the More button (![icon]) in the Task bar and choose Custom Workspace; then choose Window > Reset Panels. Drag the Layers panel out of the Panel Bin; then, hide the Panel Bin by un-checking its name in the Window menu. Hide the Photo Bin or Tool Options pane; then, choose View > Fit On Screen.

3   Drag the Background layer to the New Layer button (![icon]) at the top of the Layers panel to create a duplicate layer; then, repeat the process to create a third layer. If necessary, resize the Layers panel by dragging its lower edge so that you can see your three layers. Use the Zoom tool (![icon]) to zoom in on the upper half of the photo, as you'll be retouching the skin around the woman's eyes first.

This photo is quite a challenging candidate for retouching; the harsh flash lighting has caused strong reflections on the skin that only serve to accentuate the wrinkles.

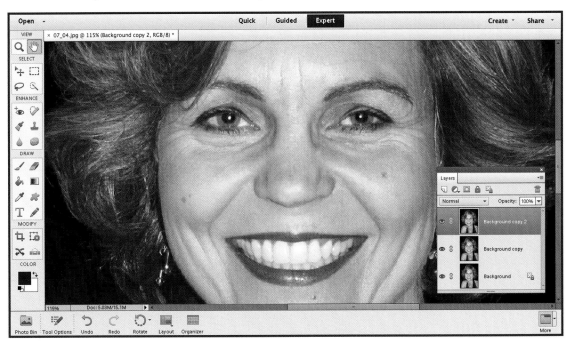

Fixing blemishes

There are three main tools in Photoshop Elements for fixing flaws in your photos:

The Spot Healing Brush tool

The Spot Healing Brush is the easiest way to remove wrinkles in skin and other small imperfections in your photos. Either click once on a blemish or click and drag to smooth it away. By blending the information of the surrounding area into the problem spot, imperfections are made indistinguishable.

The Healing Brush tool

The Healing Brush can fix larger imperfections with ease. You can define one part of your photo as a source to be sampled and blended into another area. The Healing Brush is so flexible you can even remove large objects from a detailed background—such as a snack packet from a lawn.

The Clone Stamp tool

Rather than blending the source and target areas, the Clone Stamp tool paints directly with a sample of an image. You can use the Clone Stamp tool to remove or duplicate objects in your photo. This tool is great for getting rid of garbage, power lines, or a signpost that may be spoiling a view.

Using the Healing Brush tool

You'll begin by using the Healing Brush to smooth the texture of the subject's skin.

1 Click to select the Healing Brush tool () or its variant, the Spot Healing Brush tool (—)—whichever is currently visible beside the Red Eye Removal tool in the toolbar—then, open the tool options pane at the bottom of the workspace.

2 Make sure that the tool is in Healing Brush mode, and then set the brush size to **20** px. The Source option should be set to Sampled and the Mode to Normal. Make sure that the Aligned and Sample All Layers options are both disabled.

3 Make sure that the top layer, Background copy 2, is still active (selected). First, you need to define the area in the image that will be sampled as a reference texture for the Healing Brush operation; Alt-click / Option-click a smooth area on the left cheek. If you were to switch to another tool and then back to the Healing Brush, you would need to repeat this step.

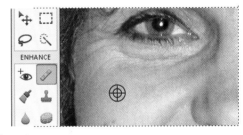

4 Draw a short horizontal stroke under the left eye. As you drag, it may appear that the brush is creating a strange effect, but when you release the mouse button, the color will be blended and natural skin tones will fill the area.

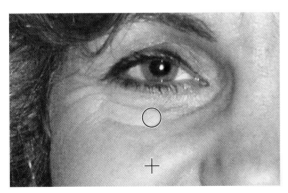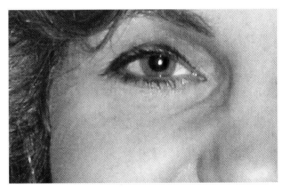

5 Continue to smooth the skin on the face with the Healing Brush. Avoid areas very close to the eyes, shadowed areas, and the hair-line. You can also reduce the worst of the shine caused by the harsh flash. As you work, re-establish the reference area occasionally by Alt-clicking / Option-clicking in new areas of the face to sample appropriate skin tone and texture. Press the left and right bracket keys ([,]) to decrease or increase the brush size as you work. Be sure to remove the moles on the woman's right cheek and the spots on her left cheek and just below the lower lip. You can use the same techniques on the neck.

▶ **Tip:** Use short brush strokes. Try just clicking rather than dragging, taking care to overlap your clicks to avoid a spotty effect. If you see results you don't like, check that the Aligned option is disabled in the tool options pane.

Long strokes may produce unacceptable results—especially near shaded areas where the darker tones may spread. If that happens, choose Edit > Undo Healing Brush. Try setting the brush to a smaller size or reversing the direction of your strokes. If the problem is related to the shadowed areas beside the nose or at the sides of the face, try stroking towards the shadows rather than away from them, or temporarily changing the mode for the Healing Brush tool from Normal to Lighten in the tool options pane.

6   Choose Window > History. In the History Panel, every action you perform is recorded in chronological order, from the earliest at the top to the most recent at the bottom of the list. You can use the History panel to quickly undo a series of steps or to assess the success of your edits. To restore the file to an earlier state, simply select an earlier (higher) action in the History list.

Until you make further changes to the file, you can still return the image to a more recent state by selecting a step lower in the list. Once you've used the History panel to restore a photo to an earlier state, any change you make to the image will replace all the actions in the more recent history.

Refining the Healing Brush results

The Healing Brush tool copies *texture* from the source area, not color. It samples the colors in the target area—the area that you're brushing—and arranges those colors according to the texture sampled from the reference area. Consequently, the Healing Brush tool appears to be smoothing the skin. So far however, the results are not convincingly realistic.

In this exercise, you'll make your retouching work look a little more natural by altering the opacity of the layer you've been working on, and then use another of the texture tools to refine the resulting blend.

1   Click the Navigator tab, beside the History tab in the floating panel group. In the Navigator panel, use the zoom slider and drag the red frame in the preview to focus the view in the image window on the area around the woman's eyes and mouth.

Extensive retouching can leave skin looking artificially smooth, looking a little like molded plastic. Reducing the opacity of the retouched layer will give the skin a more realistic look by allowing some of the wrinkles on the un-edited Background layer to show through.

2   In the Layers panel, change the Opacity of the layer "Background copy 2" to about 50%, using your own judgment to set the exact percentage.

We opted for quite a low setting, intending a fairly natural look for this photo of a friend, but the opacity value you set will depend on the extent of your retouching and the purpose for which the edited image is intended.

The opacity change restores some realism, but three noticeable blemishes have also made a reappearance—one on each cheek and one just below the lower lip.

3   In the Layers panel, select the layer "Background copy" to make it active.

4   Set the brush size for the Healing Brush tool to **20** px and click once or twice on each blemish. Gone!

5   In the toolbar, select the Blur tool ( ). In the tool options pane, set the brush size to approximately **13** px and set the Blur tool's Strength to **50**%.

6   With the layer "Background copy" still active, drag the Blur tool over some of the deeper lines around the eyes and brow. Use the Navigator panel to change the zoom level and shift the focus as needed. Reduce the Blur tool brush diameter to **7** px and smooth the lips a little, avoiding the edges.

▶ **Tip:** To remove spots and small blemishes in your photo, try the Spot Healing Brush in Proximity Match mode as an alternative to the Healing Brush. With the Spot Healing Brush, you can either click or drag to smooth away imperfections without needing to set a reference point.

Compare your results to those below—the original, the version retouched with the Healing Brush, and final refined version. Toggle the visibility of your retouched layers to compare the original image in your Background layer with the edited results.

Original

Healing Brush 100% Opacity

Healing Brush 50% Opacity over Blur tool

7   Choose File > Save As. Make sure that the new file will be included in the Organizer, but not in a Version Set. Name the edited image **07_04_Retouch**, to be saved to your My CIB Work folder in Photoshop (PSD) format.

8   Make sure that the Layers option is activated, and then click Save.

9   Choose File > Close.

In this exercise, you've learned how to set an appropriate source reference for the Healing Brush tool, and then sample the texture of the source area to repair flaws in another part of the photograph. You also used the Blur tool to smooth textures, and an opacity change to achieve a more realistic look. You've also gained a little experience in working with both the History and Navigator panels.

▶ **Tip:** For a quick and easy solution to portrait retouching, try the Perfect Portrait procedure listed under Touchups in the Guided edit mode, where you'll be stepped through smoothing skin, removing spots, fixing red eye, increasing definition in facial features, whitening teeth, and even slimming your subject!

Removing unwanted objects from images

The impact of a photo can easily be spoiled by an unwanted object in the frame. In the modern world, it's often difficult to photograph even a remote landscape without capturing a fence, power lines, satellite dishes, or litter—mundane clutter that can reduce the drama of an otherwise perfect shot.

Photoshop Elements offers several tools to help you improve an image by getting rid of extraneous detail. As you've seen, the Recompose tool lets you remove areas as you scale a photo. In this set of exercises you'll use the Spot Healing Brush tool to remove an object *without* altering the overall composition.

1 If you're still in the Editor, switch to the Organizer by clicking the Organizer button (⊞) in the Task Bar at the bottom of the workspace. If necessary, click the arrow beside the Lesson 07 tag in the Tags panel, to isolate the Lesson 7 images in the Media Browser. Right-click / Control-click the photo 07_05.jpg and choose Edit With Photoshop Elements Editor.

2 Make sure the Editor is in Expert mode; then, choose Window > Reset Panels. Press Shift+Tab on your keyboard to hide everything but the image window and the toolbar; then, select the Healing Brush tool (🖊) or its variant, the Spot Healing Brush tool (🖊)—whichever is currently visible in the toolbar—then, click the Tool Options button (🖊) in the Task bar open the tool options pane.

Using the Content-Aware healing feature

In the last project, you may have used the Spot Healing Brush in Proximity Match mode to help smooth skin blemishes in a portrait photo. In this exercise you'll set the Spot Healing Brush to Content-Aware mode.

In Content-Aware mode, the Spot Healing Brush tool compares nearby image content to fill the area under the pointer, seamlessly matching details such as shadows, object edges, and even man-made patterns like brick-work or wooden decking shot in perspective, as shown in the illustration at the left.

1 In the tool options pane, check the header and buttons at the left to make sure the Spot Healing Brush tool (🖊) is the active variant, and see that the tool is set to Content-Aware mode. Set the brush size to **100** pixels.

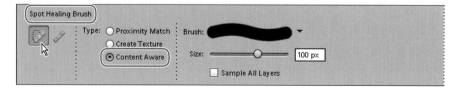

2   Press the Z key to switch to the Zoom tool, and then drag a zoom marquee to zoom in on the signpost and a little of the sky above it. Press the J key to reactivate the Spot Healing Brush. Center the circular cursor over the top of the signpost and drag downwards, stopping just before you reach the yellow sign.

3   Press the right bracket key ( ]) six times to increase the brush size to 300 pixels. Center the cursor over the yellow sign (the horizon should bisect the circle) and click once; then, center the cursor over the smaller sign and click again.

4   Press the left bracket key ([ ) ten times to reduce the brush size to 60 pixels; then, make a short downward stroke to remove the remnants of the signpost, stopping just before you reach the top of the litter bin.

5   Use the Zoom and Hand tools to focus on the area previously occupied by the late signpost. If you see any noticeable artifacts, such as blurring or misaligned texture, press the J key to reactivate the Spot Healing Brush and click or make very short strokes to remove them. If a stroke fails, or makes things worse, undo and try again, resizing the brush and varying the stroke direction as needed.

▷ **Tip:** Try to limit yourself to as few of these repairs as possible; two or three should suffice. The more you interfere, the more likely you are to introduce problems.

6   In the Tool Options pane, set the brush size to **100** pixels. Focus your view on the shadow of the litter bin. Starting at the right, make a series of overlapping clicks, keeping the brush on the grass. Don't be concerned about a little repeated detail, but undo and try again if you introduce any of the rocky foreshore.

● **Note:** It may take more than the six spot healing clicks illustrated here to clear the litter bin's shadow smoothly; we used ten overlapping clicks to achieve a satisfactory result.

7 If your overlapping spots have produced noticeable blurs or obvious repetition of detail, reduce the brush size to around 50 pixels and remove them; very short strokes should do the trick, if single clicks are not enough. You can remove the scraps of white litter at the roadside while you're at it, if you don't mind.

8 In the Tool Options pane, set the brush size to **350** pixels. Drag down over the litter bin, starting below the crest of the wave behind it and ending your stroke before you reach the gold band near the base as shown at the left, below.

9 Make a short horizontal stroke with a 250-pixel brush to remove the base of the bin; then break up any misplaced detail using a few clicks with a smaller brush.

As you've just discovered, the Spot Healing Brush in content-aware mode enables you to remove even a very prominent, irregularly-shaped, shadowed object from a complex background quickly and easily, without the need to make fussy selections.

10 When you're done, choose View > Fit On Screen. Choose File > Save As. Name the new file **07_05_DumpingOK**, to be saved to your My CIB Work folder in JPEG format, and included in the Organizer, but not in a Version Set. Click Save. Click OK to accept the JPEG Options settings; then, close the file.

Creative fun with Guided Edit

The Guided Edit panel offers far more than just correction, adjustment, and retouching tasks. In the Photo Effects and Photo Play categories you'll find guided procedures that let you experiment with a range of striking and unusual creative treatments for your photos, presented with step-by-step instructions.

1   In the Media Browser, isolate the Lesson 7 images, if necessary, and select the image 07_06.jpg, a photograph of two girls riding unicycles. Click the Editor button () in the Task bar.

2   In the Editor, switch to Guided edit mode by clicking Guided in the mode picker at the top of the workspace. Hide the Photo Bin, if it's open below the edit window; then choose View > Fit On Screen. In the Guided Edits panel at the right, click Out Of Bounds—the first guided project in the Photo Play category.

3   Follow the instructions in the Guided Edit panel. Start by clicking Add A Frame, and then let Guided Edit step you through the process of setting up the frame as you see in the illustration below. When you're happy with the frame, click the green Commit button (✓) at the lower right corner.

Tip: Remember these pointers when you're using the Quick Selection tool during this guided edit:
• Use Ctrl / Command+[to decrease the brush size, Ctrl / Command+] to increase it.
• Hold down the Alt / Option key to subtract from the selection.
• Difficult selections can be made much easier by making use of the Auto-Enhance and Refine Edge options in the tool options pane below the Edit window.

4   Continue with the guided steps until you can replicate something similar to what you see in the illustration below; then, click Done. Don't be discouraged if you need a few attempts—with a little practice you'll get great results.

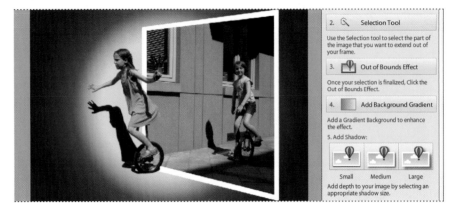

5   Choose File > Save As. Activate the Include In The Elements Organizer option and disable Save In Version Set With Original. Name the file appropriately, and then save it to your My CIB Work folder. Close the file.

Accelerating an action shot

Photoshop Elements 12 introduces several new step-by-step photo treatments across all three of the Guided Edit categories. In this exercise we'll look at the Zoom Burst effect from the Photo Effects category.

Traditionally produced by manually zooming in on a subject while the shutter is open, the Zoom Burst effect creates an impression of speedy motion, while the limited area of focus draws attention to the central object in the photograph. This photographic technique requires a very practiced hand—and even then, the results can be hit-and-miss.

Now you can easily replicate the effect digitally with just a few clicks in the new Zoom Burst Effect Guided Edit, where you can make even a playground swing look like an extreme sport.

1   In the Organizer, select the image 07_07.jpg; then, click the Editor button (⬜). If you're not in Guided edit mode from the last exercise, switch modes now.

2   In the Guided Edits panel at the right, click Zoom Burst Effect—the last guided project in the Photo Effects category.

The Zoom Burst Effect treatment consists of four steps: cropping the photo to center the subject, applying the zoom burst, defining an area of focus where the radial blur is reduced, and adding a vignette to intensify the effect. For the best results with this photo treatment, the subject of interest should be at the center of the image. Our lesson photo, however, is already very tightly framed; little can be done with the crop tool to center the girl, so we'll skip the first step.

Despite the girl's animated expression, this action photograph looks surprisingly static; let's see if we can add a sense of *speed*.

3   In the panel at the right, click the Add Zoom Burst button. You can click the button multiple times to increase the effect, but for our lesson image, where the background is already very unfocused, once will be enough.

4   Click the Add Focus Area button; then, drag a line in the image window from the tip of the girl's nose to her shoulder. Repeat the process to clear even more of the blur from the girl's face and hair.

5   Drag one more short line, starting at the gray strap that crosses the girl's right arm and extending through her hand, all the way to the edge of the photo. The objective is to add *some* focus to the hand, without entirely removing the motion blur. If you're unhappy with your first attempt, simply undo the last stroke and try again.

6   Click the Apply Vignette button; then, click Done at the bottom of the panel.

7   Choose File > Save As. Name the file **07_07_Zoom**, and save it to your My CIB Work folder in Photoshop (PSD) format, with the Layers option enabled. Included the new image in the Organizer but not in a Version Set. Close the file.

Making a picture into a puzzle

The latest addition to the Photo Play category, the Puzzle Effect Guided Edit lets you turn a photo into a jigsaw puzzle; you can even move the pieces around to make it look as though the puzzle has not yet been completed.

1   In the Organizer, select the image 07_08.jpg; then, click the Editor button (). If you're not in Guided edit mode from the last exercise, switch modes now.

2   In the Guided Edits panel, click Puzzle Effect in the Photo Play category.

3   At the top of the Puzzle Effect pane, click the Large puzzle piece button.

4   Click the Select Puzzle Piece button and click inside a piece you'd like to move; then, click the Extract Piece button. Your selected piece is extracted from the image and the Move tool becomes active.

5   Drag the extracted piece to a new position. Move the cursor just outside any of the handles on the bounding box surrounding the repositioned piece and drag to rotate it. Click the green check mark to confirm the transformation.

6   Repeat the process with as many puzzle pieces as you wish to create a pleasing arrangement. You can't delete a piece, but you can drag it off the image, behind the gray artboard, which serves the same purpose. If you remove adjacent pieces, you'll need to use the Eraser tool to remove the outlines that remain. Use the square bracket keys on your keyboard to change the size of the eraser.

7   When you're happy with the arrangement, click Done. Choose File > Save As. Name the file **07_08_Jigsaw**, and save it to your My CIB Work folder in Photoshop (PSD) format, with the Layers option enabled. Include the new image in the Organizer but not in a Version Set; then, close the file.

> **Tip:** To produce this effect, with puzzle pieces scattered outside the borders of the photo, open your saved file in the Expert mode, increase the canvas size, and then experiment with the separate layers. Have fun!

Creating effects with filters

The guided edits in the Photo Effects and Photo Play category give an image a completely new look by applying several adjustments and filters in combination. You can have a lot of fun devising your own special effects and sophisticated photo treatments in the Filter Gallery, where you can combine multiple filters and tweak the way that they work together to create unique new custom effects.

You can use the Filter Gallery to reinterpret an image and present it in an entirely new light. This can be a great way to redeem a technically inferior photo, enabling you to turn even a flawed or uninteresting image into a work of art. The possibilities are limitless!

Before exploring the Filter Gallery, you can set up a work file with some extra layers for working copies of the image.

1 In the Organizer, isolate the images for this lesson, if necessary, by clicking either the Lesson 7 folder in the left panel's My Folders list or the arrow beside the Lesson 07 keyword in the Tags panel. Right-click / Control-click the image 07_09.jpg in the Media Browser and choose Edit With Photoshop Elements Editor from the context menu. Make sure that the Editor is in Expert mode, and then choose Window > Reset Panels.

2 Many filters make use of the foreground and background colors set in the toolbar to create effects, so you can start by resetting them to the default black and white. Click the Default Foreground And Background Colors button beside the overlapping swatches at the bottom of the toolbox; then, click the arrows to switch the foreground and background colors.

3 Drag the Background layer to the New Layer button (⬜) at the left of the Layers panel's header to create a second layer. Drag the Background copy layer to the New Layer button to create a third layer. Click the eye icon (👁) beside the top layer, Background copy 2, to hide it from view in the image window. Click the middle layer, Background copy, to make it active for editing.

4 If you don't see the Quick Selection tool (🖊) at the right of the Lasso tool in the toolbar's Select category, Alt-click / Option click whichever tool is currently active to cycle through the variants until the Quick Selection tool is foremost.

5 With the Quick Selection tool, select the girl's lips, and also the wreath of flowers and leaves on her head. Use the left and right square bracket keys ([,]) to decrease or increase the brush size as you work. Hold down the Alt / Option key as you paint to subtract from your selection.

6 When the selection is complete, choose Select > Refine Edge or click the Refine Edge button in the Tool Options bar. In the Refine Edge dialog box, set both the Smooth and Contrast values to **0**, the Feather amount to **1** px, and the Shift Edge value to **1**%. These settings will soften the edges of the selection, without reducing its effective area. Click OK.

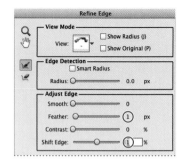

7 Choose Select > Save Selection. Name the new selection **color details**. Under Operation, activate New Selection; then, click OK. Choose Select > Deselect.

8 Choose File > Save As. Name the file **07_09_Work**, to be saved to your My CIB Work folder in Photoshop format, with layers intact. Make sure the image will be included in the Organizer, but not as part of a Version Set; then, click Save.

Using the Filter Gallery

Tip: The most reliable way to assess the effects of the filters as you work is to set the zoom level to 100%.

1 Choose Filter > Filter Gallery. If necessary, use the menu at the lower left of the Filter Gallery window to set the magnification to 100%. If you can't see the whole photo, drag in the preview pane so that most of the girl's face is visible.

2 If you don't see the center pane with its list of filter categories, click the blue button beside the OK button at the upper right.

3 If you see more than one filter listed in the right pane, select the top filter and click the Trash icon to delete it. In the center pane, expand the Artistic category and choose the Watercolor filter. Experiment with the full range of the sliders. Set the Brush Detail to **5**, the Shadow Intensity to **3**, and the Texture to **2**.

Tip: If you try a filter and see little effect, your image may be too big; although many of the filters include a brush size control, or a slider affecting the magnitude at which the filter is applied, if your file has too high a resolution the effect may not be discernible even at the maximum setting. Use the File > Image Size command to create a smaller copy of your file; then, try the filter again.

4 Click the New Effect layer button (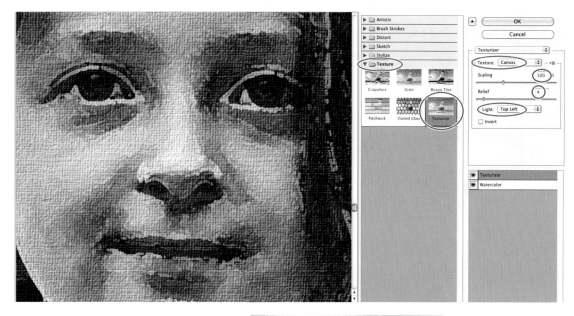) below the right pane in the Filter Gallery dialog box. Collapse the Artistic category; then, expand the Texture category and choose the Texturizer filter. The Watercolor and Texturizer filters are applied simultaneously. Choose Canvas from the Texture menu; then, set the Scaling value to **100%** and the Relief to **4**. From the Light menu, choose Top Left.

▶ **Tip:** In the Filter Gallery, you can combine as many filters as you wish, building up your own complex custom effects.

5 Click OK. The combined Watercolor and Texturizer filters are applied to the layer Background copy. From the Enhance menu, choose Adjust Color > Remove Color; then, choose Adjust Lighting > Brightness/Contrast. Set the values for both Brightness and Contrast to **50**, and then click OK.

Layering filters and effects

Although the Filter gallery offers endless possibilities for combining filters at varied settings, you can achieve even more and sophisticated results by using the Filter Gallery in tandem with the Layers panel—applying different combinations of filters to multiple duplicate layers of the same image, and then blending the layers using partial transparency, blending modes, or masks.

1 Click the eye icon beside the layer Background copy 2 to make it visible again; then, click the layer thumbnail to make the layer active. Choose Filter > Filter Gallery. Be careful to choose the second listing for the Filter Gallery—the first listing simply applies the previous settings without opening the Filter Gallery.

▶ **Tip:** If you've set up an effect that looks great in the background, but makes the faces of your subjects unrecognizable, use layer masks to separate the subjects from the background, and then apply the same set of filters to each part of the image at different settings.

Note: The stacking order of filters in the list in the Filter Gallery will alter the way they interact, though this may be more noticeable with some filters than others. You can change the order of the filters by simply dragging them in the list.

2 The Filter Gallery window opens with your previous filters, and all their settings, exactly as you left them. Click the New Effect Layer button again. Expand the Distort category and choose the Diffuse Glow filter. Set the Graininess value to **10**, and both the Glow Amount and Clear Amount to **15**. Click OK.

3 In the Layers panel, select the layer Background copy. At the top of the panel, decrease the layer's opacity to **70**%. Select the top layer, Background copy 2. Choose Overlay from the Blending Mode menu and then set the opacity to **30**%.

4 Right-click / Control-click the layer Background copy 2 and choose Duplicate Layer from the context menu. In the Duplicate Layer dialog box, type **Color Details** as the name for the new layer, and then click OK. Change the new layer's blending mode to Multiply, and its opacity to **70**%.

5 Choose Select > Load Selection. In the Load Selection dialog box, choose your saved selection, color details, from the Selection menu under Source. Make sure the New Selection option is activated under Operation, and then click OK. With the top layer selected in the Layers panel, click the Add Layer Mask button ( ) at the top of the panel. The selection is converted to a layer mask.

In the Layers panel, a layer mask icon is added to the top layer, color details, which is now masked so that only the girl's lips and the flowers on her head remain visible.

6 Toggle the visibility of each layer in turn, watching the effect in the Edit window. Choose File > Save, and then close the file.

Review questions

1   By default, dragging in a tilted image with the Straighten tool produces a horizontal reference in relation to which the your photo will be rotated. What do you do if you can't find any horizontal element in the image to provide a true level?

2   What is the purpose of the grid overlays offered in the Overlay menu in the tool options pane when you select the Crop tool?

3   How do you use the different brushes and erasers that appear in the tool options pane when you select the Recompose tool?

4   How can you quickly undo a whole series of edit steps at once?

5   What are the similarities and differences between the Healing Brush tool and the Spot Healing Brush tool for retouching photos?

Review answers

1   To designate a vertical element in your tilted photo as reference, you need to hold down the Ctrl / Command key while you drag in the photo with the Straighten tool.

2   The Crop tool's grid overlays can guide you in framing a balanced composition. The Rule Of Thirds overlay divides the image horizontally and vertically into three equal parts; according to this rule, objects look more balanced when aligned with the lines and intersections of the grid. The Golden Ratio overlay works within a rectangle of set proportions, within which the intersection of two diagonals defines a focus. The Grid overlay provides a simple grid to help you with basic alignment.

3   Use the Mark For Protection brush to define areas in the image that you wish to protect from a scaling operation. Use the Mark For Removal brush to define any areas that you want removed from the image; the Recompose tool will cut those areas before compressing others. Each of the Recompose brushes has its associated eraser.

4   The History panel lists every action performed in chronological order. To restore the file to an earlier state, select an action higher in the list. Until you make further changes, you can restore the image to a later state by selecting a step lower in the list.

5   Both healing tools blend pixels from one part of an image into another. Although the Spot Healing Brush tool enables you to remove blemishes quicker than is possible with the Healing Brush, the Healing Brush can be customized, and enables you to specify the source reference area, giving you more control.

8 COMBINING IMAGES

Lesson overview

Although you can do a lot to improve a photo with tonal adjustments, color corrections and retouching, sometimes the best way to produce the perfect image is simply to fake it! Photoshop Elements delivers powerful tools that enable you to do just that by combining images. Merge ordinary scenic photos into a stunning panoramas that truly recaptures the feel of the location—or combine a series of shots to produce the perfect group photo, where everybody is smiling and there are no closed eyes. Deal with difficult lighting conditions by blending differently exposed pictures.

In this lesson you'll learn some of the tricks you'll need for combining images to put together the perfect shot that you didn't actually get:

- Merging a series of photos into a panorama
- Assembling the perfect group shot
- Removing unwanted elements
- Blending differently exposed photographs
- Combining images using layers
- Resizing, repositioning, and defringing selections
- Creating a gradient clipping mask

 You'll probably need between one and two hours to complete this lesson. If you haven't already done so, download the Lesson 8 work files from the Lesson & Update Files tab of your Account page at www.peachpit.com.

If you're ready to go beyond fixing pictures in conventional ways, this lesson is for you. Why settle for that scenic photo that just doesn't capture the way it really looked? Or that group portrait where Dad's looking away and Mom's eyes are closed? Combine images to produce the perfect shot. Merge photos to make a stunning panorama, remove obstructions from the view, and even get little Jimmy to stop making faces.

Getting started

● **Note:** Before you start this lesson, make sure that you've set up a folder for your lesson files and downloaded the Lesson 8 folder from your Account page at www.peachpit.com, as detailed in "Accessing the Classroom in a Book files" in the chapter "Getting Started" at the beginning of this book. You should also have created a new work catalog (see "Creating a catalog for working with this book" in Lesson 1).

You'll begin by importing the sample images for this lesson to your CIB Catalog.

1   Start Photoshop Elements and click Organize in the Welcome Screen. In the Organizer, check the lower right corner of the workspace to make sure that your CIB Catalog is loaded—if not, choose File > Manage Catalogs and load it.

2   Click the Import button at the upper left of the Organizer workspace and choose From Files And Folders from the drop-down menu. In the Get Photos And Videos From Files And Folders dialog box, locate and select the Lesson 8 folder. Disable the automatic processing options; then, click Get Media.

3   In the Import Attached Keyword Tags dialog box, click Select All; then, click OK.

Combining images automatically

The Photomerge tools offer a variety of ways to combine photos. These tools not only deliver effective solutions to some tricky photographic problems, but are also great fun to use creatively, enabling you to produce striking and unusual images.

In this lesson, you'll use the Photomerge Exposure tool to combine exposures made in difficult lighting conditions into a composite image that would have been virtually impossible to capture in a single shot. You'll compose a group photo from two single-subject images with the Photomerge Group Shot tool, combine photos from a busy scene to produce an unobstructed view using the Photomerge Scene Cleaner, and blend a series of scenic photographs into a dramatic panorama.

Merging photos into a panorama

A common problem for many of us when taking photos at a scenic location is that standard lenses do not have a wide enough angle to capture the entire scene. The Photomerge Panorama tool provides the solution: you can capture a series of overlapping shots, and then merge them to create a panorama. In the following pages you'll learn how to have Photoshop Elements do most of the work for you.

You could start the Photomerge Panorama process from the Organizer, but for this exercise, you'll open the lesson photos in the Editor and set up the workspace.

1   In the Organizer, Ctrl-click / Command-click to select the images 08_01a.jpg through 08_01d.jpg in the Media Browser; then, right-click / Control-click any of the selected thumbnails and choose Edit With Photoshop Elements Editor.

2   If necessary, switch the Editor to Expert mode by clicking Expert in the mode picker at the top of the workspace. If you see only the Layers panel in the Panel Bin at the right, rather than the grouped Layers, Effects, Graphics, and Favorites panels, click the arrow beside the More button (▣) at the right of the Task bar and choose Custom Workspace from the menu.

3   Drag the Layers panel out of the Panel Bin by its name tab, and then hide the Panel Bin by un-checking its name in the Window menu. Drag the lower edge of the Layers panel to make it deep enough to show four layers; then, position the panel at the lower right of the workspace. If you don't see the Photo Bin, click the Photo Bin button (▣) at the left of the Task bar.

4   Choose Enhance > Photomerge > Photomerge Panorama.

Tip: If you don't see file names displayed below the thumbnails in the Media Browser, make sure that the Details and File Names options are activated in the View menu.

Setting up Photomerge Panorama options

The Photomerge dialog box offers a choice of layout methods that will affect the way the source images will be stitched together to create your panorama.

1   In the Photomerge dialog box, choose Cylindrical from the layout options at the left. Under Source Files, select Files from the Use menu. Click Add Open Files.

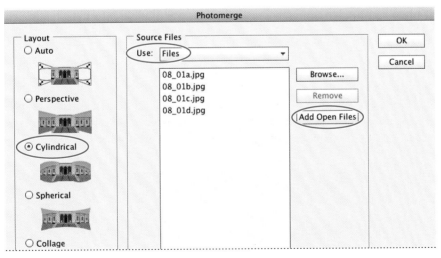

Tip: You can click Browse to find more images to add to the source files selection. To remove a photo from the source list, select the file, and then click Remove. To include all the photos in a specific folder on your hard disk in a panorama, select Folder from the Use menu rather than Files, and then click Browse to locate the source folder.

Not all of the panorama Layout options—methods for matching, aligning, and blending your source images—will work for every series of photos. Experiment with your own photos to get a feel for the differences between the layout options and which will work best for a given set of source images.

2   In the Photomerge dialog box, make sure that the Blend Images Together option is activated below the source files list, and then click OK.

3   Watch the Layers panel while Photoshop Elements creates a new file for the panorama, and then places each source image on its own layer. Photomerge calculates the overlaps, adds a blending mask to each image layer accordingly, and then color-matches adjacent images as it blends the seams. When the Clean Edges dialog box appears, drag it aside so that you can see the edges of all the source images, and the checker-board transparency around them.

For this combination of photos, cropping away the transparent areas would not remove any really significant detail; however, substantial slices of the image would be lost, making the composition somewhat cramped. Photoshop Elements can help you solve this problem, by using content-aware healing to fill in the missing areas.

4   In the Clean Edges dialog box, click Yes.

The content-aware fill usually does a great job with non-specific or organic content, such as foliage, clouds, or water—and even with regular patterns like brickwork, but cannot deal with too much man-made detail. Let's check over the results.

5   Press Ctrl+Z / Command+Z. This will not undo the healing operation, only the last step in the process—the de-selection of the area that was filled. Use the Zoom and Hand tools (🔍 , ✋) to examine the extended image; the re-instated selection will help you to look in the right places to spot the anomalies.

The results at the top of the photo are very good, but the content-aware fill has produced artefacts right across the bottom of the merged image. You may see slightly different results to those pictured in the illustration below; the content-aware fill operates with a degree of randomness in selecting areas for sampling in its attempt to reduce repetition of image detail.

 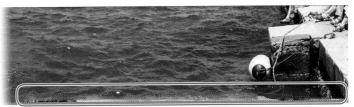

6   (Optional) If you wish to see if Photomerge will produce a better result on its second attempt, repeat the process, clicking past the warning about unsaved images. If you choose, you can retouch the unwelcome blend artifacts before moving on. It would not take a lot of work with the Spot Healing Brush and the Clone Stamp to fix the problems; even the lower left corner is manageable.

7   When you're done, press Ctrl+D / Command+D, or choose Select > Deselect.

Now let's have a closer look at how well Photoshop Elements matched the areas where the source images are overlapped.

8   In the Layers panel, click the eye icon (👁) for Layer 1—the merged panorama, including the content-aware fill—to hide it. Hold down Alt+Shift / Option+Shift and click the black and white layer mask thumbnail for the third layer. In the edit window, the mask associated with the layer appears as a semi-transparent red overlay, enabling you to see which part of the image 08_01b.jpg has contributed to the panorama. The unused portion is hidden by the layer mask.

9 Use the Zoom and Hand tools to focus on the areas where the blend borders pass through the strip of waterfront buildings. Hold Alt+Shift / Option+Shift and click the layer mask thumbnail repeatedly to show and hide the red mask overlay as you inspect the seams.

10 Hide the red mask overlay; then, Alt-click / Option-click the black and white layer mask thumbnail. The layer mask is displayed in opaque black and white. Black represents the masked portions of the layer; white represents the areas that have contributed to the blend.

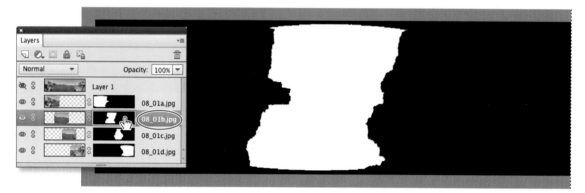

If you wished to edit any portion of the seam between images, you could alternate between the opaque and semi-transparent views of the layer mask and adjust the blend by painting (or erasing) directly onto the mask. If your panorama is extended by content-aware fill, you'll need to erase the corresponding area of the top layer, creating a "window" so that your changes to the lower layers are visible.

11 Use the same technique to inspect the blended seams between the other source layers. When you're done, make Layer 1 visible once more.

12 Choose View > Fit On Screen, and then choose Image > Crop. Drag the handles of the cropping rectangle to make it as large as possible without including the blurred image artefacts at the sides of the photo and along the its lower edge; then, click the Commit button (✓) at the lower right to commit the crop.

The finished composite panorama presents a well-composed, natural-looking view, with no more distortion than is apparent at the outside edges of the source series.

13 Choose File > Save. Name the merged image **08_01_Panorama**, to be saved to your My CIB Work folder in Photoshop format with Layers activated. Saving your file in Photoshop format enables you to preserve the layers, so that you can always return to adjust them if necessary. If you saved in JPEG format the image would be flattened and layer information lost. Make sure that the file will be included in the Organizer. Click Save; then, choose File > Close All.

Not every set of images will perform the same way in a Photomerge panorama. Different sets of source images can produce very different results, even at the same panorama layout option setting. The way a given series of photos will combine to form a panorama depends on many factors, from lighting that varies markedly across the series to issues of perspective, foreshortening, and lens distortion.

Our sample photos feature even lighting and few foreground elements, but a series of images taken close to a building or other large object—like photos shot indoors or in a confined urban space—would present different challenges. Try creating panoramas in a variety of locations; the results can be both striking and surprising.

Creating a composite group shot

Shooting the perfect group photo is a difficult task, especially if you have a large family of squirmy kids. Fortunately, Photoshop Elements offers a solution: a powerful photo blending tool called Photomerge Group Shot.

No longer do you need to put up with family photos where someone has turned away, frowned, or closed their eyes at the wrong moment. Photomerge Group Shot lets you merge the best parts of several images to create the perfect group photo.

A Photomerge Group Shot also makes a great solution to another common group photo problem, letting you put the person behind the camera back in the frame.

1   If you're still in the Editor, click the Organizer button (⊞) in the Task Bar.

2   If necessary, use the Lesson 08 tag in the Tags panel to isolate the images for this lesson, and then Ctrl-click / Command-click to select the images 08_02a.jpg and 08_02b.jpg in the Media Browser.

3   Choose Edit > Photomerge > Photomerge Group Shot.

The Photomerge Group Shot panel opens at the right, with tools and tips for merging photos; the toolbox now offers only the Zoom and Hand tools. By default, Photoshop Elements has designated the first photo in the Photo Bin as the *source* image and placed it in the Source pane on the left. The Photomerge tools will let you extract the figure from the Source image and blend it into the Final image.

▶ **Tip:** If what you see in the Photomerge preview differs from the illustration at the right, click Cancel, close both images without saving, and quit the Editor; then, start again from step 2.

Before you begin merging photos for a composite group shot, you need to consider your choice for the Final image—the "target" image into which the figures from your source images will be blended. You may choose the image with the most balanced composition, a photo with more background detail than the others, or the image with the most room for the additions you're planning.

4　Click the second thumbnail in the Photo Bin to replace the default source photo with the image 08_02b.jpg. Drag the first thumbnail (08_02a.jpg) from the Project Bin into the Final image pane on the right.

For this demonstration, with only two images in the operation, we chose the image 08_02a.jpg as the Final image (the base for the composite) because the exposure and composition are better, with more clearance at the subjects' feet. Also, you'll notice that the other shot has been skewed slightly in the alignment process.

5　In the Photomerge Group Shot panel at the right, select the Pencil tool (✏), if it's not already active; then, make sure that Show Strokes is activated and the Show Regions option is disabled. Click the Hide Panel button (⬛▶) at the right of the Task bar to hide the right panel, and then choose View > Fit On Screen.

6　In the Source image, start at the top of the man's head and draw an uninterrupted line as shown in the illustration below, passing through his face, looping across the torso, and then tracing the outside line of his leg as closely as possible from the knee down, making sure that you stay just inside the edge of his jeans. If you go off track, press Ctrl+Z / Command+Z and start again.

▷ **Tip:** Try to copy the yellow line in the illustration as closely as you can, so that you'll see results very similar to those described in this exercise. In normal circumstances, you can be much more casual with your pencil stroke.

When you release the mouse button, the man is copied into the Final image, along with a patch of the stone stairs that covers parts of the woman's forearm, leg, and shadow. Some of the hair at the right of the man's face has been left behind.

With a practiced stroke, it's actually possible to merge the man to the Final image without the unwelcome extras and missing detail; however, one objective of this exercise is to demonstrate techniques that will help you to combine more complex source images, where it can be challenging to make the perfect selection.

Whenever you have difficulty defining the element you wish to copy from the Source image, it's preferable to make a stroke that picks up extra detail from the background, rather than one that leaves portions of the subject behind. The missing hair will be easy to deal with, but where objects touch or overlap, it's much easier to remove extraneous elements than it is to add missing detail.

7   With the Pencil tool, click once in the Source image to pick up the area of hair that was not merged to the Final image.

8   Press Ctrl / Command, together with the plus sign key (+) to zoom in; then hold the spacebar and drag the Source image to center your view on the man's left leg. Make sure that you have a clear view from the knee to the foot.

9   Press the left bracket key ([ ) twice to reduce the default brush (or pencil) size; then, draw a short stroke just a little outside the line of the knee, as shown in the illustration at the right.

10 Click the Show Panel button ( ) at the right of the Task bar to show the Photomerge Group Shot controls. Select the Eraser tool ( ); then, press the left bracket key ([ ) twice to reduce the brush size. Carefully erase the short line, taking care to keep the Eraser tool cursor clear of the edge of the blue jeans. The original line will protect the edge of the man's jeans while the extraneous detail is removed, revealing the woman's leg and its shadow.

When you're working with an object that's particularly difficult to isolate, try varying your strokes with the Pencil and Eraser tools. Use a combination of long lines, short strokes, and clicks. Both the brush size and the stroke direction can also make a difference to the area that will be affected by either tool.

The Advanced Options button in the Photomerge Grooup Shot panel gives you access to controls that let you edit a blended composite by adjusting the way the images are aligned. You'll look at the Show Regions option in the next exercise.

11 Click the Done button at the bottom of the right panel to commit the merge. The merged image needs to be cropped. Choose Image > Crop, and then drag the handles of the cropping rectangle to trim off the empty areas of the photo. Click the green check mark icon at the lower right to commit the crop.

12 Choose File > Save. Name the merged image **08_02_GroupMerge**, to be saved to your My CIB Work folder in Photoshop (PSD) format with Layers activated, and included in the Organizer. Click Save; then, choose File > Close All.

Like all the Photomerge tools, the Group Shot not only provides useful solutions to a variety of photographic problems, but can also be a lot of fun to use creatively— making it easy to add a touch of humor and fancy to your shots with a little photo magic.

Removing unwelcome intruders

The Photomerge Scene Cleaner enables you combine the unobstructed areas from several photos of the same scene to produce a clear view—without the tourists, traffic, or uninvited extras that can draw attention away from your subject.

When you're sightseeing, it's a great idea to take extra shots of any busy scene so that you can use the Scene Cleaner to put together an uncluttered image later.

It's not necessary to use a tripod; as long as all your photos were shot from roughly the same viewpoint, Photoshop Elements will align the static content in the images automatically. Sequences shot with burst mode are ideal.

You can use up to ten images in a single Scene Cleaner operation; the more source images, the more chance that you'll produce a perfect result. In this exercise, you'll clear a busy scene completely by combining just four photos.

1   Select the images 08_03a.jpg, 08_03b.jpg, 08_03c.jpg, and 08_03d.jpg in the Media Browser; then, choose Edit > Photomerge > Photomerge Scene Cleaner.

2   By default, 08_03a.jpg (framed in blue), is loaded as the Source image. Click the thumbnail framed in yellow (08_03b.jpg) to replace it; then drag the thumbnail with the blue frame to the Final pane. This is the photo you will "clean"—the base image for your composite. In the Photomerge Scene Cleaner panel, make sure that the Show Strokes option is activated.

▷ **Tip:** If what you see on screen differs from the illustration below, click Cancel, close the images, quit the Editor, and return to step 1.

The tools and options in the right panel are very similar to those in the Photomerge Group Shot panel. The principle difference is that in the Scene Cleaner, the Pencil and Eraser tools can be used in both the Source image and the Final image.

3 Compare the photos in the Source and Final panes. Use the Zoom and Hand tools to focus on the lower right quadrant of the image. Note that the Source image (08_03a) has several clear areas where the Final image has obstructions. Select the Pencil tool (✐) in the Photomerge Scene Cleaner panel.

4 In the Final image, draw a line through the man in the white shirt near the top of the steps, as shown at the right. Make sure your stroke covers both the leading hand and the trailing foot, but try not to extend it beyond his form. When you release the mouse button, the man is removed from the Final image—replaced by detail copied from the Source image. Move the pointer off the Final image onto the surrounding gray background; the yellow line remains visible only in the Source image.

5 In the Final image, draw a second line through the man on the tricycle. Clip the arms and gloves, but don't move further forward, or you'll copy the man in red from the Source image. If that happens, or you don't remove as much of the tricycle as is shown at the right below, undo your stroke and try again.

▶ **Tip:** Don't worry about the disembodied head of the broom; you'll remove that with another Source image.

6 If necessary, choose View Fit On Screen to see the entire image. You can see that this Source image has nothing more to contribute to our composite scene; the left of the photo and the area at the top of the steps are as populated as the Final image. In the Photo Bin, click the third photo (the thumbnail with the green border) to make it the new Source image.

The new Source image has a clear area at the lower left that will enable you to remove three (and a half) more figures from the Final image. You can also copy the area in front of church door at the right to clear another, but we won't use this Source photo to remove the people at the left of the facade—any stroke in that area of this image picks up the girl sitting on the wall.

▶ **Tip:** If your view of the new Source image is obscured by the strokes you made earlier, move the pointer outside the edit window.

7 In the Final image, draw a line down through the young man at the far left, extending your stroke to catch the trailing foot as shown below. A mirror of the same stroke should remove the next customer. Draw a short line straight down through the third man; don't go too far at this point, or you'll introduce new problems. Click once to remove the extraneous shadow at the lower left, and once more to clear the figure from in front of the church door at the right.

8 Choose View Fit On Screen to see the entire image. In the Photo Bin, click the thumbnail with the red border to make it the new Source image.

9 Draw in either image to remove the one-and-a-half people from the central foreground, together with the wreckage of the street-sweeper's tricycle. If you intend to draw in the Source image, refer to the illustration below before making your stroke. A short horizontal stroke will get rid of the stragglers loitering at the top of the stairs, and a single click will clear the heavy shadow in the foreground. If you need to edit a stroke, use the Eraser tool (in the right panel.

10 Double-click the Hand tool or choose View > Fit On Screen. To see which part of each image has contributed to the cleared and blended composite, activate the Show Regions option in the Photomerge Scene Cleaner panel.

11 Click the Done button at the bottom of the Photomerge Scene Cleaner panel.

In the process of matching detail to align the four photos, Photoshop Elements has shifted the image so that there are empty and patched areas around the edges.

12 Choose Image > Crop. Drag the handles of the cropping rectangle to trim the incomplete parts of the image; then, click the check mark to commit the crop.

13 Choose File > Save. Name the file **08_03_Depopulated**, to be saved to your My CIB Work folder, in Photoshop (PSD) format. Make sure that the Layers option is activated, and that the file will be included in the Organizer. Click Save, and then close all five files.

Blending differently exposed photos

There are many common situations where we (or our cameras in automatic mode) are forced to choose between properly exposing the foreground or the background.

Interior shots often feature overexposed window views where the scene outside is washed-out or lost completely. Subjects captured in front of a brightly lit scene or backlit by a window are often underexposed, and therefore appear dull and dark.

Capturing outdoor night shots is another problematic situation; we need to use a flash to light our subject in the foreground, but a background such as a neon-lit street scene, a city skyline, or a moonlit vista is usually better exposed without it.

Photomerge Exposure provides a great new way to deal with photos captured in difficult lighting conditions, enabling you to combine the best-lit areas from two or more images to make a perfectly exposed shot.

For this exercise you'll work with two photos of a mother and daughter posed in front of stained-glass windows in a dim interior, captured with and without flash.

The photo shot with flash has been correctly exposed to capture the figures in the foreground, but the windows appear "burnt out" so that all color and detail have been lost. The second photo has captured the glowing colors in the stained glass reasonably well, but the rest of the image is too dark, dull, and lacking in detail.

1   If you're still in the Editor, switch to the Organizer now by clicking the Organizer button (▦) in the Task Bar.

2   Click the arrow beside the Lesson 08 tag in the Tags panel, if necessary, to isolate the images for this lesson. Ctrl-click / Command-click to select the images 08_04a.jpg and 08_04b.jpg.

3   Right-click / Control-click either of the selected images. From the context menu, choose Edit With Photoshop Elements Editor.

Using the Photomerge Exposure tool

Whenever you're faced with difficult lighting conditions, you should keep the Photomerge Exposure tool in mind; make a point of shooting two or more photos at different exposure settings, and then let Photoshop Elements align them and blend them together when you get home.

Photoshop Elements can detect whether the images you've chosen to combine are a pair shot with and without flash, or photos taken with different exposure settings; for example, a series captured using the your camera's exposure bracketing feature.

The Photomerge Exposure tool has two working modes; it will default to Manual mode for photos captured with and without flash, or open in Automatic mode for a series of exposure-bracketed shots.

Merging exposures manually

1 Ctrl-click / Command-click to select both of the photos in the Photo Bin, and then choose Enhance > Photomerge > Photomerge Exposure. Photoshop Elements displays a progress bar as it matches details in the source photos, and then aligns them accordingly.

The Photomerge tools will let you extract content from the Source image and blend it into the Final image. By default, Photoshop Elements places the first photo in the Photo Bin in the Source pane on the left of the Photomerge Exposure workspace.

2 Click the second thumbnail in the Photo Bin to replace the default source photo with the image 08_04b.jpg. Drag the first thumbnail (08_04a.jpg) from the Project Bin into the Final image pane on the right. Make sure that the option Show Strokes is activated, and then activate the Edge Blending option.

Tip: If what you see in the Photomerge preview window differs from the illustration at the left, click Cancel, close both images without saving, and quit the Editor; then, start again from step 2 on the previous page.

3 Use the Zoom and Hand tools to focus your view on the figures in the foreground; then, select the Pencil tool (✐) in the right panel. You won't need to change the default brush diameter of 10 pixels.

4 Starting near the woman's right eye, draw carefully around the top of her head, staying as close to the outline of the hair as possible without moving the brush outside it, and then drag down the line between mother and daughter.

▶ **Tip:** If you've copied unwanted background detail from around the woman's head into the Final image, use the Eraser tool from the right panel to remove that part of the line. Reduce the brush size for the Pencil tool by pressing the left bracket key ([) and try again, making sure that you stay within the outline of the woman's hair.

5 Zoom in on the daughter's head. Reduce the brush size a little, if you haven't done so already, and draw around the top of the girl's head, taking care not to move the brush outside the outline, but making sure that you pick up the highlighted areas of the hair. If your stroke introduces unwanted background detail, click or make short strokes with the Eraser tool ( ) to correct it.

▶ **Tip:** To move the cropping handles by small increments, press the Ctrl / Command key together with the plus sign key to zoom in, and press the spacebar to switch to the Hand tool.

6 Double-click the Hand tool or choose View > Fit On Screen. Don't be concerned about the legs of our subjects' jeans—you'll crop that part of the image in the next step. Click the Done button at the bottom of the right panel.

7 Double-click the Hand tool, and then choose Image > Crop. Drag the handles of the cropping rectangle to trim the incomplete parts of the image; then, click the check mark to commit the crop.

The merged image is a far better exposure than either of the original photos, but there is still plenty of room for improvement.

If we had much more time, we could add some detail from the flash-lit photo to the wall and columns, or try reversing the process by making the underexposed shot the Source image and copying the stained glass into the flash-lit photo instead.

8   Choose File > Save. Name the file **08_04_Merge_Manual**, to be saved to your My CIB Work folder, in Photoshop (PSD) format with Layers activated, and included in the Organizer. Click Save. Keep the file open for the moment.

Merging exposures automatically

Even in Automatic mode, Photomerge Exposure gives you a degree of control over the way that the source images are combined.

1   Click an empty area in the Photo Bin to deselect all the thumbnails; then, Ctrl-click / Command-click to select the two original source photos in the Photo Bin and choose Enhance > Photomerge > Photomerge Exposure.

2   Click the Automatic tab at the top of the Photomerge Exposure panel.

3   In the Photomerge Exposure panel in Automatic mode, drag the Shadows slider all the way to the right to set a new value of 100. This will lighten the shadows in the blended image, improving definition. Click Done at the bottom of the panel.

4   Crop the image as you did in the previous exercise, and then choose File > Save. Name the file **08_04_Merge_Auto**, to be saved to your My CIB Work folder, in Photoshop (PSD) format with Layers activated, and included in the Organizer. Click Save. Keep the file open for the moment.

5   At the top of the Edit pane, click back and forth between the name tabs for the two merged images, 08_04_Merge_Manual and 08_04_Merge_Auto, to compare the results of the two blending modes. For our base images, the manual blend achieved a better exposure for the foreground subjects, while the automatically merged image reveals much more of the architectural detail.

6   In the Photo Bin, deselect all the thumbnails; then, Ctrl-click / Command-click to select the last two images, 08_04_Merge_Manual and 08_04_Merge_Auto. Choose Enhance > Photomerge > Photomerge Exposure.

7   Click the Manual tab at the top of the Photomerge Exposure panel and drag the image 08_04_Merge_Auto.psd from the Photo Bin into the Final pane. Use the Pencil tool to copy the figures from the manually merged photo to the automatically generated image; you won't need to be as careful as you were earlier. When you're done, click Done. Crop the file; then save it as **08_04_Merge_Remix**.

8   Click back and forth between the name tabs for the three merged images you've produced to compare them. When you're done, choose File > Close All.

Photomerge Exposure - Manual

Photomerge Exposure - Automatic

Photomerge Exposure - Mixed methods

Using layers to combine photographs

In this lesson so far, you've used the various Photomerge tools to automate the process of combining photos. In this project, you'll take a more hands-on approach, using layers, selections, and masks to give you full control over the way several source photos are combined to create a complex composite image.

1 In the Organizer, locate and select the images 08_05b.jpg and 08_05c.jpg, a scenic view of the ruins of a Scottish castle, and a photo of a seagull in flight.

2 Click click the Editor button (⬛) in the Task bar. In the Editor click in the mode picker at the top of the workspace, if necessary, to switch to Expert mode.

Arranging the image layers

In the first part of this project, you'll arrange these two images on separate layers, and then blend them to create a composite background.

1 Click the Layout button (⬛) in the Task bar and choose the All Row layout to tile the open image windows horizontally. Click the name tab of the image 08_05c.jpg (the seagull) to make it the active window.

2 Select the Move tool (⬦) and hold down Alt / Option as you drag the seagull onto the coastal view. Release the mouse button, and then the Alt / Option key. Holding the Alt / Option key as you drag a layer to another file ensures that the layer is aligned the same way in the target file as it is in the source, so that the image appears in the same position in the window. Close the image 08_05c.jpg.

3 If the Layers panel is not already visible, choose Window > Layers. In the Layers panel, make sure that the layer Background Copy (the gull) is selected; then, choose Image > Resize > Scale. Click the Tool Options button (⬛) in the Task bar to show the tool options pane; then, choose View > Fit On Screen.

4 In the tool options pane, make sure that the option Constrain Proportions is activated, and then type **50%** in the W (width) field.

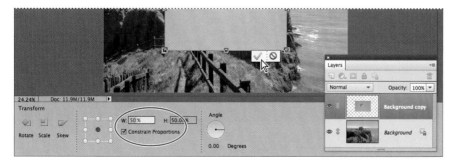

5 With the Move tool (⊹), drag the seagull photo to the upper right corner of the image; then, drag the lower left handle of the bounding box upwards and to the right to reduce the image further. Keep your eye on the width (W) and height (H) values in the tool options pane; stop when both values reach 40%. Click the green Commit button on the bounding box to accept the changes.

Creating a feathered layer mask

A layer mask allows only part of the image on a layer to show and hides the rest by making it transparent. Layers lower in the stacking order will be visible through the transparent areas in the masked layer. In the next steps you'll make a feathered selection and use it to create a soft-edged mask that will make it possible to blend the seagull into the sky in the background scene without a visible edge.

1 Select the Rectangular Marquee Tool (⌷) in the toolbar. In the Tool Options pane activate the elliptical variant of the marquee selection tool, and then use the slider or type of the default value to set the Feather amount to **50** px.

2 Starting from a point below the bird's body, drag an elliptical selection marquee, holding down the Alt / Option key as you drag to draw the marquee from its center. Release the mouse button when you have as much clearance around the seagull as shown at the right. If necessary, drag the selection in the image window to center it on the bird.

3 With the Background copy layer selected, click the Add Layer Mask button () at the top of the Layers panel to convert the selection to a layer mask. In the Layers panel, the layer with the gull now has a black and white mask icon; only the part of the image corresponding to the white area still shows in the image.

4 To see the layer mask displayed in the image window as a semi-transparent overlay, hold down the Shift key, and then Alt-click / Option-click the layer mask thumbnail. Repeat the action to hide the overlay.

As you can see, the center of the mask is completely clear; the soft edge created by the feathered selection allows just enough clearance for the seagull. Though the selection is no longer active, you could edit the mask, if necessary, by painting directly onto it in black or white

Although the feathered mask blends the image smoothly into the layer below it, the color in our wildlife photo still needs to be adjusted to match the background.

Matching the colors of blended images

Every color-matching problem will have its own solution, but this exercise should at least give you an idea of what kinds of things you can try. In this case you'll use a blending mode together with several different adjustments to color and lighting.

1 Click the colored thumbnail (not the layer mask) on the Background copy layer to select the image, rather than the mask; then, choose Enhance > Adjust Color > Adjust Hue/Saturation. In the Hue/Saturation dialog box, use the sliders or type new values to set both the Hue and Saturation, to **-12** and the Lightness to **-2**.

2 Use the menu above the sliders to switch from the Master channel to the Cyans channel. Set the Saturation value for the Cyans channel to **−20**. Switch to the Blues channel and set the Saturation to **−20**; then click OK.

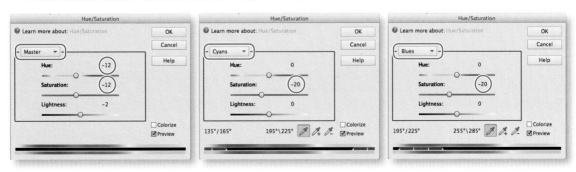

As you can see in the before and after illustration below, this combination of adjustments has not only matched the colors in the blended images, but has also reduced the contrast and made the seagull a little brighter, helping it to fit in better with the slightly hazy aerial perspective in the background image.

Tip: If you wish to tweak the position of the seagull, make sure its layer is active; then, select the Move tool and drag the bird by its center; the Move tool will not work if you try to drag a part of the image that is masked (invisible). Alternatively, once the Move tool is activated, you can nudge the selected layer with the arrow keys on your keyboard.

3   Choose File > Save As. Save the file to your work folder, in the Photoshop format with Layers enabled. Make sure that the image will be included in the Organizer, but not in a Version Set. Name the new file **08_05_Composite**, and then click Save. Keep the blended image open for the next exercise.

Cleaning up selection edges

Defringing removes the halo of residual color that often surrounds a selection copied and pasted from one image to another. In this exercise you'll add a foreground image of four sisters; then select and delete the background from that photo and use the Defringe feature to blend the selection halo into the background.

1   Choose View > Fit On Screen; then, choose File > Open. Navigate to and open your Lesson 8 folder. Select the file 08_05a.jpg, and then click Open.

2   With the image 08_05a.jpg selected as the active window in the Edit pane, choose Select > All. Choose Edit > Copy, and then File > Close. Make sure the top layer is still selected; then, choose Edit > Paste. The image of the four sisters is placed on a new layer named Layer 1, right above the layer that was selected.

3   With the new layer selected in the Layers panel, select the Move tool ( ) and drag the photo of the girls to the lower right corner of the image.

4   Click any of the handles on the bounding box. In the tool options pane, make sure that Constrain Proportions is activated; then, drag the upper left handle of the bounding box upwards and to the left to meet the left border of the image.

5 Click the Commit button at the lower right of the bounding box; then, use the left and down arrow keys to nudge Layer 1 just a fraction down and to the right.

6 Click the Quick Selection tool, or whichever of its variants is currently visible at the right of the Lasso tool (⟳) in the Select tools category. At the left of the tool options pane, activate the The Magic Wand tool (✳). Set the Tolerance for the tool to 5, activate Anti-aliasing and disable Contiguous and Sample All Layers. Select the yellow background on Layer 1 with the Magic Wand tool.

7 Press the Delete key to delete the yellow background, and then press Ctrl+D / Command+D, or choose Select > Deselect to clear the selection.

8 Zoom in to the space between the heads of the two sisters in the middle of the group. A yellowish fringe or halo is clearly visible around the girls' hair.

9 Choose Enhance > Adjust Color > Defringe Layer. In the Defringe dialog box, type 5 pixels for the width and click OK. Most of the fringe is eliminated.

▶ **Tip:** The Magic Wand tool (✳) is grouped together with the Quick Selection tool (✎) and the Selection Brush (✐) in the Select category at the top of the toolbar.

10 Double-click the Hand tool in the toolbox, or choose View > Fit On Screen to see the whole image in the edit window.

11 Select the Magic Wand tool (✴) once more, and click anywhere in the cleared area surrounding the girls. Choose Select > Modify > Border and set a border width of 4 pixels; then, click OK.

12 Choose Filter > Blur > Blur More, and then repeat the command to soften the harder edges of the pasted image. Press Ctrl+D / Command+D, or choose Select > Deselect to clear the selection.

13 Choose File > Save, and then close the document.

Congratulations, you've completed the last exercise in this lesson. You've learned how to create a stunning composite panorama, how to merge multiple photos into the perfect group shot, how to remove obstructions from a view, and how to compose several photos into a single image by arranging layers and using a selection to define a layer mask. You've also gained some experience with solving difficult lighting problems by combining shots taken at different exposures.

Take a moment to work through the lesson review on the next page before you move on to the next chapter, where you'll explore opportunities for unleashing your creativity with Photoshop Elements.

Review questions

1 What does the Photomerge Group Shot tool do?

2 How does the Photomerge Scene Cleaner work?

3 Why is it that sometimes when you think you're finished with a transformation in Photoshop Elements you cannot select another tool or perform other actions?

4 Why does Photomerge Exposure sometimes open in Automatic mode and at other times in Manual mode?

5 What is a fringe and how can you remove it?

6 What are the Photomerge tools that are not covered in this lesson?

Review answers

1 With the Photomerge Group Shot tool you can pick and choose the best parts of several similar photos, and merge them together to form one perfect picture.

2 The Photomerge Scene Cleaner helps you improve a photo by removing passing cars, tourists, and other unwanted elements. The Scene Cleaner works best when you have several shots of the same scene, so that you can combine the unobstructed areas from each source picture to produce a photograph free of traffic and tourists.

3 Photoshop Elements is waiting for you to confirm the transformation by clicking the Commit button, or by double-clicking inside the transformation boundary.

4 Photomerge Exposure detects whether your source photos were taken with exposure bracketing or with and without flash and defaults to Automatic or Manual mode accordingly. Manual mode works better for source files taken with flash/no flash.

5 A fringe is the annoying halo of color that often surrounds a selection pasted into another image. When the copied area is pasted onto another background color, or the selected background is deleted, pixels of the original background color show around the edges of your selection. The Defringe Layer command (Enhance > Adjust Color > Defringe Layer) blends the halo away so you won't see an artificial-looking edge.

6 The Photomerge Faces and Photomerge Style Match tools are not treated in this lesson. Photomerge Faces works similarly to the Photomerge Group Shot tool, except that it's specialized for working with faces. The Photomerge Style Match tool lets you merge the developing style—the tone and color settings—from one image to another.

9 GETTING CREATIVE

Lesson overview

Once you've adjusted and polished your photos, Photoshop Elements offers a multitude of ways to add your own artistic touches. You've already experimented with some of the creative possibilities of the Recompose and Photomerge tools and designed your own custom effects in the Filter Gallery; in this lesson you'll have some fun with text and explore the Create mode.

Photoshop Elements makes it simple to create stylish, professional-looking projects to showcase your photos, from greeting cards and Photo Books to calendars and animated slide shows.

This lesson introduces some fun type tools and steps you through the basic techniques you'll use to build projects in Create mode:

- Locating artwork in the Graphics library
- Setting up a photo project in Create mode
- Adding a creative touch with text and graphics
- Fitting text to an image
- Working with layers, blend modes, layer styles, and effects
- Creating layer masks and type masks

 You'll probably need between one and two hours to complete this lesson. If you haven't already done so, download the Lesson 9 work files from the Lesson & Update Files tab of your Account page at www.peachpit.com.

Photoshop elements offers a huge library of layout
templates and clip graphics, and a whole family of
text tools, that make it easy to produce eye-catching
projects using your own photos. Show loved ones
how much you care with stylish personalized greeting
cards; preserve and share your precious memories in
a sophisticated Photo Book, or combine pictures, text,
and effects to fit your photos to a practical purpose or
tell an evocative story in an artistic photo collage.

241

Getting started

● **Note:** Before you start this lesson, make sure that you've set up a folder for your lesson files and downloaded the Lesson 9 folder from your Account page at www.peachpit.com, as detailed in "Accessing the Classroom in a Book files" in the chapter "Getting Started" at the beginning of this book. You should also have created a new work catalog (see "Creating a catalog for working with this book" in Lesson 1).

You'll begin by importing the sample images for this lesson to your CIB Catalog.

1   Start Photoshop Elements and click Organize in the Welcome Screen.

2   In the Organizer, check the lower right corner of the workspace to make sure that your CIB Catalog is loaded—if not, choose File > Manage Catalogs and select it from the list.

3   Click the Import button at the upper left of the Organizer workspace and choose From Files And Folders from the drop-down menu. In the Get Photos And Videos From Files And Folders dialog box, locate and select the Lesson 9 folder inside your PSE12CIB folder.

4   Disable the option Get Photos From Subfolders; then, click Get Media.

5   In the Import Attached Keyword Tags dialog box, click Select All; then, click OK.

On the arty side of the Editor

The Photoshop Elements Editor is much more than just a digital darkroom; when you're ready to go beyond simply improving your photos technically, you'll find that the Editor is also a versatile desktop design studio equipped with everything you'll need to give free rein to your creativity.

In Lessons 4, 5, and 6 you saw how even the standard tools for correcting color and lighting can also be used to achieve striking, evocative effects. In Lessons 7 and 8, you discovered ways to reinvent and reinterpret your photos with the image editing magic of state-of-the-art content-aware editing and Photomerge technologies, and by creating your own unique photo effects in the Filter Gallery.

In this lesson, you'll have a little fun with the type tools, practice some interesting creative techniques using layers and masks, and take a look at the Editor's Create mode, where Photoshop Elements can guide you through the process of designing stylish photo projects and presentations, from animated slide shows (Windows only) and photo books to calendars, greeting cards, and even customized CD labels.

Exploring the artwork library

Whether you're working with a preset project template in Create mode, or building up a photo-illustration layer by layer in Expert mode, Photoshop Elements makes it quick and easy to create distinctive photo projects by providing an extensive collection of, backgrounds, frames, text styles, clip-art shapes and graphics in the Graphics library. Although this artwork is also available in the Create mode, we'll start by exploring the Graphics panel in Expert mode.

1   In the Organizer, press Ctrl+Shift+A / Command+Shift+A, or choose Deselect from the Edit menu to make sure you have no images selected in the Media Browser, and then click the Editor button (▦) in the Task bar.

2   If the Editor is not already in Expert mode, click Expert in the mode picker at the top of the workspace, and then choose Window > Reset Panels. If you don't see tabs for the Layers, Effects, Graphics, and Favorites panels at the top of the Panel Bin, click the arrow beside the More button (▣) at the right of the Task bar and choose Custom Workspace at the bottom of the menu.

3   Click the Graphics tab at the top of the Panel Bin to bring the Graphics panel to the front.

4   Click the menu icon (▼≡) at the far right of the Panel Bin's header bar and make sure the option Large Thumbnail View is activated.

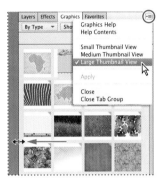

5   Move the pointer over the left edge of the Graphics panel; when the double-arrow cursor appears, drag the edge of the panel bin to the left to increase it to its maximum width.

What you see displayed in the Graphics panel depends on the options set in the sorting menus above the thumbnail swatches. By default, the sorting menu at the left is set to "By Type." At this setting, the content of the library is sorted by functional category. The second sorting menu lists the categories—Backgrounds, Frames, Graphics, Shapes, and Text—as well as the default option, Show All.

6   In the header of the Graphics panel, choose each category in turn from the second menu and scroll down to see thumbnails of the artwork available.

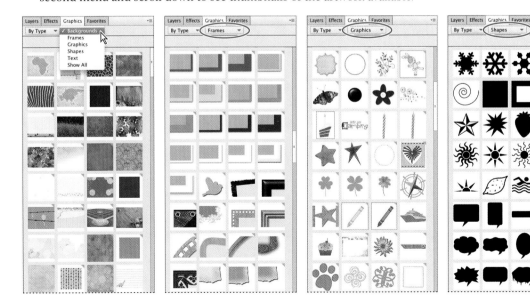

Using the Favorites panel

At first, the large number of choices in the Graphics panel may seem a little overwhelming, but you can easily locate the artwork you need by using the sorting and filtering menus at the top of the panel. These search functions are not available on the Graphics tab in Create mode, so it can save you time to do a little advance planning and assemble the items you want for a project while you're in Expert mode, using the Graphics and Favorites panels in tandem.

▶ **Tip:** If you wish to clear the default items from the Favorites panel, select each swatch in turn and click the trashcan icon in the header.

1 Drag the Favorites tab from the header to the bottom of the Panel Bin and release the mouse button when you see a blue line indicating an insertion point between the Graphics panel and the Task bar. Move the pointer over the upper edge of the repositioned Favorites panel; then, drag upwards with the double-arrow cursor until the Favorites panel occupies about half of the space in the Panel Bin. The Favorites panel already contains a small sample selection of popular graphics and image effects.

▶ **Tip:** If you don't see the filter menu below the sorting menu and the Find button, change the sorting option temporarily to By Style, and then switch back to By Word. Hold the pointer over a swatch to see the item's name.

2 Choose By Word from the sorting menu in the header of the Graphics panel; then, type **paper** in the search box. Choose Backgrounds from the filter menu in the bar below the sorting menu, and then click Find. Drag the backgrounds "Handmade Paper 03" and "Handmade Paper 04" into the Favorites panel. You'll need these items later in this lesson for your Create mode project.

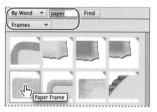

3 Set the filter to Frames. Locate the "Paper Frame" swatch and drag it into the Favorites panel.

4 Swipe over the word "paper" in the search box and type **travel**. Choose Graphics from the filter menu in the bar below the sorting menu, and then click Find. Drag the graphics "Compass 02" and "Cruise Ship" into the Favorites panel.

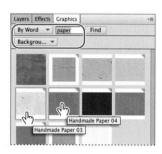

5 Choose By Color from the sorting menu, and then select Black from the colors menu. Set the filter to Backgrounds and locate "Black Folded Paper." Reset the filter for Frames and add the "Basic Black 40px" frame to your Favorites.

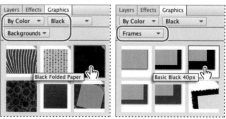

6 From the sorting menu, choose By Style; then, select Comic Book from the adjacent styles menu. Set the filter for Graphics; then drag the graphic named Speech Bubble 03 to the Favorites panel.

7 Change the style from Comic Book to Vintage. Collect the background "Blue Swirly" and the frames "Gold Frame 1," "Gold Frame Ornate," "Gold Frame Round 2," and "Old Black & Gold Frame." Change the style filter from Vintage to Decorative and add the graphics "Brass Leaves" and "Silver Flower Spray" to your favorites. Check through the preceding steps to make sure that you've added all fifteen of the artwork items in the illustration at the right.

Note: At installation, the Graphics library contains only a small selection of items. Swatches marked with blue in the upper right corner are "online assets" that will be downloaded to your computer automatically as soon as you place them in a project, so that your hard disk is not cluttered with unwanted items.

The Favorites panel can also store items from the Effects panel. To complete this exercise, you can add a few effects that you'll use to refine your photo projects later.

8 Click the Effects tab at the top of the Panel Bin. In the Effects panel's header, click Styles in the effects picker; then, choose Bevels from the effect categories menu. Drag the bevel style Simple Sharp Inner to the Favorites panel. Change the Styles category to Drop Shadows and add both the "High" and "Low" drop shadow effects.

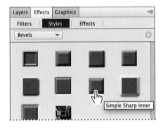

9 Click the Organizer button ( ) in the Task bar to return to the Organizer.

Producing a Photo Book

Our exploration of the Create mode will focus on the Photo Book project—the most involved of those offered in the Create menu. The skills and techniques you'll learn for your Photo Book are applicable to all of the other Create mode projects.

A sophisticated, attractive way to present and share your memories, and an ideal output medium for digital scrap-booking, a Photo Book also makes the perfect personalized gift for a loved one. You can either have your Photo Book printed and bound professionally by ordering through an online service, or print it yourself at home. However, unless you have high-quality, double-sided paper in a large enough size you may have to make some design compromises and possibly scale your layout in the printer dialog box to fit standard paper sizes.

1 Click the Lesson 9 folder in the My Folders list to isolate the images for this lesson. Make sure that the Sort By menu in the action bar above the thumbnails is set to Oldest. In the Media Browser, select the image photobook_01.jpg; then Shift-click the image photobook_26.jpg to select all the images in the series.

Tip: If you don't see file names below the thumbnails in the Media Browser, activate the Details and File Names options in the View menu.

2 Click the Create tab above the right panel group and choose Photo Book from the Create menu. The Photo Book setup dialog box opens.

3 At the left, the Sizes pane lists various printing and size options. Choose the Print Locally > 11.00 x 8.50 inches option. Scroll down to see the options in the Themes menu; then, choose the Colorful template. At the bottom of the dialog box, set the number of pages for the photo book to **8**. For the purposes of this exercise, disable the option Autofill With Selected Images; then, click OK.

● **Note:** The formats listed for the Shutterfly online printing service can also be printed from your home printer.

You'll see a series of progress bars as Photoshop Elements downloads online artwork assets, builds pages, and generates previews, and then the title page of the photo book appears in the Edit window. The Pages panel at the right displays thumbnail previews for the title page and four two-page spreads.

4 Show the Photo Bin by clicking the Photo Bin button () in the Task bar.

▶ **Tip:** If you don't see thumbnails for a cover page and four two-page spreads in the Pages panel at the right, you may need to refresh the view. Click the Layouts button (▦) at the right of the Task bar; then, click the Pages button (▢) to re-open the Pages panel.

Changing page layouts

When Photoshop Elements generates Photo Book pages automatically, it applies a different layout to each page randomly, varying the number, size, and positioning of photos so that every spread has a unique design, as reflected in the Pages preview.

You could, of course, accept the automatic layout as is, but for the purposes of this project, we'll customise the design page by page. To save time in this exercise, we've prepared a tweaked layout designed to fit the lesson images, leaving it up to you to finalize the page layout for the final spread.

1   Choose File > Close, and then click No / Don't Save to discard the default layout. Choose File > Open. Navigate to and open your Lesson 9 folder; then, select the file Venice_Book.pse and click Open. On Windows, you'll need to select the nested file Venice_Book.pse, and then click Open.

2   In the Pages panel at the right, click to select the last spread, pages 7 and 8.

3   Click the Layouts button () in the Task bar below the right panel. In the first category, Different Layouts, locate the design named "4 Up Photobook Landscape" and drag it onto the left page of the Page 7/8 spread in the Edit window.

Tip: You may see a warning that text layers might need to be updated for output. Activate the option Don't Show Again, and then click Update.

4   Scroll down the Layouts menu to the One Photo category and locate the template Photobook Landscape at the left in the bottom row. Drag the Photobook Landscape swatch to the right page of the spread in the Edit window.

5   Click the Pages button ( ) in the Task bar below the right panel and examine the completed base layout in the Pages preview. Including the cover page, the design now includes placeholders for all 26 of the lesson photos.

6   When you're done, click to select the Title Page at the top of the Pages preview.

Tip: Three of the place-holder frames may be hard to spot as they fill whole pages (pages 2, 4, and 5), with smaller frames arranged on top of them.

Rearranging the order of images in a project

When you create a photo book—or any other photo project—and have Photoshop Elements place your photos automatically, the images are arranged in the layout template in the same order in which they appear in the Photo Bin.

For a multiple-page project such as a photo book, you can save time and effort by arranging your photos before you begin. In the Organizer, you can establish a custom sorting order by creating an Album. Once you're in the Editor, the easiest way to change the order of your images is by simply shuffling them in the Photo Bin.

1   If necessary, click the Photo Bin button () in the Task bar to show the Photo Bin. Make sure the menu at the left of the Photo Bin header is set to Show Files Selected In Organizer. If you don't see file names, right-click / Control-click in the Photo Bin and choose the option Show Filenames from the context menu.

Tip: If you can't drag a thumbnail to a new position, you may have all of the images in the Photo Bin selected.

2   Drag the image photobook_05.jpg to a new position to the left of the image photobook_02.jpg, so that it becomes the second image in the Photo Bin.

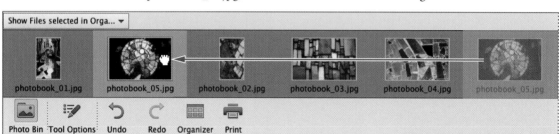

3   Right-click / Control-click any of the thumbnails in the Photo Bin and choose Auto Fill With Photo Bin Photos. Wait while Photoshop Elements places the images that you selected in the Organizer inside the frames in your book layout and regenerates the page previews.

4   Hide the Photo Bin by clicking the Photo Bin button at the left of the Task bar. Choose File > Save.

Working with backgrounds

You can change the background, like any other element in a preset theme template, as easily as you changed the page layout. You can move, rotate, scale, or even delete the preset background, just as you can with a frame or clip-art graphic. Unlike an image in a frame however, you can't simply select and drag the background image. As the "foundation" of the file, the locked Background layer is a special case: for some operations, it will need to be "simplified"—unlocked and converted to standard bit-mapped data—before it can be edited as other layers can.

1   In the Pages panel, click the first two-page spread, pages 1 and 2; then, click the Advanced Mode button at the left of the actions bar above the Edit window. Click the Layers button () in the Task bar to open the Layers panel. Choose Window > Favorites to open the Favorites panel. Drag the Favorites panel by its header to position it where it won't obstruct your view of the layers in the Layers panel or too much of the working preview in Edit window.

2 Double-click the background swatch, Black Folded Paper in the Favorites panel. Wait while Photoshop Elements downloads this online asset to your computer; then, watch both the Layers panel and the preview spread in the Edit window as the Background layer is updated.

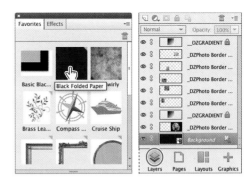

The new background graphic has been scaled to fit right across the width of the two-page spread, but at this point the right half is obscured by the full-page image on page 2.

3 With the Move tool (✛) selected in the toolbar, right-click / Control-click the full-page image on the right page of the spread and choose Clear Frame from the context menu. You now have a clear view of the line where the inside edges of the facing pages meet at the center of the spread.

We could make more of the subtle textural detail in this background by reducing it to cover only the left page. To move, scale, or rotate the background, you first need to use the Move Background command to unlock it on the Background layer.

4 Right-click / Control-click the background where it's visible on the left page and choose Move Background from the context menu. A bounding box now surrounds the background graphic, though most if it is out of view because the image is larger than the two-page spread. Test this by dragging the background downwards; then, drag the image back to its original position.

5 In order to scale or rotate the background manually, you could drag the image for access to the control handles, but in this case it will be more convenient to use the controls in the tool options pane. Click the Tool Options button (🖉) in the Task bar. In the tool options pane, type **50**% in the Width (W) text box; with the Constrain Proportions option activated, the Height (H) value will be updated automatically. The background image is scaled by 50% from its center.

6   Drag the reduced background artwork and position it flush with the left edge of page 1. Move the image up and down until you're pleased with the placement of the detail, and then click the Commit button (✔) to commit the changes.

7   Without the background covering the entire spread, there is a thin margin of white showing around the large photo on the right page. Click the image; then, click once on any of the bounding box handles. Rather than drag the handles to scale the image and its containing frame, type **101**% in either the W or H text box in the tool options pane; then, commit the change.

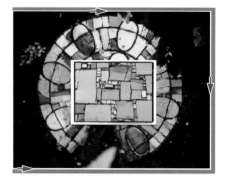

8   Drag the Basic Black 40px frame swatch from the Favorites panel onto each of the five framed photos in the layout; then, click on the background.

9   Choose File > Save; then, click the button at the left of the actions bar to return to Advanced mode. If necessary, click the Pages button (▢) in the Task bar to open the Pages panel. In the Pages preview, click the third spread in the photo book: pages 5 and 6. Alternatively, you can navigate to the page 5 and 6 spread by clicking twice on the right-facing arrow above the Edit window.

Working with photos and frames

You've already replaced photo frames in a page layout by substituting artwork from the Graphics library; in this exercise you'll learn how to manipulate a photo and its frame as a single grouped design element, and how to modify a photo's position and orientation independently of the frame with which it's grouped.

1   You can start by replacing all seven frames in the page 5 and 6 spread. Drag the Old Black & Gold Frame from the Favorites panel onto each of the four small images on the left page, and the Paper Frame onto the three photos on the right.

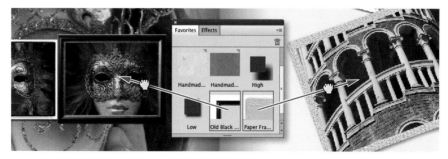

2 Double-click the Handmade Paper 04 swatch to replace the background; then, right-click / Control-click the full-page image on the left of the spread and choose Clear Frame from the context menu.

3 To move a framed photo in the layout, simply drag it with the Move tool (⊹). Shift-click to select all four of the small images on the left page. Hold down the shift key to constrain the movement and drag the row of photos downwards to position them half-way between the girl's eyes and the mouth of her mask.

▶ **Tip:** When the Move tool is active, you can use the arrow keys on your keyboard to move a selected project element in small steps instead of dragging them with the mouse.

4 Click the background to deselect the four photos, and then re-select the image at the left. Hold down the Shift key as you drag the framed photo about halfway to the left edge of the page. Move the photo on the right end of the row the same distance in the opposite direction. Select all four images; then, click the Tool Options button (📝), if necessary, to show the tool options pane. Click the Middle button in the right-hand column under Distribute to automatically space the second and third photos evenly between the first and fourth images.

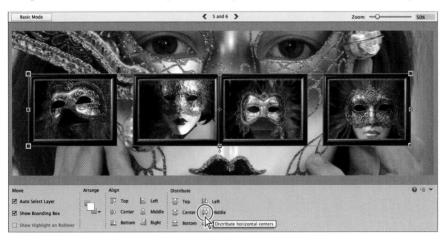

5 Right-click / Control-click each of the three photos on the right page in turn and choose Fit Frame To Photo from the context menu. The frames are re-sized so that their outside borders conform to the edges of the images.

6 Click to select the image at the right; then, drag the handle at the lower right of the bounding box to enlarge it—together with its frame—until the right edge of the image extends beyond the boundary of the page. You don't need to use the Shift key; the proportions of the frame group are constrained by default. Click the Commit button (✓).

7 Drag or nudge the three tilted photos into a pleasing arrangement, scaling or rotating them as you wish. To rotate a framed photo manually, select the photo; then, move the pointer close to one of the corner handles, staying just outside the bounding box. When the curved double-arrow cursor appears, drag to rotate the image. Hold down the Shift key as you drag to constrain the rotation to 15° increments. Always click the Commit button (✓) to commit the changes.

▶ **Tip:** If a photo does not fill its frame properly when scaled or rotated, right-click/Control-click the photo and choose Fit Frame To Photo. Alternatively, double-click the photo and resize it within its frame by using the slider, as discussed in the next exercise, "Adjusting a photo inside a frame."

8 Choose File > Save; then, click the Advanced Mode button in the actions bar. Click the right-facing arrow above the Edit pane to move on to pages 7 and 8.

Adjusting a photo inside a frame

Although a photo frame appears to be overlaid on the image it surrounds, the two elements actually occupy the same layer (by default, a layer for a framed photo even takes its name from the frame graphic). As a result, the standard moving, scaling, and rotating operations affect the photo and frame as if they were a single object. In this exercise, you'll learn how to transform a photo independently of its frame; but first, you'll change the background and frames for the last spread in your book.

1 Double-click the Handmade Paper 03 swatch in the Favorites panel to replace the background for the page 7 and 8 spread; then, drag the Basic Black 40px frame swatch onto each of the four images on page 7. You can keep the default frame for the large photo on page 8.

There are two preset text frames below the lower left corner of the image on page 8. The white place-holder text is a little difficult to see, but even if the background was also white, you could easily locate and select the text frames in the Layers panel.

2 If necessary, click the Layers button (▧) in the Task bar to show the Layers panel. Shift-click to select both _TXTFrame layers and press Backspace / Delete on your keyboard. Click Yes to confirm the deletion.

When you move a framed photo, or use its bounding box handles to scale or rotate it, the photo and frame are transformed together.

To move or transform a photo inside its frame, right-click/Control-click the image and choose Position Photo In Frame from the menu—or alternatively, double-click the photo with the Move tool (✛). A control bar appears above the photo, with a scaling slider and buttons to re-orient the image or replace it with another.

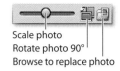

Scale photo
Rotate photo 90°
Browse to replace photo

3   Right-click / Control-click the image on the right page and choose Position Photo In Frame from the context menu. Hold down the Shift key to constrain the movement as you drag the image to the left within its frame, so that the gondolier on the right is no longer cut off by the border. Commit the change.

4   Use the Zoom tool (🔍) to focus on the photos on the left page. We'll deal with the image at the lower right in the next step; for the other three, right-click / Control-click each image in turn and choose Position Photo In Frame. Use the scaling slider to reveal as much of each image as possible, without resizing the frames. Drag each photo within its frame to arrange the most interesting crop; then commit the changes.

5   You can rotate the last of the four photos within its frame to straighten the blue and white gondola poles. Right-click / Control-click the image and choose Position Photo In Frame. To rotate the photo inside its frame, move the pointer close to any bounding box handle; when the pointer becomes a curved double-arrow cursor, drag the handle in either direction. Scale and position the photo within its frame as you did with its three neighbors; then, commit the changes.

6 Move the large photo on the right, together with its frame, downwards to center it on the page. Double-click the Hand tool to see the entire spread.

7 Click the left-facing arrow above the Edit pane twice to move to pages 3 and 4.

Refining your Photo Book layout using layers and effects

In this exercise you'll begin to polish your Photo Book design while you refresh some of the skills that you've picked up in the course of this lesson.

You'll start by customizing pages 3 and 4—the last un-treated spread—then, add some sophistication to the layout using a little layer magic.

Tip: After you've cleared the frame from the large image, you can enlarge the image by 1% to remove the pale border as you did in step 7 on page 248.

1 Double-click the Handmade Paper 03 swatch to replace the background; then, drag the Paper Frame swatch from the Favorites panel onto each of the three images on the left page. Drag the Gold Frame Ornate swatch from the Favorites panel onto the photo of an antique interior on the right page, and the Gold Frame Round 2 swatch onto the photo of the couple. Right-click / Control-click the large image on the right and choose Clear Frame from the context menu.

2   Right-click / Control-click each of the three photos on the left page and choose Fit Frame To Photo from the context menu. Drag or nudge the three tilted photos to position them, and scale or rotate them as you wish. If you want to change the stacking order of a photo, right-click / Control-click the image and choose Bring To Front, Bring Forward, Send Backwards, or Send To Back from the context menu. Scale, move or rotate each photo within its frame as needed, referring to the previous exercises if you need to refresh your memory.

3   For each of the two gold-framed photos, first make sure you are happy with scaling and placement; then, select the framed image, right-click / Control-click its layer in the Layers panel, and choose Simplify Layer. Without this step, it would not be possible to apply layer styles to these particular framing groups.

4   Drag the High drop shadow swatch from the Favorites panel onto both of the gold-framed images on page 4. In the Layers panel, double-click the *fx* icon at the right of the listing for each of the simplified layers in turn to open the Style Settings dialog box where you can adjust the settings for the drop shadow effect. For both of the simplified gold-framed images, reduce the Distance setting to **55** px, and then click OK.

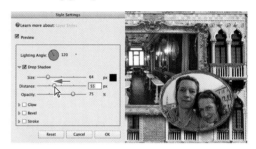

5   Click to select the full-page image on the right of the spread. At the top of the Layers panel, use the slider to reduce the selected layer's opacity to 40%.

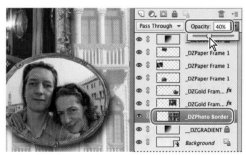

Although this image is no longer grouped with a frame graphic, it is still contained in an invisible photo-holder frame, within which it can be moved, scaled, and rotated, just as you did with the other photos

6   Revisit the Page 5/6 spread and apply the High drop shadow effect to the four small photos on the left page, first simplifying the respective layers in the Layers panel, as you did in step 3, and then editing the effect as you did in step 4.

Re-ordering the pages in a Photo Book

If you feel that a particular spread would look better placed at a different point in your photo book, it's very easy to change the page order.

1 You can start by revisiting the first spread; pages 1 and 2. Move, tilt and scale the upper right photo of the group on page 1 to add variety by breaking up the regular arrangement a little (*see the illustration below step 3*).

2 Double-click the smaller image on page 2; then, click the button to the right of the slider at the upper left of the frame to rotate this portrait-format photo to suit its horizontal frame. Click the button twice more to flip the image, and then use the slider to reduce it to fit the frame. When you're done, click the green check mark to commit the change.

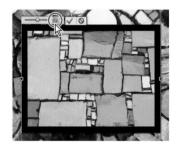

3 Rotate and move the image, together with its frame, to reveal more of the full-page image and hide the out-of-focus foliage at the bottom. Commit the changes.

▶ **Tip:** While you're working on a complex project like a Photo Book you should save regularly to avoid losing time and effort. After saving, you'll need to click the Advanced Mode button in the actions bar to return to Advanced mode.

4 Click the Pages button (⬚) in the Task bar to show the Pages preview. Drag the first spread downwards. Release the mouse button when you see an insertion line appear between the page 3 and 4 and page 5 and 6 spreads. The first and second spreads change places and the pages are renumbered. If the Pages panel previews are slow to re-draw, click each of the thumbnails in turn.

Adding graphics to a project

Before adding text, you can liven up the design with a judicious use of graphics from the content library. You can start by adding some atmosphere to the title page, so that the front cover of your photo book will create an evocative first impression.

1   Use the left arrow button in the bar above the Edit pane, or click the top thumbnail in the Pages preview, to move to the title page; then, click the Layers button (🍃) in the Task bar to open the Layers panel.

2   The preset text frames included in many page layout templates are useful for simple titles and captioning, but for this project you'll create your own text layers from scratch. Shift-click to select both of the text frames below the framed image, or select the two TXTFrame layers in the Layers panel; then, press Backspace / Delete on your keyboard and click Yes to confirm the deletions.

3   Click the Tool Options button (✏️), if necessary, to show the tool options pane. Select the framed photo, and then click any of the bounding box handles. In the tool options bar, type **30**% in the Width (W) text box; with Constrain Proportions activated, the Height (H) value is updated automatically. Click the Commit button under the image frame.

4   While the framed photo is still selected, double-click the Gold Frame Ornate swatch in the Favorites panel; then, right-click / Control-click the image and choose Fit Frame To Photo.

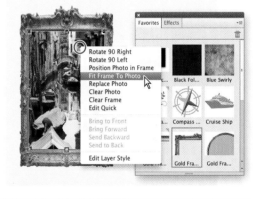

5   In the Favorites panel, double-click the Blue Swirly swatch to replace the background. In the Layers panel, right-click / Control click the Background layer and choose Duplicate Layer from the context menu. Click OK to accept Background copy as the default name for the duplicate layer.

6   At the top of the Layers panel, set the layer blending mode to Multiply, and the opacity to **50**%. In the Edit window, hold down the Shift key to constrain the movement as you drag the new layer downwards until it covers a little more than one third of the cover page.

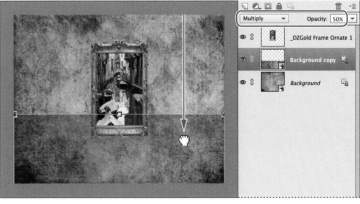

7 Drag the swatch for the graphic Cruise Ship from the Favorites panel to the right side of the page. Watch the W (width) and H (Height) values in the Tool Options pane as you drag one of the corner bounding box handles to enlarge the graphic to around 200%. Choose Image > Rotate > Flip Layer Horizontal; then, click the check mark below the bounding box mark to commit the change.

8 Drag the ship to position it as shown in the illustration at the right. To move the ship behind the photo frame, right-click / Control-click the graphic and choose Send Backward from the context menu.

▶ **Tip:** While you're working on a complex project like a Photo Book you should save regularly to avoid losing time and effort. After saving, you'll need to click the Advanced Mode button in the actions bar to return to Advanced mode.

9 Drag the graphic Compass 02 from the Favorites panel to the upper left of the page, placing it as shown below. At the top of the Layers panel, change the blending mode for the new layer to Difference, and set the layer's opacity to **70**%. Change the opacity for the Cruise Ship layer to the same value.

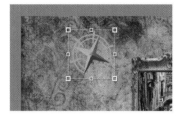

Placing text in a layout

In this exercise you'll add a title on the cover, and a message on the last page.

1 Select the Horizontal Type tool (T); then, choose Bickham Script Pro from the font menu in the Tool Options pane. Set the style to Regular and type **460** pt in the font size text box. Click the Center Text option and ensure that Anti-aliasing is activated so that the letters are smoothed. Click the text color swatch below the font menus and sample Light Green Cyan.

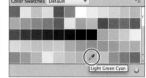

2 Click below the photo and Type **Venice**, then commit the text. At the top of the Layers panel, change the blending mode for the text layer to Difference and the opacity to **90**%; then drag the text layer downwards in the layer order to position it below (behind) the framed photo. Drag the title, or use the arrow keys on your keyboard, to center it horizontally. Select the compass and the photo together and drag them to the right to center the frame above the "n" in Venice.

3 Right-click / Control-click the layer "_DZGold Frame Ornate 1" in the Layers panel and choose Simplify Layer from the context menu; then, drag the High drop shadow effect from the Favorites panel onto the framed photo. In the Layers panel, double-click the *fx* icon on the frame layer and reduce the drop shadow's Distance setting to 55px; then, click OK.

4 Navigate to the last spread in the layout. Drag the Speech Bubble 03 swatch from the Favorites panel onto page 8. Choose Image > Rotate > Flip Layer Horizontal. Use the handles on the bounding box to scale the shape and position it as shown in the illustration at the right.

5 With the speech bubble graphic still selected, switch to the Type tool. Keep the same font, but change the font size to 36 pt, the font style to Semibold, and the text color to black. Click the arrow beside the Leading text box—to the right of the text color swatch—and change the setting from Auto to 30 pt. Click in the center of the speech bubble and type **Gondola: mid 16th century**; then, Press Enter / Return, and then type **"to rock and roll."** (include the quote marks and period). Click the Confirm button and drag the text to adjust its position.

6   Just two more flourishes and you're done! Use the navigation buttons above the Edit window preview, or the Pages panel, to move to the page 1 and 2 spread. Drag the graphic Silver Flower Spray onto the left page. Rotate the artwork 90° counter-clockwise, and scale it to almost the width of the page. Move the flower spray so that it extends off the top edge of the page. In the Layers panel, move the layer Silver Flower Spray down in the order, so that it lies below (behind) at least one of the paper-framed photos, and above (in front of) at least one other.

7   Drag the Brass Leaves graphic onto the right page of the page 5 and 6 spread *twice*. Scale and rotate each copy so that plenty of the leaves lie in areas not occupied by framed photos, particularly at the right side of the page. In the Layers panel, move both Brass Leaves layers below (behind) all of the Paper Frame layers. Change the blending mode for both Brass Leaves layers to Screen.

8　The Photo Book is complete; choose File > Save. By default photo projects are saved in Photo Project Format, a multi-page document format that preserves text and layers so that they can be edited later. You could also choose to save the project as a PDF file that can be shared as an e-mail attachment.

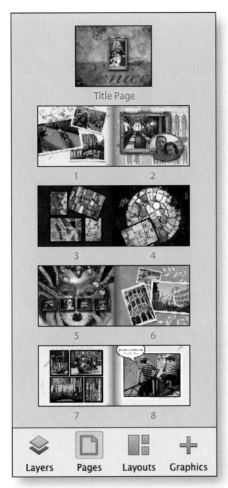

9　Choose File > Export Photobook. In the Export Photobook dialog box, choose the PDF format. Click Browse to specify your My CIB Work folder as the Save To Location; then, click OK. Choose File > Close and close without re-saving.

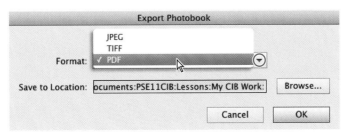

Creative framing with layer masks

There are endless ways to use layer masks to edit, blend, and combine photos. In this exercise you'll paint directly into a layer mask to produce a free-form cutout frame—another great way to add creative flair to an everyday image.

1   In the Organizer, isolate the images for this lesson, if necessary, by clicking the Lesson 9 folder in the My Folders list. Select the image 09_Girls.jpg in the Media Browser; then, click the Editor button (▦) in the Task bar.

2   If the Editor is not in Expert mode, click Expert in the mode picker, and then choose Window > Reset Panels. If you don't see tabs for the Layers, Effects, Graphics, and Favorites panels at the top of the Panel Bin, click the arrow beside the More button (▣) at the right of the Task bar and choose Custom Workspace from the menu. Drag the Layers panel out of the Panel Bin by its name tab and position it where it won't block your view of the Edit pane.

3   Right-click / Control-click the image's single layer, the Background layer, and choose Duplicate Layer from the context menu. In the Duplicate Layer dialog box, click OK to accept the default layer name, Background copy.

4   Click the eye icon (👁) beside the Background layer to hide it. With the new layer, Background copy, selected in the Layers panel, click the Add Layer Mask button (◎) at the top of the panel.

The new Layer Mask thumbnail on the Background copy layer is highlighted by a blue border, indicating that it is selected—or active—ready for editing.

5   Choose Edit > Fill Layer. In the Fill Layer dialog box, choose Black From the Use menu under Contents; then, click OK.

The solid black fill in the layer mask obscures the photo on the Background copy layer completely. With the Background layer also hidden from view, the image window shows only the checkerboard pattern that indicates layer transparency.

6   Click the barred eye icon (👁) beside the Background layer make the layer visible again. Hold down the Shift key; then, Alt-click / Option-click the layer mask thumbnail to show the mask as a semi-transparent red overlay.

7   Double-click the Eraser tool (✐) in the toolbar to select the tool and access the tool settings. In the Tool Options pane, make sure that Brush is selected in the eraser's Type options at the right and make sure that the Opacity is set to 100%.

8 Click the arrow beside the sample brush stroke to open the Brush Picker and choose Thick Heavy Brushes from the Brushes menu. The name of each brush appears in a tooltip when you hold the pointer over the swatch. Double-click the second brush in the set, the Rough Flat Bristle brush: then, press the right bracket key (]) six times to increase the brush size to 300 pixels.

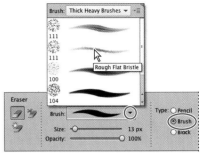

9 With the Eraser tool, scribble a rough line in the image window to quickly clear the red overlay from the faces of all four girls.

10 Hold down Shift+Alt / Shift+Option and click the layer mask thumbnail to hide the mask overlay; then, click the eye icon to hide the Background layer again. As you can see, the Rough Flat Bristle brush is partly transparent. In the image window, make another short stroke or two over each girl's face.

▶ **Tip:** When you wish to make a hard-edged mask, you can use any of the mechanical selection tools (either the Rectangular or Elliptical Marquee tool, or the Polygonal Lasso tool) rather than a brush or an eraser. You could also use any of the bit-mapped Shapes from the Graphics library as the basis for your clipping mask.

By using a layer mask in this way, you've effectively created your own ragged-edged photo frame. Now, you need a new background.

11 Click the Graphics tab at the top of the Panel Bin. Choose By Seasons from the sorting menu in the header of the Graphics panel; then, choose Winter from the adjacent menu. Choose Backgrounds from the filter menu in the bar below the sorting menu. Scroll down in the Graphics menu, if necessary, and double-click the "Snow" swatch. Photoshop Elements displays progress bars as this online graphic is downloaded and placed, replacing the original Background layer.

12 Choose Enhance > Adjust Color > Adjust Hue/Saturation. Reduce the value for Saturation to -15, and increase the Lightness setting to +30; then, click OK.

13 In the Layers panel, select the Background copy layer. Click the Effects tab at the top of the Panel Bin. Click Styles in the header of the Effects panel; then, choose Inner Shadows from the styles menu. Double-click the Low inner shadow swatch, or drag it onto the image in the Edit window. The inner shadow emphasizes the cut-out effect.

14 Choose File > Save As. Name the new file **09_Girls_BrushMask**, to be saved to your work folder in Photoshop format with layers enabled. Include the image in the Organizer, but not as part of a Version Set. Click Save; then, close the file.

Getting creative with text

Adding a title or caption is a great way fit an image to a specific purpose, such as a cover page for a printed document or a title screen for a slideshow, but text can also be used imaginatively to suggest meaning, emphasize context, add humour, or evoke emotion. Photoshop Elements delivers a suite of type tools that provide limitless creative possibilities for fitting text to your images, whatever the purpose.

Fitting text to a selection

One of several type tool variants that enable you to shape your text creatively to image elements in your photos, the Text On Selection tool makes it easy to wrap your message around any pictured object.

1   In the Organizer, select the images 09_Type1.jpg and 09_Type2.jpg in the Media Browser, and then click the Editor button (▦) in the Task bar. Make sure the Editor is in Expert mode; then, choose Window > Reset Panels. If you don't see tabs for the Layers, Effects, Graphics, and Favorites panels at the top of the Panel Bin, click the arrow beside the More button (◼) at the right of the Task bar and choose Custom Workspace from the menu. At the top of the Edit pane, click the name tab for 09_Type1.jpg to bring its image window to the front.

The Text On Selection tool (T) can make its own selections, but it can also be used with a selection that is already established. For this exercise, you'll first create and fine-tune a selection so that you can have your text follow a path well outside the edge of the selected object, rather than wrapping tightly to its outline.

2   In the toolbar, click the Quick Selection tool (🔍), beside the Lasso tool. If you don't see Quick Selection tool, Alt-click / Option-click its variant, the Selection Brush (✏) to switch tools; then drag inside the sculpture to select the figure, together with his seat. You don't need to be very precise, but if you go too far, hold down the Alt / Option key as you paint to subtract from the selection.

3   When you're done, choose Select > Modify > Expand. In the Expand Selection dialog box, set the Expand By value to **40** pixels; then click OK. Alt-click / Option-click the Quick Selection tool to switch to the Selection Brush (✏). Use a medium brush to round out any tight angles on the selection outline. Hold the Alt / Option key as you paint to remove any obvious lumps and bumps along the edge.

For the sake of comparison, the illustration at right shows the expanded Quick Selection as a dashed line, and the smoothed outline as a red overlay, which is just as you'll see it if you switch the Selection Brush to Mask mode.

4 In the toolbar, double-click whichever variant of the Type tool is currently visible. In the Tool Options pane, select the Text On Selection tool (⊤) from the seven tool variants at the left. Set the font to Arial, the style to Bold, the size to 18 pt, and change the text color to white.

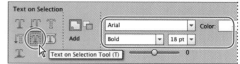

5 Move the tool over the image in the Edit window; the pointer changes to the Quick Selection cursor. Click inside the active selection; then click the green check mark to convert the selection into a path for your text.

6 Move the tool over the newly created path; the pointer becomes a text insertion cursor. Click above the figure's neck and type this quote from Leonardo da Vinci: **men of lofty genius are most active when they are doing the least work**.

7 The tool options pane now shows the full suite of options for horizontal type. If necessary, activate the Center Text (≡) alignment option.

▷ **Tip:** When you're dragging to reposition the text, be careful to keep your cursor on the outside of the outline; otherwise, the text will flip to wrap around the inside of the path. You can add extra spaces between words or letters, where needed, to reduce clumping.

8 Click in the text near your starting point the text insertion tool. Release the mouse button; then, hold the Ctrl / Command key and drag the text left or right to fine-tune its placement on the path, referring to the illustration below. When you're happy with the result, click the green check mark to commit the text.

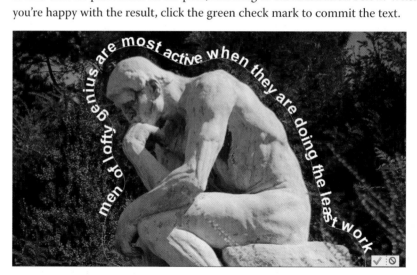

9 Choose File > Save. Name the file **09_Thinker**, to be saved to your work folder in Photoshop format with Layers enabled, and included in the Organizer, but not as part of a Version Set. Click Save, and then close the file.

Wrapping text around a shape

The Text On Shape tool (⊤) works in much the same way as the Text On Selection tool, except that the first step is to draw a vector shape with one of a selection of shape tools, rather than to make a selection.

1   With the image 09_Type2.jpg in the Edit pane, hold Ctrl / Command and press the minus sign key three or four times, so that you can see a lot of empty gray space around the photo, as shown in the illustration for step 3.

2   In the toolbar, double-click the Text On Selection tool, or whichever Type tool variant is currently active. In the tool options pane select the Text On Shape tool () from the variants at the left. Set the font to Brush Script Std and the size to 36 pt. Choose the Ellipse tool from the shape options. You'll apply color to the type in the next exercise.

Tip: If you don't have the Brush Script font, choose another script typeface, or any font of comparable weight that has a similarly organic feel.

3   Hold down the Alt / Option key so that your shape will be drawn from the center outwards. Drag with the Ellipse tool, starting from a point in they gray 'artboard' well below the image, and a little right of center. Match the ellipse to the upper curve of the rainbow, making sure to allow clearance so that your text will run parallel to the rainbow, rather than interfering with its edge.

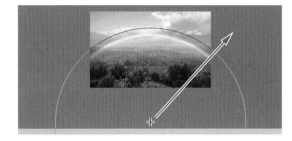

4   Hold Ctrl / Command and press the plus sign key three or four times, so that the photo fils your view. Move the Text On Shape tool over the upper edge of the ellipse and click with the text insertion cursor at the highest point of the curve. Type **Somewhere, under the Rainbow**. Click the green check mark.

Once you've committed the text, the Move tool becomes active by default, and the text becomes selected as an abject that can be moved, scaled, and rotated on its own layer, just like any other graphic. To edit the content of the text, you would first need to activate one of the Type tools.

5   Drag the text, or use the arrow keys on your keyboard, to adjust its placement.

Using preset text styles

You can apply any of the filters and layer styles from the Effects panel to your text, adding bevels, shadows, glows, textures, and gradients to create your own text effects. Some editing operations require that you first "simplify" the text layer to a bit-mapped graphic that can no longer be edited as live text. In this exercise, you'll apply a preset text style from the Graphics panel instead.

1   Click the Graphics tab at the top of the Panel Bin. Set the Graphics panel's sorting menu to By Type, and then choose Text from the adjacent categories menu. Scroll down through the swatches to see the many preset styles available in the Graphics library.

2 Drag the Gradient Blue Medium style from the fourth row of text presets onto the text in the Edit pane; then, click the green check mark to commit the change.

3 Click the Layers tab at the top of the Panel Bin to show the Layers panel. Double-click the *fx* icon on the text layer to open the Style Settings dialog box. Set the Lighting angle to **-90**. Check the box to activate the Drop Shadow effect. Increase the drop shadow Size to **10** px, and the Opacity to **85**%. Click the small color swatch beside the Drop Shadow settings and change the color from black to a deep, saturated blue; then, click OK to close the Style Settings dialog box.

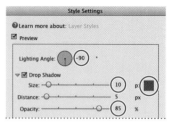

4 As a final touch, you can soften the effect a little by using the slider at the upper right of the Layers panel to reduce the opacity of the text layer to 85%.

▶ **Tip:** Your text is still "live" and editable. Simply double-click the text to activate the text tool; then swipe over the words you wish to edit, or place the text insertion point and start typing to add to the message.

5 Save the file as **09_Somewhere**, and then close it.

More fun with type

As its name suggests, the Text On Custom Path tool—the last of this group of Type tools—lets you draw and tweak a freehand path for your text to follow, providing the perfect solution for images like the example at the right, where creating a path automatically from a selection is not an option.

Try clicking the Create Warped Text button at the right of the Type tool controls in the tool options pane to discover how you can warp, bloat, pinch, twist, and otherwise torture your type.

Creating a type mask

The Type Mask tool (⊤) turns text outlines into a layer mask through which an underlying image is visible, effectively filling the letter shapes with image detail. This can create far more visual impact than using plain text filled with a solid color.

● **Note:** The Type Mask tool has one variant for horizontal type and another for vertical type.

1 In the Organizer, isolate the lesson images, if necessary, by clicking the Lesson 9 folder in the My Folders list. Right-click / Control-click the image 09_Runners.jpg and choose Edit With Photoshop Elements Editor from the context menu.

2 Make sure the Editor is in Expert mode; then, choose Window > Reset Panels. If you don't see tabs for the Layers, Effects, Graphics, and Favorites panels at the top of the Panel Bin, click the arrow beside the More button (▨) at the right of the Task bar and choose Custom Workspace from the menu.

3 Drag the Layers and Favorites panels out of the Panel Bin by their name tabs and position them where they won't block your view of the Edit pane. Choose Window > Panel Bin to hide the Panel Bin., and then double-click the Hand tool or choose View > Fit On Screen.

4 In the toolbar, double-click whichever variant of the Type tool is currently visible in the bottom row of the Draw category. In the Tool Options pane, click to select the Horizontal Type Mask tool (⊤) from the tool variants at the left.

5   Set up the text attributes in the tool options pane: Choose a font from the Font Family menu. We chose Mercurius CT Std, Black Italic, but if you don't have that font, choose any typeface that's blocky enough to let plenty of the image show through the letter forms. Type a new value of **950** pt for the font Size (you may need to adjust that for a different font). Choose Center Text (☰) from the paragraph alignment options. You don't need to worry about a color for the text; the type will be filled with detail from our marathon image.

6   Click at a horizontally centered point low in the image and type **RUN!**

7   Hold down the Ctrl / Command key on your keyboard; a bounding box surrounds the text in the image window. Drag inside the bounding box to reposition the type mask.

8   If you wish to resize the text, hold down the Ctrl / Command key and drag a corner handle of the bounding box. The operation is automatically constrained so that the text is scaled proportionally. Alternatively, you can double-click the text with the Type Mask tool to select it, and then type a new font size in the tool options bar.

9   When you're satisfied with the result, click the green Commit button in the tool options bar. The outline of the text becomes an active selection. If you're not happy with the placement of the selection, use the arrow keys on your keyboard to nudge it into place.

10 Choose Edit > Copy, and then Edit > Paste. In the Layers panel, you can see that the cutout type image has been placed onto a new layer, surrounded by transparency.

11 Hide the Background layer by clicking the eye icon beside the layer thumbnail.

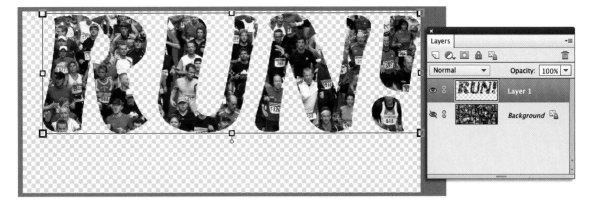

Adding impact to a type mask

The text is no longer live—the mask was converted to a selection outline, so it can no longer be edited with a text tool; however, you can still apply a layer style or an effect to enhance it or make it more prominent.

1 If necessary, select Layer 1 in the Layers panel to make it active. With the Move tool (✛), drag the type to center it in the image window; then, press the up arrow and right arrow keys eight times each.

2 In the Favorites panel, double-click the swatch for the High drop-shadow effect.

3 In the Layers panel, double-click the *fx* icon on Layer 1. In the Style Settings dialog box, set the Lighting Angle to **45**°. Increase the Drop Shadow Size to **40** px, the Distance to **50** px, and the Opacity to **80**%; then, click OK.

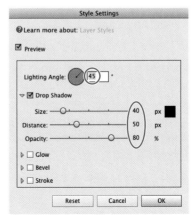

4 In the Layers panel, select the Background Layer. Make the layer visible; then, choose Image > Rotate > Flip Layer Horizontal. Click OK to confirm the conversion of the background, and then click OK to accept the default name.

5 Choose Enhance > Adjust Color > Adjust Hue/Saturation. In the Hue/Saturation dialog box, reduce the Saturation value to **–60**, increase the Lightness to **+60**, and then click OK.

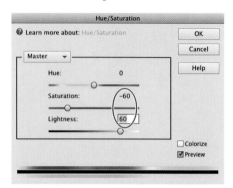

6 Choose File > Save As. In the Save As dialog box, choose Photoshop (PSD) as the file format, enable layers, and save the file to your My CIB Work folder. Make sure that the new file will be included in the Organizer, but not in a Version Set; then, name the file **09_runners_mask** and click Save. Close the file.

Congratulations! You've completed the lesson. You've explored the Graphics library and become familiar with a variety of methods for locating the artwork you need. You've also learned how set up a project in Create mode, how to replace and manipulate backgrounds, frames, and text, and the basics of working with layers and layer styles. You've had some fun with type and gained more experience with layer masks.

Before you move on to the next lesson, take a moment to refresh your new skills by reading through the review on the facing page.

Review questions

1   How do you begin a new project such as a greeting card or Photo Book?

2   How do you scale and reposition a photo in a photo project?

3   How do you change the order of the pictures in a photo book?

4   How can you find the items you want amongst all the choices in the Graphics library?

5   What are layers, how do they work, and how do you work with them?

Review answers

1   To create a project, select the photos you want to use in the Organizer, or open them from the Editor; then, choose a project option on the Create at the upper right of either workspace. Once you've chosen a theme, the right panel group presents page previews and provides access to layers layout templates, graphics and effects.

2   You can scale or rotate a framed photo by dragging the bounding box handles and move it by dragging. To scale, rotate, or move a photo within its frame you need to double-click the image to isolate it before using the same techniques, so that the changes affect the photo independently of its frame.

3   You can change the order of images in a photo book by dragging them to new positions in the Photo Bin below the Edit pane.

4   You can sort and search the items in the Graphics library by using the menus and text box at the top of the Content panel. You can sort the content by type, activity, mood, season, color, keywords and other attributes. Use the Favorites panel to assemble a collection of the items you're most likely to use, rather than looking through the entire library every time you want to add an artwork item to a project.

5   Layers are like transparent overlays on which you can paint or place photos, artwork, or text. Each element in a photo project occupies its own layer—the background is at the bottom and the other elements are overlaid in the order in which they are added to the project. You work with layers in the Layers panel, where you can toggle their visibility, drag to change their order, and add layer styles, effects, and masks. To make changes to a layer mask rather than the image on that layer, first select the black and white mask thumbnail to the right of the image thumbnail. The checkerboard grid areas in the layer thumbnails represent the transparent parts of the layers through which you can see the layers below.

10 PRINTING, SHARING, AND EXPORTING

Lesson overview

In previous lessons you've imported images from a range of sources, explored a variety of ways to organize and find your files, learned how to correct and enhance photos, and then created projects and presentations to showcase them.

In this lesson, you'll learn about outputting your images and creations so that you can share them with family, friends, or the world at large:

- Printing at home

- Ordering prints online

- Fine-tuning the composition of an image in the print preview

- Sharing photos by e-mail and Photo Mail

- Backing up your catalog and media files

- Sharing your photos online

- Exporting images for use on the Web

 You'll probably need between one and two hours to complete this lesson. If you haven't already done so, download the Lesson 10 work files from the Lesson & Update Files tab of your Account page at www.peachpit.com.

Now that you've organized and searched the images in your growing collection, corrected and enhanced your photos, and created presentations to showcase them, you're ready to let Photoshop Elements help you share your images and creations with the world —as printed output, by e-mail, or online.

Getting started

● **Note:** Before you start this lesson, make sure that you've set up a folder for your lesson files and downloaded the Lesson 10 folder from your Account page at www.peachpit.com, as detailed in "Accessing the Classroom in a Book files" in the chapter "Getting Started" at the beginning of this book. You should also have created a new work catalog (see "Creating a catalog for working with this book" in Lesson 1).

You'll begin by importing the sample images for this lesson to your CIB Catalog.

1   Start Photoshop Elements and click Organize in the Welcome Screen. In the Organizer, check the lower right corner of the workspace to make sure that your CIB Catalog is loaded—if not, choose File > Manage Catalogs and load it.

2   Click the Import button at the upper left of the workspace and choose From Files And Folders from the drop-down menu; then, locate and select the Lesson 10 folder. Activate the option Get Photos From Subfolders and disable all of the automatic processing options; then, click Get Media.

3   In the Import Attached Keyword Tags dialog box, click Select All; then, click OK.

Thumbnails of the images you've just imported appear in the Media Browser. The bar above the thumbnails indicates that you are viewing newly imported files.

About printing

Photoshop Elements offers a range of options for printing your photographs and projects such as photo books, greeting cards, and photo collages. You can output any Photoshop Elements print job from your home printer, or take advantage of Adobe partner services to order professional prints online.

You can print photos individually—in batches or one at a time, have Photoshop Elements generate a picture package layout that repeats the same image at a variety of sizes on the same page, or preview a multiple selection of photos as thumbnail images arranged on a printed contact sheet.

Printing a contact sheet

Before the advent of digital photography, a *contact sheet* or *contact proof* was produced by laying strips of film negatives directly onto a sheet of photographic paper, which was then exposed in the darkroom to create a printed preview of every shot on the roll. Photoshop Elements offers the option of printing a digital contact sheet—an effective and economical way to print-preview a selection of images at thumbnail size, arranged in a grid layout on a single sheet of paper.

To learn how to set up a contact sheet on Mac OS, skip ahead to the next exercise.

Printing a contact sheet on Windows

1   Click the Back button (◀ Back) in the actions bar above the thumbnail grid, so that the Media Browser displays all the images in your catalog.

2   In the left panel, click in the My Folders list to select the folder To_Print, and then press Ctrl+A to select all the images in the source folder.

3   Choose File > Print.

The Prints dialog box opens. The column on the left displays thumbnails of all the photos you selected for this print job. At center stage is the print preview.

▶ **Tip:** You can also open the Prints dialog box in contact sheet mode from the Create tab above the right panel group. Choose Photo Prints from the Create menu, and then click Contact Sheet. If you cancel a print job that was launched from the Create menu, you'll also need to click Cancel in the Task bar below the Create panel.

4   In the Prints dialog box, choose a printer from the Select Printer menu. For the purposes of this demonstration set the paper size to Letter. From the Select Type Of Print menu, choose Contact Sheet, Make sure that the Crop To Fit option is disabled. Under Select A Layout, the number of columns should be set to 4 so that all twenty photos will fit neatly on a single page.

▶ **Tip:** To remove a photo from the contact sheet, select its thumb-nail in the column at the left and click the Remove button (➖) below the menu pane.

The contact sheet layout includes all the images in the thumbnail column at the left. A page count below the print preview indicates that you are viewing page 1 of 1.

5   Under Select A Layout, click the down arrow button beside the Columns number or type **3** in the text box: With only three columns the images are larger, but only nine photos will fit on a single page at this paper size; the page count below the print preview now indicates that you are viewing page 1 of 3. Use the Next Page and Previous page buttons on either side of the page count to navigate between the pages. Change the number of columns to nine, which is the maximum. You can see that a single letter page can accommodate many photos at this setting. Return the layout to four columns.

6   Click to select any photo in the print preview; then, use the slider below the preview pane to zoom in. Drag the photo to reposition it within the frame of its image cell. Select another image, and then use the Rotate buttons to the left of the zoom slider to change the photo's orientation.

● **Note:** Some words in the text label may be truncated, depending on the page setup and column layout.

7   To print information extracted from the images' metadata below each photo on the contact sheet, first click to activate Show Print Options (just below the Columns setting), and then activate any or all of the text label options.

8   Click Print or Cancel and skip to "Printing a Picture Package" on the next page.

Printing a contact sheet on Mac OS

On Mac OS, you need to initiate a contact sheet print from the Editor. For this demonstration, in which we'll use all the photos in a single folder; it will be quicker to open the Editor without first making a selection in the Organizer. If you want to print a contact sheet with photos drawn from multiple folders, you'll need to select the images in the Media Browser, and then switch to the Editor.

1   Press Shift+Command+A to deselect any images that are currently selected in the Media Browser; then, click the Editor button (⌨) in the Task bar. If necessary, click Expert in the mode picker to switch the Editor to Expert mode.

▶ **Tip:** The alternative option in the Use menu under Source Images fills your contact sheet with whatever images are already open in the Editor. This is the setting you would use if you had made a selection of images in the Media Browser before switching to the Editor.

2   Choose File > Contact Sheet II. Set up the Contact Sheet dialog box as shown in the illustration at the right. Choose Folder from the Use menu under Source Images. Click Choose and locate your Lesson 10 / To_Print folder. Click Open. In the Document, settings, specify a size for your contact sheet. Under Thumbnails, specify the order in which the images will be placed. Activate Use Auto-Spacing; then, type **4** and **5** in the Columns and Rows boxes respectively. Your

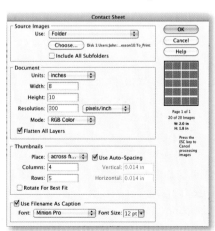

Columns and Rows settings are reflected in the layout preview at the right. Disable Rotate For Best Fit, and activate Use Filename As Caption.

3 Click OK, and then wait while Photoshop Elements places the images and captions.

In our example, all twenty images fit onto a single page. When the number of images selected for printing exceeds the capacity of a single page at the layout settings specified, Photoshop Elements will generate more pages to accommodate the extra photos.

4 Select the contact sheet page(s) in the Project Bin. Choose File > Print if you wish to print the contact sheet. If not, choose File > Close; then, click Don't Save.

Tip: You can also open the Prints dialog box in contact sheet mode from the Create tab above the right panel group. Choose Photo Prints from the Create menu, and then click Contact Sheet. If you do this from the Organizer, you'll see a message asking if you'd like to open the Editor to initiate printing. If you cancel a print job that was launched from the Create menu, you'll also need to click Cancel in the Task bar below the Create panel.

Printing a Picture Package

A Picture Package layout lets you print a photo repeated at a choice of sizes on the same page, much as professional portrait studios do. You can choose from a variety of layout options and range of image sizes to customize your picture package print.

To set up a picture package print on Mac OS, skip ahead to the next exercise.

Printing a Picture Package on Windows

1 Select two or more pictures in the Media Browser, and then choose File > Print.

2 In the Prints dialog box, choose a printer from the Select Printer menu and a paper size from the Select Paper Size menu. Which layout options are available for your picture package depends on your choice of paper size; for the purposes of this exercise, choose Letter.

3 Choose Picture Package from the Select Type Of Print menu. If a Printing Warning dialog box cautioning against enlarging pictures appears, click OK; for this exercise you'll print multiple images at smaller sizes.

4 Choose a layout from the Select A Layout menu, and then activate the option Fill Page With First Photo. This will result in a page with a single photo repeated at a variety of sizes, according to the layout you have chosen. If you selected more than one photo in the Media browser, a separate Print Package page will be generated for each photo selected; you can see the print preview for each page by clicking the page navigation buttons below the preview pane.

The layout options available for a Picture Package depend on the paper size specified in the Prints dialog box, the page setup, and the printer preferences. To change the paper size, choose from the Select Paper Size menu or click either the Page Setup button at the lower left of the Prints dialog box or the Change Settings button under Printer Settings. Depending on your printer, you may need to look for the paper size options in the Advanced preferences settings.

Tip: You can also open the Prints dialog box in picture package mode from the Create tab in the Task pane. Click Photo Prints, and then click the Picture Package button. If you cancel a print job that was launched from the Create menu, you'll also need to click Cancel in the Task bar below the Create panel.

5 Try some of the options in the Select A Frame menu. We selected the Icicles border to suit the winter holiday theme of our selection. You can choose only one frame per picture package; it will be applied to every picture in the layout.

6 Toggle the Crop To Fit option and assess the result; the Crop To Fit option may fit the multiple images more closely to the layout to better fill the printable area, especially when your photo is of non-standard proportions.

Note: The images in a Picture Package layout are automatically oriented to make the best use of the printable paper area for the layout you have chosen. You cannot manually rotate the image cells (or *photoholders*) in a picture package layout; however, you can still zoom or rotate each image within its print well using the zoom slider and orientation buttons below the preview. Drag any image in the picture package to adjust its position within its print well.

7 Click the Add button (➕) below the thumbnail menu at the left. In the Add Media dialog box, you can choose from your entire catalog or from those photos currently visible in the Media Browser. More sources can be accessed by expanding the Advanced options. Choose one or more photos from any of these sets, and then click Done; the selected images are added to the print job and now appear in the thumbnails column in the Prints dialog box.

8 Drag the thumbnail of one of your newly acquired photos from the thumbnails column onto any image cell in the print preview; the original image is replaced.

9 Click Print or Cancel and skip ahead to the exercise "Printing individual photos."

Printing a Picture Package on Mac OS

1   If necessary, switch to the Organizer by clicking the Organizer button (▦) in the Task bar, leaving the Editor window open. Select two or more photos in the Media Browser; then, click the Editor button (🖼) in the Task bar. If necessary, click Expert in the mode picker to switch the Editor to Expert mode.

2   In the Photo Bin, double-click whichever photo that you'd like to print first to make it the active image; then, Choose File > Picture Package.

3   Under Document in the Picture Package dialog box, make a selection from the Page Size and Layout menus, and then click the Edit Layout button below the Layout preview box.

4   In the Picture Package Edit Layout dialog box, click to select an image in the layout preview, and then click the Delete Zone button in the Image Zones options at the left. Select another image in the preview and drag it to a new position on the page preview. Drag the handles on the image's bounding box to scale it or change its orientation.

> **Tip:** You can open the Picture Package dialog box from the Create tab in the Task pane. Click Photo Prints, and then click the Picture Package button. If you do this from the Organizer, you'll see a message asking if you'd like to open the Editor to initiate printing.

5   Right-click an image in the Edit Layout preview and try out some of the menu choices; then experiment with the other settings and buttons in the Image Zones options. Click Cancel, and then click No to avoid overwriting the default settings for the layout preset you selected.

6   Click OK in the Picture Package dialog box, and then wait while Photoshop Elements creates a new document and places the images for your Picture Package. If you wish to see the Picture Package printed choose File > Print; otherwise choose File > Close All, and then click Don't Save.

> **Tip:** If you cancel a print job that was launched from the Create menu, you'll also need to click Cancel in the Task bar below the Create panel.

Printing individual photos

The Photoshop Elements Prints dialog box presents all your printing options in one convenient place and also enables you to fine-tune the placement of each image within its own *photoholder* (its frame in the print preview). You can zoom or rotate an image with the controls beneath the preview and drag to reposition it, enabling you to get the image placed just right for printing without first editing it.

1 In the Organizer, Ctrl-click / Command-click to select eight or more images.

2 Choose File > Print. Alternatively, click the Create tab in the Task pane, click Photo Prints, and then click the Local Printer button. On Mac OS, click Yes to continue to the Editor, where printing will be initiated.

3 In the Prints / Print dialog box, select a printer, paper size and print size from the menus at the right. On Windows, choose Individual Prints from the Select Type Of Print menu. If you see a print resolution alert, click OK to dismiss it.

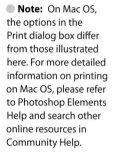 **Note:** On Mac OS, the options in the Print dialog box differ from those illustrated here. For more detailed information on printing on Mac OS, please refer to Photoshop Elements Help and search other online resources in Community Help.

4 Experiment with the controls below the Print preview. Click to select an image in the preview and zoom in and out inside the image cell using the zoom slider. Use the Rotate Left and Rotate Right buttons beside the zoom slider to change the orientation of the image within its print well frame. Drag the selected image to reposition it within the frame. Toggle the Crop To Fit option below the Select Print Size menu and observe the effect in the print preview.

5 Select any image thumbnail in the menu column on the left side of the dialog box and click the Remove Selected Item(s) button (━).

6 Click the Add Photos button (✚) below the thumbnails menu. In the Add Media dialog box, select an image source; you can choose from your entire catalog, or from those photos currently visible in the Media Browser. Choose one or more photos from any of these sets, and then click Add Selected Media. The selected images are added to the thumbnails column in the Print dialog box and the Add Media dialog box remains open. Expand the Advanced source options and choose a different source. Select one or more photos; then, click Done to add the photos to your print job and dismiss the Add Media dialog box.

Note: You can add images to the selection to be printed only if they are part of the currently active catalog.

If you've selected more pictures than will fit on one page at the image dimensions you specified, Photoshop Elements automatically generates extra pages.

7 Check the page count below the Print Preview. If your print job has more than one page, preview the other pages by clicking the arrow buttons at either side of the page count.

8 Click the More Options button at the bottom of the Prints dialog box and explore the settings available in the More Options dialog box. In the Printing Choices section, you can choose to print text details with your images, add image borders or a background color, and print crop marks to help you trim your images. The More Options dialog box also offers Custom Print Size and Color Management settings. Click Cancel to close the More Options dialog box.

9 In the Prints / Print dialog box, click Print if you wish to see these images printed; otherwise, click Cancel to save your ink and paper for your own prints. On Mac OS, choose File > Close All.

Ordering professionally printed photos online

If you want high quality prints of your photos and photo projects, you can order professional prints from an online service. Photoshop Elements provides integrated links to online printing partners that you can conveniently access from anywhere in the workspace.

● **Note:** Users who purchased Photoshop Elements at Costco® can also order directly from Costco 1 Hour Photo.

For users in the United States and Canada, Photoshop Elements offers a direct link to the Shutterfly online printing service. For a list of services available outside the United States and Canada, please refer to Photoshop Elements help.

To ensure faster delivery and lower shipping costs from partner services, you need to set your location. Unless you change location, you'll only need to do this once.

1   In the Organizer, do one of the following:

   • On Windows, choose Edit > Preferences > Adobe Partner Services, and then click the Choose button under Location in the Adobe Partner Services pane of the Preferences dialog box. In the Choose Location dialog box, choose your country from the menu, and then click OK. Click OK once more to dismiss the Choose Location dialog box; then, click OK to confirm the change and close the Preferences dialog box.

   • On Mac OS, choose Adobe Partner Services Location from the Elements Organizer menu. In the Choose Location dialog box, choose your country from the menu, and then click OK. Click OK once more to dismiss the Choose Location dialog box. If you see a message confirming your changed settings, click OK to acknowledge and dismiss the message.

2   In the Organizer, select one or more photos in the Media Browser, and then do one of the following:

   • Choose File > Order Prints > Order Shutterfly Prints.

   • Click the Create tab at the top of the Task pane. On the Create tab, click the Photo Prints button, and then click Order Prints From Shutterfly.

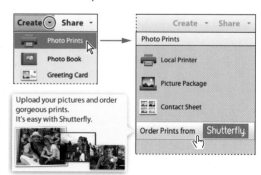

3 In the Order Shutterfly Prints dialog box, do one of the following:

- If you're already a Shutterfly member, click the "Already a member? Sign in" link, enter your e-mail address and password and click Sign In.

- If you're not already a Shutterfly member, create a new account by entering your name, e-mail address, and a password of at least six characters. If you accept the Shutterfly Terms and Conditions, click the check box below the personal details fields, and then click Join Now / Next.

Once you've signed up, the Order Shutterfly Prints dialog box leads you through the ordering process in easy-to-follow steps, which are laid out in a workflow diagram at the top of the dialog box.

4 In the first step—Size/Qty—you can specify print sizes and quantities for the each of the photos you selected. Click Remove under a thumbnail image in the list on the left side of the dialog box to remove that photo from your order.

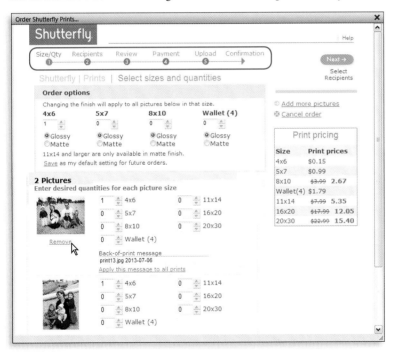

5 When you've set up the print sizes and quantities for your order, click Next.

In the next two steps of the order process, you'll add the names and delivery addresses of recipients for your prints, and then review your order—making changes as necessary. In the remaining steps you can provide credit card details in the Payment / Billing dialog box; then upload your images and confirm your order.

6 For now, click Cancel. A dialog box appears to ask if you want to stop using this service. Click OK. Click Cancel in the Task bar below the right panel group.

Sharing pictures

In this section we'll look at a variety of ways to share your pictures with friends, family, clients, or the world at large.

Sharing photos by e-mail

Perhaps the most basic way to share a photo is by attaching it to an e-mail. The Organizer's e-mail function makes it easy—automatically optimizing your images specifically for sending via e-mail.

● **Note:** The first time you access this feature you may be presented with the E-mail dialog box. Choose your e-mail client (such as Outlook Express or Adobe E-mail Service, Mail, or Microsoft Entourage) from the menu, and then click Continue. You can review or change your settings later by choosing Sharing from the Preferences menu.

1 In the Media Browser, select a photo to attach to an e-mail. Click the Share tab at the top of the Task Pane; then click the E-mail Attachments button.

2 Drag another image from the Media Browser to the Email Attachments pane to add it to the selection to be e-mailed.

3 Choose one of the smaller size options from the Maximum Photo Size menu, and then adjust the image quality using the Quality slider. The higher the quality setting, the larger the file size will be— and therefore, the longer the download time. The estimated file size is displayed for your reference at the bottom of the Email Attachments panel.

At this stage, you could generate your e-mail without specifying recipients in Photoshop Elements, but for the purposes of this exercise we'll make a start on setting up an e-mail contacts list. Populating your Photoshop Elements address book can save time, especially if you often e-mail photo attachments to the same people.

4 Click the Edit Recipients In Contact Book button (👤) below the Quality slider to create a new listing. In the Contact Book dialog box, click New Contact.

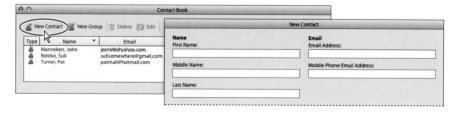

5   In the New Contact dialog box, type in the personal details and e-mail address of the person to whom you wish to e-mail the pictures. Click OK to close the New Contact dialog box, and then inspect the other options in the Contact Book dialog box.

The New Group button lets you arrange your contacts in groups, so that with just one click, you can e-mail your favorite vacation shots to all your family and friends, or send a photo-update to all of your colleagues. On Windows, the Contact Book dialog box also enables you to import your Outlook Express or vCard contacts list.

6   In the Select Recipients box, make sure that there is a check mark beside each contact that you wish to receive your e-mailed photos, and then click Next in the Task bar. Photoshop Elements automatically launches your default e-mail application and opens a new message, complete with the images that you selected earlier, addressed to all of your intended recipients. You can edit the default subject line and text as you wish. When you're done, either click Send if you want to go ahead and send this example e-mail, or close the message without saving or sending it.

Using Photo Mail

Photo Mail is not supported on Mac OS; if you're working on Mac OS, you can skip this exercise and move ahead to "Sharing photos online."

On Windows, another way to share your images by e-mail is to use the Photo Mail feature, which embeds photos in the body of an e-mail, within a customized layout.

1   In the Organizer, select two or three of the photos from the To_Print folder in the Media Browser; then, click the Photo Mail button on the Share tab.

2   Click the check box just below the Photo Mail thumbnails pane to activate the Include Caption option.

3   Choose the recipient(s) for your Photo Mail. If your contact list is still empty, click the Edit Recipients In Contact Book button ( ) and create a new entry in the Contact Book dialog box (*see steps 4, 5, and 6 in the preceding exercise*).

4 Click Next in the Task bar. In the Stationery & Layouts Wizard dialog box, click each category in the list at the left in turn to see the range of stationery template designs that are available.

5 Choose a stationery style appropriate to your selected photos. Keep in mind that each Photo Mail stationery template includes certain elements that can be customized such as backgrounds, graphics, borders, and frames. When you're done, click Next Step at the lower right.

6 Customize the layout by choosing a Photo Size, Layout option. Choose a font; then click the color swatch beside the font menu and choose a text color. To edit a message or caption, first click the text to make it active. Depending on your choice of stationery template, you may see options and controls that differ from those illustrated below. When you're done, click Next.

7 You may be asked to verify your sender address; then, Photoshop Elements opens your default e-mail application and embeds your layout in a new message addressed to the recipients you selected. Click Send if you want to go ahead and send this example Photo Mail, or close the message without saving it.

Sharing photos and videos online

From within Photoshop Elements, you can upload your photos, videos and presentations directly to social networking or photo and video sharing web sites by choosing from the Share tab menu in either the Organizer or the Editor. You can also use these services to download media and even to collaborate on shared content.

On the Share tab in both modules, you'll find integrated links to Adobe Revel (Private Web Album), Facebook, Flickr, Twitter, and SmugMug,

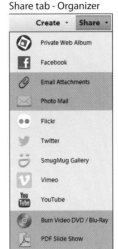

In the Organizer, the Share tab also offers buttons for posting video clips directly to Vimeo and YouTube.

Depending on whether you already have an account with the service you wish to use, you may first need to sign up. Some services, such as Flickr, Twitter and Facebook, will also ask you to authorize Photoshop Elements to connect to your online account.

Although the procedure for logging in and sharing may differ slightly for each of these services, the process is essentially similar, and you'll be guided step by step.

Sharing photos via Adobe Revel

In this part of the lesson, we'll look at sharing images to and from Adobe Revel, the latest addition to Photoshop Elements' integrated online sharing services.

Before you begin the exercises in this section, you need to set up the Organizer to link to Adobe Revel and create some Mobile Albums as detailed in the two exercises in "Access your photos anywhere with Mobile Albums" in Lesson 3.

1 If you're currently signed in to Adobe Revel on one of your mobile devices, or in your desktop web browser, sign out now.

2 In the Organizer, choose File > Manage Catalogs; then, select your personal catalog (the catalog you linked to your Adobe Revel account in Lesson 3) from the Catalogs list and click Open.

You should see an orange alert icon beside the Mobile Albums header in the left panel; this indicates that your catalog has already been linked to Adobe Revel, but is not currently connected.

3   Choose File > Sign In To Adobe Revel. Enter your Adobe ID and password in the Elements Mobile Albums screen, and then click Sign In.

4   If necessary, expand the Mobile Albums category in the left panel, and then expand your Revel library to see the Mobile Albums nested inside it.

5   Move the pointer over the listing for the Mobile Album that you'd like to share. Click the Share icon ([icon]) to the right of the album name; then, click Start Sharing in the Album Web Share dialog box. Specify whether you'd like to allow downloads from your shared album, and then click Copy This Link.

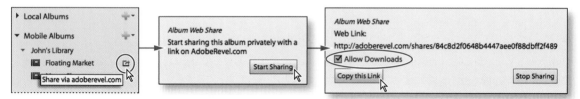

6   Move the pointer over the Mobile Album you've just enabled for sharing; the Share icon beside the shared album's name has turned blue.

7   To see how your shared Mobile Album will look to your invited viewers, paste the copied URL into your web browser. If you wish to share the album with friends or family, go to your e-mail application and paste the copied URL into as many invitation messages as you like; then, return to the Elements Organizer.

Creating a Private Web Album

By default, your Mobile Albums in Adobe Revel are private until you enable sharing, and then issue invitations, as you did in the preceding exercise. When you wish to upload a selection of photos to Revel for the express purpose of sharing them, you can use the Private Web Album button on the Share tab in either module to create a new Revel album, share it, and initiate an e-mail invitation in a single procedure.

1   If the Media Browser is displaying the contents of a selected album or folder, click the All Media button in the actions bar to see all the photos in your catalog.

▶ **Tip:** You can make a selection of media for a Private Web Album by choosing from the Media Browser, by selecting an album in the Local Albums category, or even by selecting a subset of the images in an existing Mobile Album.

2   Ctrl-click / Command-click to select a small group of images in the Media Browser; then, open the Share tab at the upper right of the workspace and click the Private Web Album button.

3   Click the button at the bottom of the Private Web Album dialog box to sign in with your Adobe ID. Your web browser opens to a sign-in page; enter your Adobe ID and password, and then click Sign In. When you see the "thank you" message, close the web page and return to the Elements Organizer.

4   Click the Complete Authorization button in the Private Web Album dialog box to move on to the next step in the procedure.

5 Your Private Web Album needs to be associated with a Revel album; in the Private Web Album dialog box, click the plus sign beside the album name, and then enter a name for the new album. Specify whether you wish to allow downloads; then, click Start Sharing. You'll see a progress bar as your photos are uploaded to Revel, and then a "Successfully Shared!" message.

6 Click the words "Email link," just below the URL for your shared album; your e-mail application automatically opens a new e-mail message containing an invitation and link to your new Private Web Album. Address and send the invitation; then, return to the Elements Organizer and click Done.

Collaborating on a shared Revel library

You can invite others to contribute to and collaborate on any of your Revel libraries. This can be a great way to put together a shared record of a family event, to collate different viewpoints on a common project, or to share travel experiences. You'll start by creating a new Revel library, separate from your personal albums.

> **Note:** Collaborators will be able to add photos to your shared library, but they can't delete your photos or add more collaborators.

1 Click the arrow beside the green plus sign icon ( ) to the right of the Mobile Albums header and choose Settings from the menu to open the Adobe Revel tab in the Elements Organizer Preferences dialog box. Click the plus sign (+) at the top of the Libraries list; then, enter a name for the new library and press Enter / Return. Click OK to close the Preferences dialog box.

2 Your new library is listed under Mobile Albums in the Organizer. Drag an album from the Local Albums category, or a small selection of images from the Media Browser, onto the new listing.

3 Wait for a minute or so while your images are uploaded, and then move the pointer over the new library. Click the Invite Users To Collaborate button ( ) to the right of the library name. Enter the e-mail address of the person you wish to invite, and then click Add. Either add more e-mail addresses, or click Done. The icon beside your new library turns blue, indicating that it has been shared.

When you're invited to collaborate on a library, you'll receive an e-mail message as well as a notification in Elements Organizer; an envelope icon appears beside the Mobile Albums heading, indicating that you have an unanswered invitation. Click the notification icon to accept or reject the invitation. If you accept, the library you were invited to share appears in your Mobile Albums list.

> **Note:** If you invite someone who is not a Revel user, they will receive an e-mail invitation to sign up and participate.

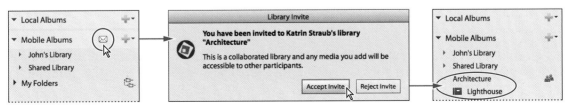

4 Choose File > Manage Catalogs. Select your CIB catalog and click Open.

Exporting copies of your photos for the Web

When you want to share your photos online, you can use the Save For Web dialog box to preview the effects of different optimization options. You can choose from a range of file formats for your exported files, resize them, specify color and compression options, and enable transparency or background matting. Use an export preset as a starting point, and then tweak the settings to fine-tune the optimization.

In this exercise you'll optimize and export a copy in JPEG format, which reduces the file size and looks good in the majority of web browsers.

1   In the Organizer, click the All Media button (☰All Media) if it's visible in the actions bar above the thumbnails grid. Select any photo in the Media Browser, and then click the Editor button (⬜) in the Task bar.

2   In the Editor, choose File > Save For Web. In the Save For Web dialog box, choose Fit On Screen from the Zoom menu, just above the Preview button in the lower left corner of the dialog box.

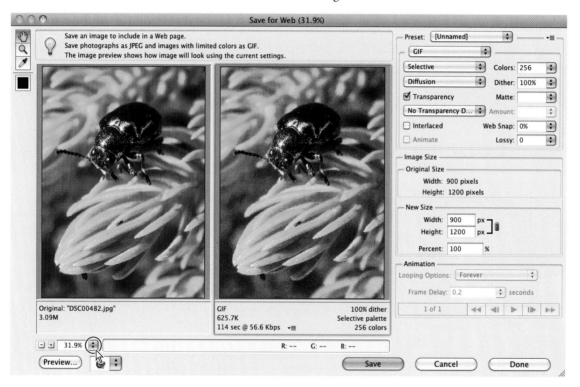

While you're previewing photos in the Save For Web dialog box, you can magnify the view with the Zoom tool (🔍) in the toolbox at the upper left of the dialog box. To zoom out, hold the Alt / Option key as you click the image with the Zoom tool. While you're zoomed in, you can drag in either window with the Hand tool (🖐); the images pan in unison so that you see the same part of the photo in both views.

3   Watch the change in the file size information displayed below the export preview on the right as you choose JPEG Medium from the Preset menu at the upper right of the dialog box.

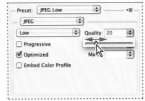

4   Select the JPEG low preset; the file size is reduced even further. Tweak the Quality setting to set a level between the two presets; the default values for the JPEG Low and JPEG Medium settings are 10 and 30, respectively.

Note: The JPEG format reduces the file size using compression, which discards some of the image data. The amount of information lost, and the resulting image quality, will vary depending on the photo you're working with and the quality settings.

5   Under New Size, type **500** in the Width field. The Height is adjusted automatically to retain the image's original proportions. Once again, notice the change in the file size displayed beneath the optimized export preview. Choose Fit On Screen from the Zoom menu to compare the reduced image to the original.

6   Click the Preview button in the lower left corner of the Save For Web dialog box to see the image displayed in your default browser at the current export settings. Scroll down the browser page, if necessary, to see a summary of the optimization settings that were applied. Return to Photoshop Elements.

7   Click Save. Add the extension **_Work** to the original and save the file to your My CIB Work folder. In the Editor, choose File > Close, without saving changes.

Backing up your catalog and media files

The importance of a good backup strategy is often only understood too late. You can't prevent a disaster from happening but you *can* reduce the risk of loss and the time and effort needed for recovery by backing up regularly.

Photoshop Elements offers several options that make it quick and easy to manage backups and safeguard your photo library.

Backing up the catalog file

The catalog file stores a great deal of information—not only the locations of your image files, but the metadata attached to them, including titles, captions, tags, ratings, and album groupings. Even if you have copies of your original images, you could lose hundreds of hours of work in the event of a hard disk failure, accidental deletion, or a corrupted catalog file—unless you back up your catalog.

One useful technique is to save as much of this information as possible back to your original image files, which serves as a partial *distributed* backup of the catalog.

1   In the Organizer, click the All Media button (**All Media**) if it's visible in the actions bar above the thumbnails grid. Press Ctrl+A / Command+A to select all the media files in your catalog. Choose File > Save Metadata To Files.

Next, you'll make a full backup of your catalog and all the associated media files.

2 Choose File > Backup Catalog. Make sure that Full Backup is selected in the Backup Options; then, click Next. Select a destination drive, name the backup **CIB Backup**, and then click the Browse button beside Backup Path to specify a destination folder. Click OK, and then click Save Backup. Photoshop Elements will notify you when the backup is complete; click ok to dismiss the message.

Doing incremental backups

In the usual course of events, the majority of the images in your library will remain unchanged between backups. An incremental backup saves you time by replacing only the catalog entries and images that have been modified since the last backup.

1 In the Media browser, add ratings to several un-rated photos by clicking the rating stars below the thumbnails. This will serve as the incremental change to the catalog since your full backup.

2 Choose File > Backup Catalog. This time, activate Incremental Backup in the Backup Options; then, click Next.

3 Select the same destination drive, name the backup **CIB_BU_2**, and then click the Browse button to navigate to and open the same destination folder. In the Specify Backup Folder dialog box, click New Folder. Name the new folder **Incremental**. Click OK to close the Specify Backup Folder dialog box, and then click the Browse button beside Previous Backup File. Navigate to the folder containing your full backup and select the file Backup.tly. Click Open, and then click save Backup. Click OK to dismiss the completion message.

Should you ever need to restore a damaged catalog file or start afresh after a hard disk failure, simply choose File > Restore Catalog and locate your backup files.

Congratulations, you've completed the last lesson in this book! Take a few moments to refresh what you've learned about printing and sharing photos from Photoshop Elements by reading through the review on the facing page.

Review questions

1 What is a Picture Package?

2 How can you fine-tune the composition of a photo for printing?

3 Do the media files for a Private Web Album first need to be grouped as an album in the Organizer?

4 How can you add collaborators to a Revel library?

5 Is the Save For Web command available only in Expert mode?

6 What is an incremental backup?

Review answers

1 A Picture Package lets you print a photo repeated at a choice of sizes on the same page. You can choose from a variety of layout options with a range of image sizes to customize your picture package print.

2 You can fine-tune the placement of each image within its own *photoholder* frame in the print preview, enabling you to get the image placed just right for printing without first editing it. Zoom or rotate an image with the controls beneath the print preview and drag to reposition it in the frame.

3 No; you can make a selection of media for a Private Web Album either by choosing separate files from the Media Browser, by selecting an album in the Local Albums category, or even by selecting a subset of the images in an existing Mobile Album.

4 To invite friends, family, or associates to collaborate on a Revel library, click the Invite Users To Collaborate button (👥) that appears when you move the pointer over the library name in the Mobile Albums list. Enter e-mail addresses of the people you wish to invite, and then click Add. The icon beside the library name turns blue, to indicate that it has been shared.

5 The Save For Web command is available from the File menu in all three Edit modes: Expert, Quick edit and Guided edit.

6 An incremental backup copies only those images and catalog entries that have changed since the last full backup.

INDEX

Production Notes

The *Adobe Photoshop Elements 12 Classroom in a Book* was created electronically using Adobe InDesign CS5. Art was produced using Adobe InDesign, Adobe Illustrator, and Adobe Photoshop.

Team credits

The following individuals contributed to the development of this edition of the *Adobe Photoshop Elements 12 Classroom in a Book*:

Project coordinators, technical writers: John Evans & Katrin Straub

Production: Manneken Pis Productions (www.manneken.be)

Copyediting & Proofreading: John Evans & Katrin Straub

Keystroker: Lisa Fridsma

Special thanks to Tracey Croom, Torsten Buck, Eric Geoffroy, Barbara Kruszyńska, Connie Jeung-Mills, Petra Laux, Berenice Seitz and Philipp Meyer, Kelly Willis, and Christine Yarrow.

Typefaces used

Adobe Myriad Pro and Adobe Warnock Pro are used throughout the lessons. For more information about OpenType and Adobe fonts, visit www.adobe.com/type/opentype/.

Photo Credits

Photographic images and illustrations supplied by Han Buck, Torsten Buck, John Evans, Katrin Straub, and Adobe Systems Incorporated. Photos are for use only with the lessons in the book.

Contributors

John Evans has worked in computer graphics and design for more than 25 years, initially as a graphic designer, and then as a multimedia author, software interface designer, and technical writer. His multimedia and digital illustration work associated with Japanese type attracted an award from Apple Computer Australia. His other projects range from music education software for children to interface design for innovative font design software. As a technical writer his work includes software design specifications, user manuals, and copy editing for *Adobe Photoshop Elements 7 Classroom in a Book*, *Adobe Photoshop Lightroom 2 Classroom in a Book*, and *Adobe Creative Suite 4 Classroom in a Book*. More recently he has authored several editions of *Adobe Photoshop Lightroom Classroom in a Book* and *Adobe Photoshop Elements Classroom in a Book*.

Katrin Straub is an artist, a graphic designer, and author. Her award-winning print, painting, and multimedia work has been exhibited worldwide. With more than 15 years experience in design, Katrin has worked as Design Director for companies such as Landor Associates and Fontworks in the United States, Hong Kong, and Japan. Her work includes packaging, promotional campaigns, multimedia, website design, and internationally recognized corporate and retail identities. She holds degrees from the FH Augsburg, ISIA Urbino, and The New School University in New York. Katrin has authored many books, from the *Adobe Creative Suite Idea Kit* to Classroom in a Book titles for Adobe Photoshop Lightroom 2, Adobe Creative Suite 4, Adobe Soundbooth, and several versions of *Adobe Photoshop Elements Classroom in a Book* and *Adobe Premiere Elements Classroom in a Book*.

Tao, Zoë, Han, and Mia Buck have been volunteering as photographic models for the last seven editions of the Photoshop Elements Classroom in a Book. Tao wants to become at least as famous as Audrey Hepburn; failing that, she's considering becoming a psychologist. Zoë loves to juggle with numbers and is a talented gymnast. She is deeply concerned about the environment and wants to study biology. Han spends her free time drawing and reading. She is interested in nature, like her twin sister Zoë, and is thinking of becoming an explorer—or else a falconer. Mia doesn't want to commit to any profession yet. She is, however, passionate about the piano and a promising dancer.

WATCH
READ
CREATE

Unlimited online access to all Peachpit, Adobe Press, Apple Training and New Riders videos and books, as well as content from other leading publishers including: O'Reilly Media, Focal Press, Sams, Que, Total Training, John Wiley & Sons, Course Technology PTR, Class on Demand, VTC and more.

No time commitment or contract required! Sign up for one month or a year. **All for $19.99 a month**

SIGN UP TODAY
peachpit.com/creativeedge